NEWS
FLASH

NEWS FLASH

Journalism, Infotainment, and the
Bottom-Line Business of Broadcast News

BONNIE M. ANDERSON
Veteran Reporter for CNN and NBC

JOSSEY-BASS
A Wiley Imprint
www.josseybass.com

Published by Jossey-Bass
A Wiley Imprint
989 Market Street, San Francisco, CA 94103-1741   www.josseybass.com

Jossey-Bass books and products are available through most bookstores. To contact
Jossey-Bass directly, call our Customer Care Department within the U.S. at
800-956-7739 or outside the U.S. at 317-572-3986, or fax to 317-572-4002.

Jossey-Bass also publishes its books in a variety of electronic formats. Some content
that appears in print may not be available in electronic books.

Library of Congress Cataloging-in-Publication Data

Anderson, Bonnie, date
    Journalism, infotainment, and the bottom-line business of broadcast news /
Bonnie M. Anderson.— 1st ed.
        p. cm.
    Includes bibliographical references and index.
    ISBN 978-0-7879-7285-1 (alk. paper)
    ISBN 978-0-470-40177-4 (paperback)
    1. Television broadcasting of news—United States. I. Title.
PN4888.T4A55 2004
070.4'3'0973—dc22   2004001684

FIRST EDITION
            10 9 8 7 6 5 4 3 2 1

CONTENTS

For all people who treasure democracy, for all journalists who are passionate about freedom of the press, and for Howard F. Anderson, who gave his life for these most basic human rights

PREFACE

"What's a journalist?"

I was so sure that the question was a joke that I laughed. After all, the man asking it was the head of programming for all the Turner Broadcasting networks, including CNN, the world's first twenty-four-hour *news* network. But the look on Garth Ancier's handsome young face left no doubt that he was serious.

It was the afternoon of April 16, 2001, and we were in Ancier's office in CNN Center, on the penthouse level where the masters of our news universe toiled. Ancier had just arrived at CNN from Hollywood, where he'd been president of NBC Entertainment. Everything in his suite looked and smelled brand new—the plush, cream-colored carpet; the sleekly upholstered furniture; the hardwood desk upon which his feet were propped. Other senior executives kept walking in to admire the bank of high-tech television sets he'd had installed against one wall.

As vice president of recruiting, I was showing him videotapes of potential news anchors. These were people I thought had the requisite combination of strong journalistic credentials and screen presence. I suppose I shouldn't have been surprised by Ancier's question. After all, he had already shocked me once at this meeting by saying he didn't want to see tapes of any more minority anchors or correspondents.

"We have enough of those people," he said, "I want to cast people viewers are more likely to want to watch."

I bit my tongue and kept my focus on what I was there for: getting CNN to hire what I considered to be the very best people.

"I think we can attract some of the top journalists in the country, who will also be compelling to watch," I said.

That's when he asked me what a journalist was.

In that moment, I realized that Ancier didn't view television reporters as news professionals—people who follow specific ethical guidelines and uphold high standards. He didn't grasp that the skills needed to research, investigate, write, shape, and report stories took years to master.

The e-mail Ancier had sent me that morning should have been the tip-off: "We need younger, more attractive anchors (male & female) who project credibility." *Project* credibility. Not *have* credibility, earned through years of training and experience. Why didn't Ancier want anchors who had earned their stripes? Because those years of experience show—on one's face.

As I began explaining who we journalists are and what we do, my mind was reeling. Of course, Ancier's use of the word *cast* to describe the hiring of a journalist should have been another tip-off. This was a man used to casting actors. You don't have to go to medical school to play a doctor on *ER*. Why not apply that same standard to television journalism? Ancier made it clear that the only things that mattered to him were whether a person was attractive and could read the news with authority. Anchors were simply actors.

When I finished speaking, Ancier shook his head, smirked, and said, "You people are too hung up on journalism."

That was the final blow. How could CNN, the network that bills itself as "the world's news leader," be too hung up on journalism? I picked up my tapes, thanked him for his time, and walked out of his office. When I got around the corner, though, I pulled out a pen and wrote down everything Ancier had just said—like a good journalist.

I took the elevator down to my office, put the tapes away, and sat down to think. It didn't take me long to realize that, on a fundamental level, Ancier didn't understand the importance of journalism, its ethics, its history, its power, and why it is one of the linchpins of a free and democratic society.

He was a proponent of infotainment, that amorphous amalgam of news and entertainment in which hooking the viewer with Hollywood-star looks, provocative lead-ins, snappy editing, and sensational, often titillating, stories is more important than delivering the news the way it should be—straight up, no chaser.

As I sat at my desk pondering my next step, I took heart in knowing that his attitude and comments would send everyone in the news division through the roof in outrage. Wouldn't they? Over the next few weeks, to my growing dismay, I got my answer. One news executive after another heard me out, usually with a look of deep concern on his face, and then told me, in effect, to keep my mouth shut.

I believe that some things in life are just too important to play the go-along-to-get-ahead game. And journalistic standards are one of them. The primary function of the news is not and should not be to entertain. It is to inform—with honesty, integrity, and objectivity. This is a responsibility that I took very seriously during my twenty years as a correspondent and five years as a news executive. It is one that I saw eroding at CNN firsthand, and that I see eroding almost every time I watch television news. I wrote this book because I believe that this is a dangerous trend, not just for journalism but for American society as a whole.

Why is a high standard of journalism so important? Because journalism not only reports the news, it reflects and affects our society. "At the end of the twentieth century and beginning of the twenty-first century, national television, international television is the critical force," said CNN war correspondent Christiane Amanpour. "What we do and say and show really matters. . . . It has an effect on our local communities, on our states, on our country, and on the state of the world."

Journalism doesn't exist in a vacuum; it is a key player in the vigorous checks and balances of a healthy democracy. People's opinions are often shaped by the news. Think of our nation's recent history. The pictures of black Americans being beaten, battered by high-pressure water from fire hoses, and lynched stirred and horrified millions of fellow citizens and contributed to the success of the Civil Rights movement. I was a young girl during this period, and I vividly remember being deeply moved, sometimes to tears, by those images. They have stayed with me, an example of how news stories can live on in viewers' hearts and minds and continue to shape opinion for decades. Footage of American soldiers dying in the jungles of Vietnam fueled the antiwar movement and led to a speedier end to that war. In my own career, a story I worked on during the Ethiopian civil war and famine in 1984 led directly to a reversal of American foreign policy that barred the sending of emergency food supplies to rebel-occupied areas, a change that the Ethiopian government later credited with saving the lives of hundreds of thousands of starving people.

There is a stark difference between that quality of television news coverage and what we're mostly being bombarded with today. I can't, for example, begin to imagine how any California voters were able to make wise, informed decisions during the 2003 recall race of Governor Gray Davis. Where was the elderly couple worried about rising costs and the state's weak economy going to find platform information on the candidates? What about the college student concerned about the increase in state university tuition bills? Or the small-business owner whose livelihood depends on a steady supply of affordable electricity? That same owner was probably wondering about whether the state's governor planned to address the hike in workman's comp insurance. And how about California residents watching their vehicle taxes almost triple? Or the tens of thousands of laid-off workers in California wanting to know what the candidates would do for them? These were just a few of the serious issues facing Californians and their governor, but many television journalists apparently thought they weren't fun to report or entertaining enough to watch.

Instead, California voters—like people across the country—were treated to infotainment: stories about the various colorful characters in the race, their personalities and backgrounds and what the reporters speculated were the candidates' strategies. For the journalists, it was more interesting to report on the wackiness of candidates such as adult magazine publisher Larry Flynt, star Gary Coleman, or the young female candidate who hawked thong underwear on her campaign Web site.

And then there was the fawning over the eventual winner, candidate Arnold Schwarzenegger, quickly dubbed the "Governator" by the media. This wealthy bodybuilder-turned-actor whose only known intellectual prowess consisted of delivering memorized movie lines instantly became the darling of journalists. Why? Because he's a movie star whose wife is also a celebrity—and a television journalist. Stories and video about him would increase ratings. Schwarzenegger's every move was reported, often live on television, earning him millions of dollars worth of free exposure despite his reluctance to provide details about his position on just about anything. So while the TV media was busy letting California know where they could buy their "Hasta la Vista, Davis" t-shirts, voters with serious concerns on their minds were left virtually on their own to search for the candidates' positions on various issues. On September 2, 2003, network newscasts, including those on ABC and NBC, even devoted a couple of minutes each to the fact that Schwarzenegger *wasn't* going to participate in the first debate. "I decide my schedule," he said on ABC. The names of the other major candidates who *would* take part in the debate were not mentioned. Instead, ABC News devoted even more time on the nightly newscast to a soundbite from Schwarzenegger saying, "Don't worry about my way of getting the message across. Let me take care of that." And he did, with little watchdogging by the news media. Not only did Schwarzenegger launch his campaign on NBC's *Tonight Show with Jay Leno* but he also chose to give his last two interviews prior to polls opening to *Entertainment Tonight* and *Access Hollywood.*

That he blatantly (and without criticism) avoided in-depth interviews with journalists who might have asked him difficult questions in those critical final hours of the campaign shows just how much entertainment has invaded hard news—and vice versa. If Ronald Reagan, another former actor, had announced his candidacy for the 1966 California governor's race while sitting in a studio next to Johnny Carson, he would never have been taken seriously. But for Schwarzenegger, it was a brilliant move. He took advantage of his stardom and the release of his latest Terminator movie to kickstart his political career. And he knew that TV stations and networks, with their current penchant for infotainment, could not resist covering him even if he gave them short shrift in favor of entertainment programs, including *The Oprah Winfrey Show.*

"As any actor would be, he was tuned in to what was going to work in California," said Joe Angotti, a former senior vice president at NBC News and the current chair of the broadcast program at Northwestern University's Medill School of Journalism. "So he knew that by going to the entertainment side he was not going to be asked the tough questions that he was asked by [Peter] Jennings or [Tom] Brokaw, so he knew he'd get an easier ride. And he also knew he'd reach the audience he wanted to reach with his message, or lack of message."

By meekly going along with this strategy instead of exposing it, the television news media deserves a great deal of the blame or credit, depending on one's position, for the election of this political neophyte. TV journalism let down these voters by infotaining them instead of informing them. This trend, seen nationwide, is exceptionally worrisome when you consider that people in this country have depended on television for most of their news since 1963. According to a 2002 survey by The Pew Research Center for the People and the Press, 57 percent of those questioned watch local newscasts on a regular basis. A 2003 Pew survey in which participants could choose two answers (out of six options: television, newspapers, radio, magazines, Internet, and other) found that more than three-quarters (79 percent) said they got their news about national and international events from television. Only 45 percent chose newspapers as one of their choices.

Still, the Pew research shows that overall television news viewership continues to decline. For the evening news broadcasts on ABC, CBS, and NBC alone, there has been a 50 percent drop over the past decade—even for newsmagazines such as NBC's *Dateline.* Among the cable networks, only Fox News has seen huge sustainable ratings successes. As a result, all news networks and divisions—some more openly than others—are now fighting to attract viewers from conservative America as well as young people from, well, *anywhere.* The ever-increasing competition for a select viewer demographic has resulted in networks catering to what they *think* these viewers want to see instead of offering news coverage that is relevant and important to everyone. And in many cases, people looking for solid news programs are voting with their off buttons. According to the Pew Research Center, Americans in 1994 watched an average of thirty-eight minutes of TV news a day. In 2000, the number dropped to twenty-eight minutes, where it remained through 2002.

Many media analysts speculate that the decline in ratings for news programs can be attributed to "compassion fatigue." On August 11, 2003, for example, the *New York Times* published an article titled "Suffering News Burnout? The Rest of America Is, Too." The comfortable explanation was that viewers were simply too tired of seeing stories about war and terrorism. But I maintain that people aren't tired of real news; they're fed up with being fed garbage that is disguised as news.

And if all of this isn't enough of a threat to the integrity of television journalism, the effort by the Federal Communications Commission to ease restrictions on the number of local news outlets a major corporation can own foretells even greater danger. In effect, consumers would have fewer diverse voices to choose from. Already, just a handful of megacorporations control much of the media in this country. And their drive for greater profits has resulted in the erosion of professional standards. *News Flash* will reveal examples of some of the more major violations of ethics in recent times. And in case we've forgotten what good television journalism looks like, I'll share some rare but recent examples of excellence—proof that despite the overall downward spiral of television journalism, some committed professionals still manage to excel now and then, against the odds. That might be the most encouraging sign of all, a sign of hope.

Still, as I write this, there is yet another threat to journalism. The Bush administration is continuing its broad-based assault on freedom of the press. It is imposing secrecy on once-public records and proceedings. President Bush issued an executive order that, critics charge, illegally curtails access to presidential records, both his own and those of his predecessors. Attorney General John Ashcroft issued a directive to all federal agency heads ordering them to deny access to a whole range of public records.

More than a thousand non-American citizens were detained secretly—their names and locations kept from the press and public. The administration is fighting to keep the press out of many of the courtroom proceedings involving suspected terrorists. They argue that opening the proceedings would jeopardize national security. This muzzling of the press is a dangerous precedent, one that has chilling echoes of the most notorious totalitarian states in history. Who gets to define national security? Since when can an administration redefine the meaning and intent of the First Amendment? If journalists are kept out of one set of proceedings, it will only lead to them being kept out of others.

Is it, therefore, a wild leap from decrying the infotaining of American broadcast news and one administration's attempts to muzzle the press to sounding an alarm for the strength and health of our democracy? I don't think so. To me, informing the public is a sacred responsibility, one that news organizations have a duty to perform with absolute integrity. When entertaining viewers with soft or sensational stories becomes more important than reporting the truth, when winning higher ratings matters more than vigorously challenging a popular administration's dangerous new policies, I think we as a society have something to worry about. And when an administration can defy a judge's show-cause order to defend its barring of the press from court proceedings, as the Bush administration has done, with nary a peep from the major news organizations, our basic freedoms are under assault—from government and from unscrupulous media executives.

Rather than being the watchdogs, the cable news networks and the news divisions of the broadcast networks have become lapdogs that program their so-called newscasts to infotain the audience. We are all the victims of this collusion. The ability of all Americans, all viewers, to make informed decisions suffers.

Yes, my respect for the power and importance of the press is profound and abiding. And it is also deeply personal. In 1961, when I was just five years old, my father became the first American executed by firing squad by Fidel Castro's dictatorship. He was accused of counterrevolutionary activities, but his worst crime was simply being a U.S. citizen. When his truncated trial was over, he had the blood drained from his body to be used in transfusions for revolutionaries. The media was barred from the proceedings, a fact that has always haunted me. Would Castro's government have been able to railroad my father that way if the press had been reporting on the trial and sentence?

When I was a teenager, my mother finally let me read the letters my father wrote to us during the last month of his life, which was spent in a series of Cuban prisons. To me, his five-year-old daughter, he stuck to the basics: "Behave yourself and study hard." To my older brother, Gary, he wrote, "Always remember that honesty is one of our greatest virtues. With that as the firm base of our character we will never lack for respect from our friends and associates." Honesty seemed to me the soul of journalism, and being a reporter became my singular goal, a way to honor my father's memory and keep his spirit alive in me.

Over the years I was able to make two trips to Cuba as a journalist. After the first trip in 1978, I wrote a magazine article about my father's murder that so angered Fidel Castro that he refused to let me return for two decades. What I didn't know until my last trip in 1998 was that he also ordered my father's remains dug up and thrown away. It was not the first time he had ordered such a desecration, but these activities have never been reported in the Cuban media.

This is the truth of communism, of fascism, of any sort of extremist government that controls what people are permitted to know. This is the reality of countries whose governments have no respect for civil rights or for basic human decency. If Cuba had had a free and open press, the conviction, torture, and execution of Howard F. Anderson and nearly twenty thousand others would not have been possible. The power of a First Amendment that authorizes and, yes, encourages the media to play a watchdog role is a powerful check on totalitarianism. And it is the heartbeat of a healthy democracy, a strong manifestation of patriotism, American style.

At the Medill School of Journalism, I learned about the Canons of Journalism, originally published in 1922 by the American Society of Newspaper Editors. They lay out a journalist's basic responsibilities: informing the public, protecting freedom of the press, being fair and objective. They state that the public's right to know is the "overriding mission of the mass media . . . Journalists who use their professional status as representatives of the public for selfish or unworthy motives violate a high trust." An updated code of ethics, added nearly fifty years later by the Society of Professional Journalists, states that journalists should "seek news that serves the public interest despite the obstacles . . . Journalists and their employers should conduct their personal lives in a manner which protects them from conflict of interest, real or apparent. Their responsibilities to the public are paramount. That is the nature of their profession." Why is it important to adhere to these strict guidelines? Because journalism is fundamental to our way of life, and for it to fulfill that role it must be practiced to the highest standards. The First Amendment affords special protection to journalists precisely because a free press is the cornerstone of any truly democratic society.

During my twenty-seven years in journalism, most of which have been in broadcast news, I've seen a profession that was once filled with idealism and passion for truth sacrifice integrity for profits. I've seen television networks and news divisions that once put the public trust above an obsession for ratings abandon the highest standards of journalism. I can't just stand by silently while it happens, nor can I stand by as those accused of crimes are denied the public accounting that only a free press can provide.

I have been privileged to work alongside men and women who believe, as I do, that journalism is a sacred responsibility. So *News Flash* includes examples of amazing heroism and respect for journalistic ethics. But it also shines a light on their opposites—cowardice and sleaze—among news people and executives alike.

I have worked in more than 125 countries, been shot at and wounded; when the number of my friends and colleagues killed in the line of duty reached eleven, I stopped counting. They all died because they fully believed in informing the public—in the United States and around the world—in an unbiased and independent manner at all cost. They upheld the highest standards of journalism, not for personal or company gain, not because they held a political agenda, but because it was the right thing to do. They embodied the spirit of the First Amendment.

As my friend, colleague and CNN war correspondent Christiane Amanpour, said, "I have often wondered why I do it, why we do it. After a few seconds the answer used to come easily: because it's worth it, because it matters, because the world will care once they see our stories. Because if we, the storytellers, don't do this, then the bad people will win. We do it because we're committed, because we're believers."

I hope that *News Flash* will provoke debate about these critical issues. Yes, I *am* hung up on journalism. I understand journalism's critical role in a strong, thriving democracy. In fact, I revere it. I have written this book to fight for it.

April 2004   Bonnie M. Anderson
                                                Atlanta, Georgia

ACKNOWLEDGMENTS

From the moment I put on my rookie reporter hat I've been fortunate to have been surrounded by some of the finest journalists our profession has ever seen. I've learned from them all, but even more important, they influenced me deeply as I was forming my own set of ethics and professional standards that would guide me throughout my career. I am grateful to them all, from my two mentors, Guillermo Martinez and Don Browne, to the photographers, sound technicians, editors, and producers with whom I've been so privileged to work. Among those who have played a particularly important part in my life in recent years are Steven Springer, a truly remarkable journalist and friend, Richard Griffiths, Andy "Dirty" Segal, David Steck, and Linda Saether. These exceptional producers helped inspire me to become a better correspondent during our coverage of issues of critical importance to our country and our world. Additional heartfelt thanks go to Steven (and his wife, Kara) for all the time and advice he graciously gave me during this project.

I am also indebted to my agent, Helen Rees, who believed in me and knew there was an important story that needed to be told. Her persistence, care, and confidence in me opened the doors to a new world. Helen is, quite frankly, the first person you want on your side if your passion is to write. She introduced me to Sebastian Stuart, who zeroed in on my deep commitment to journalism and encouraged me to follow my heart. And Joan Mazmanian helped make it happen. Thank you all.

Johanna Vondeling, my spectacular and brilliant editor at Jossey-Bass, offered invaluable guidance throughout the process. Our shared reverence for a free press and its vital role in a healthy democracy fueled a dynamic and immensely satisfying working relationship. Johanna's insight, her broad knowledge of current events, and, frankly, virtually everything we discussed, are reflected on every page. She reminds me of the finest television producers I've worked with: she knows how to encourage writers to do even better than they, themselves, believe they are capable of doing. And she does it with grace and humor. A better editor one could not ask for. (My favorite quote of all is from Sir Winston Churchill: "Ending a sentence with a preposition is something up with which I will not put.") Sometimes we try to, though. David Horne, who fine-tuned the manuscript with precision and sensitivity also deserves my sincere thanks. He's exceptional.

I am also blessed to have wonderful friends who have stood by me through thick and thin, always believing in my dream. My dearest friend John Macone, who read early drafts of a much different and rougher version, encouraged me incessantly. Coming from a modern-day Renaissance man who is, by far, the best-read person of nonfiction I know, his confidence in me has been truly inspiring. My most sincere thanks also go to Kathleen Myler Drummond, Gail O'Neill, Joe Ashkouti, John Monroe, Al Lambert, Jane Olson, The Penas (Ismael, Susana, and Candela), Dr. Fred and Joyce Svendsen, Julie Shannon, Nancy Whisenhunt, Sue Keeney, Gretchen Byrd, Julie Tallman, and Martha Stephens—all of whom have shown me the meaning of true friendship. For Karen Lynn there will never be enough words. I also can't write a book about journalism without acknowledging the people who—when I was a mere teenager—had such an influence on me becoming a journalist: Connie Rossi, Bob and Pat Chatten, and Sue Rudeen Jarrett.

I also owe a debt to the following organizations: The Reporters Committee for Freedom of the Press, The Pew Research Center for the People and the Press, Nielsen Media Research, The Committee to Protect Journalists, The Radio-Television News Directors Association, The National Association of Black Journalists, The National Association of Hispanic Journalists, and The Asian-American Journalists Association.

Finally, my family, who certainly deserve a tremendous amount of credit: My mother, Dorothy, the most remarkable woman I've ever met, and my most-patient stepfather, Mac, have influenced me in many ways and provided me with opportunities—educational and otherwise—that have given me (sometimes much to their chagrin) a different outlook on life than most people. To my brothers, Gary and Marc, and their wives, Viki and Adela, my sister Lee and her husband, Larry, les quiero con todo mi corazon.

To all, I'm most grateful.

NEWS
FLASH

THE RISE OF
THE CORPORATE
NEWS NETWORKS

S NAPSHOTS OF THE STATE of television journalism:

- On February 2, 2004, CNN Headline News led its 11 PM news-cast with the twenty-six-hour-old story about Janet Jackson's exposed breast during the Super Bowl halftime show. The onscreen graphic titled the incident "First and b . . . oops." This was followed by an update on the breaking news story that ricin, a deadly toxin, had been found in the mailroom of the Senate majority leader, causing the evacuation of Senate office buildings and prompting increased surveillance at the Pentagon for poten-tial terrorist activity.

- At ABC News, CBS News, and NBC News, anchors routinely and intentionally delude their viewers into thinking that what they are seeing is live. For example, on Aug. 19, 2003, while filling in for Tom Brokaw on the *NBC Nightly News,* John Siegenthaler introduced (or "tossed to" as we say in the business) correspondent Mike Taibbi in Afghanistan. "Mike?" he said. Taibbi, seen on camera, began his report by acknowledging the New York anchor. "John, . . ." To the untrained eye, it looked like every other live shot viewers have seen. But it wasn't. It was taped. These kinds of reports are so common they even have their own names: "look lives" or "live on tape." Oxymorons if ever there were.

- At Miami's WSVN television station, reporter Rosh Lowe proudly proclaimed he was an infotainer.

- Before, during, and after the war in Iraq, anchors and correspondents of at least three television news organizations and dozens of local affiliates wore American flag pins on the air. They and countless others also referred to American troops as "our troops" and the war as "us against them." And a 2003 survey revealed that 70 percent of the people in the United States believe it is good when news organizations take "a strong pro-American point of view."

- On Sept. 12, 2003, ABC News anchor Peter Jennings began *World News Tonight* with back-to-back stories about the deaths of country singer Johnny Cash and actor John Ritter. From 1969 to 1971, *The Johnny Cash Show* ran on ABC. Disney, the company that owns ABC, also owned Ritter's television show. And, oh yeah, two more soldiers died in Iraq that same day. But the entertainment report came first.

- In New York, from Fox affiliate Channel 5, came this story from a news writer: "One day, when I was struggling to write a story, the copyeditor told me, 'Fox it up.' You don't need a translation of that. Fox it up."

- On March 27, 2003, during the Iraq war, the new executive producer of CNN anchor Paula Zahn's morning show exploded in the Atlanta control room during a live shot with White House correspondent John King. "Look at that!" he yelled, pointing at a graphic of Iraq that was on the screen. Then, as a senior staffer in the control room confirmed, the executive producer said, "Baghdad is spelled B-A-G-H-D-A-D—that's wrong, isn't it?" Silence. "No? Well, then I'm a fucking idiot!"

IN NEWS WE TRUST(ED)

How did television journalism get to a place where showing a singer's digitalized breast for the umpteenth time is considered more important than informing Americans that the U.S. Capitol was closed due to a toxin emergency, where senior-level producers don't need to be able to spell, where it's considered acceptable—even appropriate—to take sides while covering a war? How did we go from the days when journalists caught hell for raising an eyebrow while reporting a news story—possibly telegraphing their personal feelings—to a time when anchors who baldly express their political opinions are rewarded with higher ratings? At what point did these defenders of the public trust, these believers in truth, honesty, and the First Amendment, decide it was acceptable to fake live shots and fool the public?

Television journalism is at a critical stage in its history. It has the capacity to affect more people than any other medium, but this source of news is fast losing its credibility with viewers. More than half of the people polled by the Pew Research Center for the People and the Press completely or mostly agreed that the "people who decide what to put on TV news or in the newspaper are out of touch with people like me." Granted, "more than half" isn't exactly an overwhelming condemnation, but it should sound an alarm with news programmers. And the following survey results gathered by the Pew Research Center in mid-2003 are even more disturbing for the fate of serious journalism.

- Fifty-six percent of those surveyed believe news organizations "often report inaccurately."

- Sixty-two percent believe news organizations "try to cover up mistakes."

- Fifty-three percent believe news organizations "are politically biased."

- Seventy percent believe journalists are "influenced by the power-ful." This number has been increasing every year for nearly two decades.

- Fifty-eight percent believe that reporters at all news organizations "either frequently (22 percent) or occasionally (36 percent) make up news stories." (I am *not* making this up.)

The crisis of confidence in journalism, particularly television news, applies to all levels. "It used to be that there was a different perception about network correspondents, that they were a cut above. You could rely on what was being reported on ABC, CBS, or NBC," said Robert Wiener, who as executive producer for CNN in Baghdad during the Gulf War orchestrated the coverage that put CNN on the news map. "People now can no longer tell the difference between the networks, local (stations), cable. It's all one big mish-mash." Wiener recalled being in Somalia when one of NBC's *Dateline* stories had to be retracted because employees had faked crucial video. "I had some of my young puppies there who were laughing and gloating. I said 'don't gloat.' This will tar us with the same brush."

THE WAY WE WERE—AND RARELY ARE TODAY

If television journalism in this country had never amounted to much, had never played an important role in informing the public and maintaining this democracy, then today's realities might not be seen as so worrisome or even out of character for the profession. But that's not the case. Sure, there were hiccups and screwups along the way as this "new" medium grew and matured. But it has provided people with extraordinary access to information and breathtaking events around the planet and beyond.

We watched in awe—live and in real time—as human beings walked on the surface of the moon. We heard, again live, Martin Luther King Jr. eloquently tell the world about his dream. On November 22, 1963, we watched in shock when Walter Cronkite interrupted a soap opera to be the first to report that President Kennedy had been shot. Less than an hour later, he informed the nation that the President had died. And we saw him take off his glasses and wipe his own eyes. We were able to watch continuing coverage, which meant we knew the latest developments almost as soon as the newsmen did. Through television news, viewers saw the spectacular funeral procession, complete with Charles de Gaulle and other heads of state paying their respects, and had the opportunity to grieve together as a nation. And we also watched the truly stunning: Lee Harvey Oswald shot—live—on television. Reality TV writ large.

Then there are the images of Cronkite reporting from Vietnam in 1968, saying that the best Washington could hope for was a stalemate. And the pictures of President Lyndon Johnson watching Cronkite's reports, knowing that his support for the war was waning. "If I've lost Cronkite, then I've lost middle America," the President was quoted as saying. Television journalism was showing the public that the government didn't always tell the whole truth.

A nation was glued to television sets, a presidential election hanging in the balance, during the Iranian hostage crisis in 1979. Over the years we've seen wars in real time and shuttle disasters live. We've witnessed— as it took place—over one hundred people losing their lives in a fire at the Branch Davidian complex in Waco, Texas. And, more recently, we've had a front-row seat in the impeachment hearings for another president and we saw American military crewmen who were captured by the Chinese boarding a plane to go home—all live. We've watched in horror, from our homes and offices, as the World Trade Center buildings collapsed before our eyes. And for agonizing days and weeks, we saw search-and-rescue people continue to comb through the rubble, looking first for survivors and then simply for bodies. Two years later, we saw what had once seemed unimaginable: Army doctors and medics examining a shaggy Saddam Hussein's head for lice while providing him with the quality of medical care few if any of his prisoners ever received.

These last examples are some of the shining moments of television journalism in recent times. But they are exceptions to the daily rule, the daily fare. To borrow a beer commercial's line, television news today generally looks good, but it's less filling. Reese Schonfeld, CNN's first president, said the following words specifically about CNN, but they apply across the television network news world: CNN, he said, "has become worldwide and skin-deep . . . Its coverage splashes over everything and saturates nothing."

Once *news* was the star; now the stars are the stars. And what's worse, the stars are often the news. And more and more on-air journalists are collecting multimillion dollar paychecks and being treated like celebrities rather than as journalists. It is little wonder that our moral and ethical compasses have a tough time finding true north.

NEWS PROFIT

At the heart of the problem is what drives corporate America today: money. Lots of it. For the corporations that own the major television news organizations, journalism has become exclusively a bottom-line business. When the increasingly rare example of good solid journalism is seen on television screens these days, you can be sure it is the work of nearly extinct professional newsmen and newswomen fighting the good fight for a free, responsible press against all odds.

For decades, the broadcast network news divisions were money losers on a large scale. According to author Barbara Matusow, NBC lost $12 million in 1962 while CBS lost $5 million "but nobody seemed to worry about going over budget. News employees were deliberately insulated from the more mercenary aspects of broadcasting—demographics, cost-per-thousand, share points, profits, et cetera," Matusow wrote. Still, network news chiefs (unlike their corporate counterparts) wore the red ink like badges of honor. They were serving the public in a selfless manner. That news programs also fulfilled the networks' licensing obligations to provide public service programming didn't hurt either. But more than anything, journalists who lived through the early days recall a sense of honor, a sense of pride that they were serving the public in an honorable way that kept democracy strong and vibrant.

Author James Fallows, who has written extensively on the media, blames the increasing popularity in the early 1970s of the CBS News program *60 Minutes* for changing television news forever. Why? The program made money. And to make money, CBS News made its correspondents into stars and sandwiched hard-hitting investigative pieces with profiles of celebrities and happenings in the world of entertainment. The sad irony now is that *60 Minutes,* which for the most part has remained true to its original format and style, is now considered one of the straightest, most professional news programs, if not the premier one, on the air today. The night of Sept. 3, 2003, at the annual news Emmy Awards, *60 Minutes* producer Don Hewitt and all past and president correspondents of the program were honored with lifetime achievement awards from the National Academy of Television Arts and Sciences.

It is as though life, indeed, imitates art. In the 1987 movie *Broadcast News,* television news producer Jane Craig, played by Holly Hunter, chews out reporter-anchor Tom Grunick, played by William Hurt, for faking emotion when the camera turns to him for a reaction shot during an interview. "(By) working up tears for a news piece cutaway, you totally crossed the line . . ." she yells. "It's not hard to cross," he interrupts, "They keep moving the little sucker, don't they?" Indeed, they—we—do. CBS's *60 Minutes* was one of the first, if not the first, to cross that "little sucker." But over the years the line moved faster toward infotainment, cutting professional corners, lowering standards, and ignoring once-inviolable ethics along the way. Despite where it started, *60 Minutes* is now nearly alone on the ethical side of "the little sucker."

By the mid-1970s, news was making money for all of the networks. Quoting *Variety,* author Matusow wrote that "news rose from 'a 15 percent loss position in 1972' to contribute one percent of the profits for the three networks in 1975 and 1976." When the business world saw that news could actually make money and not just spend it, which everyone knew it did exceptionally well, the die was cast. The drive for profit was furthered across the network news world by the purchase of the broadcast networks by non-news entities in rapid, almost dizzying succession. In 1985, General Electric bought NBC. A year later, Capital Cities Corporation purchased ABC and created Cap Cities-ABC. That same year, Lawrence Tisch and Loews grabbed a 25 percent stake in CBS. In 1995, Westinghouse Electric bought CBS while Disney was busy taking over Cap Cities-ABC. The next year, Time Warner merged with Turner Broadcasting, the parent company of the CNN News Group. In 1999, Viacom bought CBS. In 2001, AOL took over Time Warner. By the time you've read this, they may have all changed hands once again.

"One of our responsibilities is to keep these entities economically viable," Andrew Heyward, the president of CBS News, told a convention of Hispanic journalists in 2003. "We're way past the time as I said before where news was a loss leader to kind of placate the public. It's a businesslike part of the enterprise. We're not held necessarily to the same profit margin that a radio station might be, but we have to make a buck."

Exactly how much they're earning, however, is often difficult to pinpoint. First, the parent corporations don't report separate numbers for their news divisions. Additionally, different allocation strategies come into play as the corporations try to zero out their overhead by having news divisions pick up certain costs such as payroll and legal services. According to author Ken Auletta, who spent a few months "embedded" at the Fox News Channel, network officials put their 2002 revenue at $325 million, with profits at $70 million. At CNN, he reported, revenues rose above a billion dollars that same year, with that news network's profits at about $250 million. CNBC earned profits in the neighborhood of $300 million. Tom Wolzien, a former network executive, is the senior media analyst for Sanford C. Bernstein & Co., LLP, a Wall Street research and investment management company. His knowledge of the media industry and his estimates of revenues and profits are well regarded by many people in and out of the business. Wolzien believes CNN's profits have averaged between $100 million and $200 million, and perhaps as high as $250 million at some point. As for the broadcast networks, he says their moneymaking news shows are the prime-time magazine programs such as *Dateline, 20/20,* or *60 Minutes.* Wolzien estimates that the broadcast news divisions can earn as much as $100 million a year each, with CBS News making the least and NBC News making the most because of its partnership with Microsoft.

News can definitely be a profitable business, but it will always be *so much more* than that. It is a critical pillar of democracy, a public service.

We're not just selling airplane engines or tickets to movie theaters. We are providing a fundamental benefit that keeps the public informed and arms citizens with vital information needed to make decisions that directly affect the lives of people in this country. As journalists, it is our civic duty, our social responsibility to protect this institution. By no means is it unpatriotic to make money in the news business. But the value of a free media should never be measured in terms of dollars earned or in ratings achieved, although both can coexist with public service. Neither dollars nor ratings are ways to judge the health and value of journalism or of our society. Big news profits don't mean responsible news. And huge ratings are no guarantee that the news programming is fair and balanced—or that a particular news organization is assured of being profitable in the future. "Our parent companies and corporations are raking in the profits," said CNN's chief international correspondent Christiane Amanpour. "But let me now lay down this challenge: What is the point of having all this money and this fancy new technology and being able to go anywhere and broadcast everywhere if we are simply going to drive ourselves and our news operations into the ground? It really makes you wonder about megamergers. Yes, you are running businesses, and yes, we understand and accept that. But surely there must be a level beyond which profit from news is simply indecent."

That level, that point, is when the drive for profit forces ethical backsliding or cutbacks that compromise the quality of the content. It is when corporate bean counters demand lower costs and higher profits, even if that means sacrificing the integrity of news and the role an honest, thorough media plays in a democracy. And it is precisely the level we have reached today.

THE COST OF MAKING MONEY

To please corporate owners, all of the networks have been suffering the same fate to various degrees over the past two decades or so. Repeated cutbacks in staff. Belt tightening across the board. Early on, the broadcast networks simply closed most, if not all, of their news offices in Africa.

They and CNN have since also shut down or severely trimmed other international bureaus as well as domestic news offices. This has given rise to greater dependence on news agencies and affiliates whose professional standards might not match those of the networks. The "financial imperatives" have also resulted in cutting professional corners, adding entertainment to news, and getting rid of older correspondents in favor of younger, more attractive ones. If to achieve higher ratings also means going after the majority of viewers, who are white, by hiring white anchors and correspondents, that's considered just good business. And if easing pro-Bush politics into the newscasts appeals to more conservative viewers, why not? The single aim was, and is, this: attracting more viewers, preferably younger or more affluent ones, to the news programs for longer periods of time. That translates into higher advertising rates and more revenue. And that makes shareholders happy. So who really cares if the people delivering the news went from the likes of Edward R. Murrow and Walter Cronkite to unseasoned fluffball reporters stumbling over themselves to put on army fatigues, helmets, and gas masks in hopes that they might be launched into "stardom?" Certainly not the broadcast news divisions and cable news networks. They've learned that if they make stars, the stars make *them* more money. But there's a catch. To keep the high-paid stars they've made, all of the broadcast news divisions and cable news networks have been forced to cut back even further on news-gathering costs.

But make no mistake: when huge news breaks, the networks do spend money. Tons of it. In these situations, the aim is to "own" the big story so that people who normally watch another network or newscast turn to yours for the duration of the story and hopefully longer. So news divisions and networks blast out of the news gate paying whatever it costs to chalk up big coverage wins early on. But there's no free lunch, not even if your network did own the story and won huge ratings for the coverage. Before the end of the year, the networks will try to get back on budget by cutting expenses any way they can. There were months at a time at CNN, for example, when travel was extremely restricted. Rather than send correspondents and camera crews to cover stories, the network depended on local affiliate stations to send their material to Atlanta. The issue became truly laughable when the Travel Unit, which put together weekly travel shows and reports, wasn't allowed to spend money on air-fares, hotels, or per diems for at least a quarter of a year. The program anchors did all of their on-camera work in the Atlanta area; if the story was about waterfront vacation destinations, they'd use the Chattahoochee River as a backdrop. (While I'd never make light of the serious conse-quences to journalism, some of the cutbacks that have stemmed from the corporate buyouts and mergers had a particularly harsh impact on one staff. Tom Lubart, a colleague formerly employed at ABC News, relates how employees at the network's New York headquarters first realized the extent of the cutbacks. "ABC in the '80s wasn't the plushest place to work, but the bathrooms had very decent toilet paper," said Lubart. "Not long after Cap Cities took it over, the quality of the toilet paper changed for the worst in the employee bathrooms. The executive bathrooms still had the good stuff. After Disney took over, *everyone* had the lower-quality toi-let paper.")

Across town, the *NBC Nightly News* program nearly went *into* the toilet when executives there gave serious thought to canceling their flag-ship newscast. Joe Angotti, a former NBC senior vice president, is pub-licly sharing this story for the first time. In early 1987, Angotti filled in for NBC News president Larry Grossman at a high-level executive meet-ing called by Bob Wright, the new president and chief executive officer of the company. "Bob Wright raised all these questions to these people about things that should be continued and things that should be dropped. He raised the issue of professional football contracts. Is it worth our money to pay these outrageous rights fees when we don't make much money?" Angotti recalls Wright asking. "Should we drop *Nightly News?* Wouldn't we make more money if we turned that time over to the local stations?"

Shortly after that meeting, senior news executives Bob McFarland and Tom Roth launched an investigation into what the cost implications were of dropping *NBC Nightly News.* "Only a few of us knew this was going on. It was very secret," said Angotti. "And what they determined was there would be no financial gain to NBC to drop the *Nightly News,* because whatever you made up on the local station side in terms of giving that time back to the station, you'd lose having to keep resources that were now divided between *The Today Show* and *Nightly News*. And if that happened, *The Today Show* would have to absorb the costs all by themselves. So they decided it wasn't worth it."

What was never on Wright's table for consideration then was the concept of news being a public trust, a sacred responsibility, a key player and watchdog in a healthy democracy. "I think it took a long time for General Electric to understand that the news division of NBC was more than just a profit center, that the news division was a public service, and when we would raise that question to GE people, their response would be, 'Why is that a bigger public service than making airplane engines? People put public trust in our airplane engines. If they fail, people die. No one dies if you don't have a good news show,'" Angotti recalled, adding that the journalists in the room were stunned. "Our argument was that the basis of our government is to have this estate that keeps government honest and keeps people honest and serves a very important function in society. And that the First Amendment is hallowed ground."

Angotti says he believes Bob Wright and the other corporate leaders of General Electric now understand that. "During 9/11 they knew they were going to lose a whole lot of money, and they did, and they had to subsidize that loss. And General Electric did subsidize that loss because they realized it was a public responsibility to put on that coverage that didn't bring in revenue. And that was an honorable commitment that they made." (My firsthand experience following 9/11 at CNN was a little different. There I was present at executive meetings during which there were discussions on how soon the network could resume running commercials without angering viewers who might then turn off CNN and affect ratings, which would then lower earnings. The bottom line of these conversations was—the bottom line.)

Whether or not that specific NBC News decision was an honorable one, veteran NBC News correspondent George Lewis, who has been with the network since 1969, has seen the definite shift in priorities. "The old paradigm was that we were part of the public service of broadcasting," he said. "The new paradigm is that we're part of the profitmaking machinery. Being a news person used to be a calling. Now it's a business."

CORPORATE SYNERGY

Another part of the fallout from megacorporations owning networks and news divisions is equally disturbing. In the executive suites, it's called "synergy." In the newsrooms, it's "cross pollination." Cross pollination is an attempt to save money while getting cross promotion by having the separate entities within the corporation work together on projects. After Time Warner took over Turner Broadcasting, CNN launched programs such as *CNN and Time* and *CNN and Fortune.* The idea was to use some of Time Warner's other staff members in CNN programming and to share resources and reporting. It never really worked. Magazines work quite differently from twenty-four-hour cable news networks, and so do the reporters. Few of the print correspondents were able to make the transition successfully.

At NBC, the synergy is a clear attempt to add entertainment to programs produced by the news division. *The Today Show,* which admittedly isn't the newsiest show around, does come under the NBC News umbrella—allowing executives to justify having Katie Couric, a former news reporter, and Matt Lauer, who had no previous news experience, interview world leaders and major newsmakers. Both, frankly, do a good job for the most part. But now, on an almost weekly basis, Pat O'Brien and Billy Bush contribute stories about celebrities and the world of entertainment to *The Today Show.* O'Brien and Bush work for the *Access Hollywood* show, which is also produced by NBC News. O'Brien's 2003 interview with Jennifer Lopez and Ben Affleck was given an entire hour of *Dateline.*

And as Gail Pennington noted in the St. Louis Post-Dispatch, Julie Chen of CBS's *The Early Show* appears on the CBS entertainment program *Big Brother* three times a week. But this pales by comparison with CBS's efforts to get the first exclusive interview with former Iraq POW Jessica Lynch. "A CBS executive wrote to Lynch seeking an exclusive interview (a so-called 'get') for CBS News by suggesting, among other things, a made-for-TV movie, a book deal and a concert," Pennington reported. "The various components of the offer would have encompassed both CBS and the network's siblings in the Viacom family, including MTV."

Another example occurred after Disney bought Cap Cities-ABC. A huge controversy erupted in the ABC newsroom and among journalists elsewhere over millennium coverage planned for the ABC network that included Leonardo di Caprio interviewing President Clinton. An actor interviewed the president of the most powerful country on Earth, when dozens—probably hundreds—of well-trained journalists armed with tough, substantive questions had been turned down by the White House for interviews.

The influence of Hollywood and the world of entertainment was even more obvious after America Online bought Time Warner, which had eaten up Turner Broadcasting a couple of years earlier. Within months, the top people at Turner Broadcasting, the parent company of the CNN networks, were replaced by men who were responsible for creating much of the world of entertainment known today—men with huge accomplishments, but whose resumes were not necessarily respected in the news world.

Among them: Jamie Kellner, who became chairman and chief executive officer of Turner Broadcasting System, Inc. For seven years, he had been president of the Orion Entertainment Group. Before that, he triumphed at Viacom Enterprises. In 1993, he formed The WB Network in a joint venture with Warner Brothers, the Tribune Company, and himself. His deputy was Garth Ancier, a former president of NBC Entertainment, who also helped launch the Fox network and develop The WB with Kellner. Among his television coups was creating the Ricki Lake talk show, supervising production for shows such as *Cheers, The Cosby Show, Family Ties,* and *Golden Girls,* and helping to develop *The Simpsons, Married . . . with Children, In Living Color, Buffy the Vampire Slayer, Dawson's Creek, 7th Heaven, Felicity,* and *The Magical World of Disney.* But not a single news show. To complicate matters from a news network's point of view, Ancier was also a consultant to the Democratic National Committee for the presidential nomination in 1991 and 1992. And that's just CNN. At Fox News, Roger Ailes is chairman of the board, CEO, and president of the Fox News Network. He is also a Republican operative who was a media consultant for Richard Nixon in 1968, Ronald Reagan in 1984, and George H. W. Bush in 1988. And he continues to offer advice to the current resident of the White House.

INFOTAINMENT, CELEBRITY, AND SEX

Just take a look at what you see on cable and broadcast news programs and decide for yourself whether the people at the top (news executives and corporate officers) have changed not only how news is reported but also the definition of what *is* news. And while this might be more subtle, the ranking of news stories—which is more important, which should be told first—has also been affected. For example, the deaths of entertainers such as Bob Hope, Johnny Cash, and John Ritter were reported not only first in the evening broadcasts but also in stories lasting several minutes, while the deaths of American soldiers in Iraq and deadly monsoons in North Korea were given a fraction of the attention. "I am not alone in feeling really depressed about the state of news today," Christiane Amanpour said. "A veteran BBC reporter and a friend of mine, with supreme British understatement, said, 'News is heading down a rather curious corridor.'"

Indeed it is. But if the intrusion of entertainment into news is considered an epidemic, the infection started long ago and has taken years to become truly threatening. And I've played my own part in this. In the early 1980s, as an NBC News correspondent, I was diverted from a serious news story about Florida's citrus crops being threatened by Mediterranean fruit flies to camp out in front of a family home in central Florida. The object of our interest? A woman whose stage name was Koo Stark, who by some descriptions was called an actress-model, by others an erotic film actress. NBC News cared for one reason: she was Britain's Prince Andrew's latest fling, and any news about British royalty, especially salacious information, attracts viewers. Every other network had crews there, too, and we were all equally mortified. This was not the type of reporting we ever expected to be doing. These stories were best left to non-news programs such as *Entertainment Tonight* or *Inside Edition,* where theoretically they wouldn't be confused with real journalism. But the Prince Andrew-Koo Stark coverage simply foreshadowed the changes in news to come. Years later, when I was a national correspondent for CNN, I was dispatched to chase ice skater Tonya Harding around after it was known she was responsible for having rival Nancy Kerrigan whacked in the knee. The press corps had a joke concerning Connie Chung: it was said that she followed Harding so closely that when the skater stopped abruptly, Connie broke her nose. The truth is that the rest of us did, too, though we hated to admit it.

There have been many more of these entertainment-pseudo-news stories over the years, and since 1995 they have all been measured by the O. J. Simpson meter. From January to September of that year, all of the networks obsessed over this story. CNN, still the leading twenty-four-hour news network at the time, prided itself on gavel-to-gavel coverage of the court proceedings. As a correspondent, I did my best to hide every time the bosses in Atlanta were looking for reinforcements in Los Angeles. But I, all the other non-O. J. correspondents at all news networks, and especially the American public paid a price for this coverage. It was nearly impossible to get any other news on the air.

The Monica Lewinsky scandal was the same and more. But what happened at the beginning of this story is truly a chapter of shame for the American television media. The U.S. networks and well over a hundred local affiliates had spent millions and millions of dollars to send thousands of journalists to Cuba to cover a most historic moment: Pope John Paul II's visit to the Communist island. To give you an idea of just how much coverage was planned, the major networks chartered a huge ship to carry equipment from the United States to Cuba. CNN, alone, sent nearly a hundred people and spent over $1.2 million on the coverage. And it made sense. There are more than sixty million Roman Catholics in the United States, far more than in any other religion. And this pope in particular had touched many hearts in this nation.

I could compare what I saw in Havana that January of 1998 only to the extensive coverage afforded political conventions. News organizations literally took over hotels, with entire floors dedicated to makeshift newsrooms, with satellite dishes on rooftops and backyards, trucks of equipment lining the streets, and cables strung up the sides of buildings. When the pope arrived, we all broadcast live that amazing image of the pontiff, who had suffered so much under communism, greeting Fidel Castro, the last of his breed in this hemisphere. Television networks and local stations began running the taped stories they had spent months preparing for this visit. Though Pope John Paul II wagged his finger at Fidel Castro, warning him to change his ways, he also asked the United States to abandon its embargo of the island. It was an amazing moment.

Then came news that a former White House intern named Monica Lewinsky was claiming she had had an affair with President Bill Clinton. Within hours, Peter Jennings, Dan Rather, Tom Brokaw, Ted Koppel, and nearly every major local anchor who had traveled to Havana had packed their bags and were headed home. Never mind that the networks had more than enough people in Washington to cover a scandal that was just beginning. It's important to remember that on the day the story broke, it had not been confirmed, it was not known that the president had lied, and as far as anyone knew it was not a story. That didn't matter. This was news that would galvanize viewers. What it was, and why the networks abandoned Cuba, was a story about sex in the White House. Sex, simply put, sells. Television news executives determined that sex was a bigger audience draw than the pope in Cuba.

And it's still that way, perhaps more than ever. On August 20, 2003, while respected CNN business correspondent Rhonda Schaffler was giving a live update from the floor of the New York Stock Exchange, the Atlanta control room added music to her report. Her update was on the release of a new male impotence drug, Levitra, which the manufacturers were hoping would lure some of Viagra's market share. The music being played in the background of her report was Frank Sinatra singing "Making Whoopee." Schaffler was clearly not anticipating this and made a few comments about the music, clearly hinting to the control room that it was inappropriate, but managed to finish her report with grace. The infusion of entertainment values into news, says George Lewis, is damaging the image of journalism and journalists. "Because we are more competitive now for eyeballs and dollars, we are seen as more crass and less of a public service as we used to be."

THE COLORS OF PATRIOTISM: RED, WHITE, BLUE, AND GREEN

The past few years have seen the rise of yet another worrisome trend that is counter to the tenets of professional and responsible journalism: a new and different definition of what is considered patriotic in the media. In their wisdom, the writers of the First Amendment sought to endow a free press with the duty and responsibility of being government watchdogs. No elected official or political party should be given preference; all should be monitored with the same critical eye. Whether reporting on Nixon and Watergate or Clinton and Lewinsky, the media's role is to shine a light on darkness and inform the people. For journalists or news organizations to truly be patriotic, they must place the news itself on center stage, not the reporters. The coverage must be fair and give all sides equal voice. The only motive of the reports should be to inform viewers so that they can weigh their opinion and their response in a responsible manner. But in recent years, patriotism in the media has come to mean reporters and anchors taking sides with an administration, wearing American flags on air, and crafting newscasts and talk shows to promote a particular political position. A survey by the Pew Research Center confirms these disturbing realities:

- Seventy-seven percent of Fox viewers, 74 percent of CNN viewers, and 72 percent of the broadcast network news viewers say "it is good that news organizations take a pro-American point of view."
- Just over half believe the news agencies "stand up for America."
- Forty-six percent say the news agencies are "too critical of America."
- Nearly half believe it is good for journalists to share their strong political opinions.

Whether the Fox News Channel anticipated these latest trends or took—and is taking—a large role in creating and perpetuating them is a debate being waged in many newsrooms across the country. But either way, what is exceptionally clear is that Fox is directly programming its newscasts to appeal to this large, conservative segment of the population. And it has paid off handsomely for the new network. In early 2002, Fox overtook CNN in average daily viewership numbers and continues to lead the cable news war. According to Nielsen Media Research figures for the time period between September 2002 and July 2003, Fox averaged 1,092,000 daily viewers while CNN pulled in 758,000. MSNBC was third with 369,000 daily viewers, while CNBC came in a distant fourth with 198,000. And the day Saddam Hussein was captured in December of 2003, Fox overwhelmed its competitors with 2.32 million viewers.

B IS FOR BIAS AND FOR BIGGER AUDIENCE

The success of Fox has resulted in a fight—particularly at CNN and MSNBC—for the typical Fox viewer, at the expense of truly "fair and bal-anced" reporting. "This is very worrisome," said Lewis of NBC News. Speaking of news trends in general, he added, "If we try to adopt a bias in hopes of attracting a particular segment of the audience, that's not good journalism. I think copying them is not a good idea, and I don't think it's going to succeed in the long run."

MSNBC learned that lesson the hard way. In an extreme effort to lure conservative viewers, the cable network hired right-wing talk show host Michael Savage, who was well known for gay bashing. In July of 2003, he lived up to his reputation. When a caller identified himself as a sodomite, Savage responded with, "Oh, you're one of the sodomites. You should only get AIDS and die, you pig." The exchange was widely reported, and Savage was summarily fired. But no one in the executive suites took responsibility for hiring him. "A lot of us said, 'Why did you hire him in the first place?'" said an NBC staffer who asked not to be named for fear of retribution. "You knew that would happen." Why? Because MSNBC, the lowest-rated cable news network, was trying to out-Fox Fox. "They're so desperate to attract an audience to MSNBC and they don't have a vision to do that. So they try to play the Fox game and they fall flat on their ass trying to do it. They don't have a clue how to program that damn cable network so they try to imitate Fox and they do it badly and everyone else is scratching their heads about that."

It is an uphill battle for all of the other networks, Angotti agrees. "Fox has two things going for it," he said. "It has a political agenda that many people find attractive, and it has an entertainment value that many people find attractive. And the other networks have neither. You have Fox on a roll, and it will continue on a roll. Fox had a plan and Fox had a strategy. CNN has been all over the place. MSNBC has been all over the place."

Perhaps the only place the networks and news divisions haven't gone back to is their roots, back to doing television journalism the old-fashioned way: news that is truly fair and balanced with no political agenda; news that viewers want to know and need to know; news that is relevant to all sectors of the public, not just to a specific group. I am convinced that such reporting would draw viewers from across the spectrum—old and young, people of different races and religions, conservatives and liberals, men and women.

While the corporate honchos might not understand this, the journalists do, and in many cases they agree with the public's perception of their work. According to another Pew Research Center survey, of a cross section of journalists from reporters to executives, "lack of credibility is the single issue most often cited by the news media as the most important problem facing journalism today." The survey included local and national broadcast, cable, print, Internet, and radio media. These professional reporters also admitted, the Pew survey shows, that their news stories contain frequent factual errors that are the result of sloppy reporting. As a result, the journalists acknowledge that "lack of trust is a leading cause of declining news audiences."

Other findings include the following:

- A majority of journalists believe that bottom-line pressure hurts the quality of coverage.
- TV news journalists "are more likely than their counterparts in print to cite quality issues as journalism's top problem and to say that in order to attract new audiences, the news media crosses the line between entertainment and news."

- A majority of journalists concede they're out of touch with the public, and they blame themselves for the declining audiences.

- Two-thirds of journalists nationwide believe their news organizations have been pushed toward infotainment in an attempt to attract more viewers or readers.

- "About half of journalists and media executives say that in reporting on the personal and ethical behavior of public figures, news organizations often drive the controversies rather than merely report the facts."

- But only 38 percent of journalists in national news believe they are reaching a proper balance between what people want to know and what it is important for them to know.

The survey also highlights the dangers facing honest, unbiased, straightforward news coverage as a result of corporate buyouts of news organizations. News staffs, the people on the front line, "see more than twice as much corporate influence over news content [as] executives do." As a result, more than a third (37 percent) of those questioned admitted they sometimes avoid covering stories they believe are newsworthy. Why? Thirty percent say they "got signals from their bosses," a quarter avoided stories because they believed their bosses would disapprove, and nearly one in five simply decided on their own not to cover the story.

NBC's George Lewis, however, believes that journalists must share the blame for what has happened to television news. "The drive for profits and the drive for ratings is certainly driven by management, but we've all gone along with it. Oftentimes there's too much sloppiness and laziness in the way we news people do our jobs. We have to share the blame when things are reported wrong."

These are alarming statistics that reveal the immense power—real or perceived—of the megacorporations that own the news organizations and how that power has led to huge ethical lapses among journalists and their bosses. And the future is potentially even dimmer. In June of 2003, the Republican-controlled Federal Communications Commission (FCC) voted 3 to 2 to make it easier for corporations to buy even more news outlets, even in the same market. Congress, journalist associations, and lobbyists on all sides joined the heated and prolonged debate, but it wasn't until November that a compromise was reached between Congress and the White House. The FCC and the White House wanted to permit a single company to own stations that could reach up to 45 percent of the viewing audience, an increase from 35 percent. Opponents argued that that would give networks too much control over local programming and would provide fewer independent voices for the public. The compromise raised the percentage to 39 percent, which among other things permits News Corporation, the owner of the Fox News Channel, and Viacom, the owner of CBS, to keep all of their current stations. Had the 35 percent figure been maintained, both organizations would have been forced to reduce the number of stations they own. It was not the big win the corporations wanted, but it gave them legal access to more viewers and more control over broadcast content than ever before. The fact that more than half of the U.S. population opposed further consolidation of the news media was not a factor in this business decision.

It's all about money, a desperate attempt to hang on to the huge profits news had earned over the years. And that is far more important to the corporations than the people's right to know, even more important than a healthy democracy. "It's an example of companies trying anything to find a solution to the declining news audience," Joe Angotti explains. "And there is no solution because the declining audience is a result of fragmentation, the result [of the fact] that there are all these different outlets for news, and advertising dollars are going to all these different places rather than to what was once just the three networks. Fragmentation has reduced income for virtually all television news outlets in the country. As a result of that, people are looking for solutions." Solutions that so far have come at the expense of responsible journalism.

On-air correspondents and anchors are, indeed, part of the problem. They've colluded with management, both at the company and corporate level. But the "talent," as they're called, have very little actual clout within a news organization, and as the Pew survey shows, many on-air journalists are also disturbed about the fate of television news. The people with the real power, the real authority, are the news and corporate executives who set the priorities of a news organization and decide its direction and course. How long will they be permitted to exploit this public trust before journalism's foot soldiers and news consumers join forces to demand the return of a responsible, honorable television media? I don't know. But the institution of a free press is far too important to our country's very existence and to our way of life for any of us—citizens all—to cave in to big business, or to big politics.

As my colleague Christiane Amanpour said, "We, I believe, are in the fight of our lives to save this profession which we love. I believe we can do it, and I believe we can win this battle."

We must.

WHAT YOU DON'T KNOW CAN HURT YOU

C NN'S JUDY WOODRUFF is an exceptional journalist who has paid her dues, earned her stripes, and won respect through hard work. Her list of accomplishments is astounding. This formidable female journalist has covered every presidential campaign and convention since 1976, and was a White House correspondent for NBC News, a correspondent for the *MacNeil/Lehrer NewsHour,* and anchor of PBS's *Frontline.* For CNN, as the network's main female anchor for a decade, Woodruff has been on the main news set for virtually every major news story. In addition, her colleagues and many others have honored her with nearly every award a journalist can win.

For years, Woodruff has also hosted the weekday program *Inside Politics,* CNN's premier news program about the people, the issues, and the controversies in Washington government. Although its average ratings have never been extraordinary, *Inside Politics* is must-see-TV in the White House and on Capitol Hill. A great deal of the program's credibility is due to Woodruff. Her broad slate of sources and knowledge of what happens behind the scenes inside the beltway are legendary in the business. She has served the American public well.

In 2003, network executives assigned younger and less experienced anchor Paula Zahn to take over many of Woodruff's duties. The leaders of Turner Broadcasting at the time, men whose entire experience was in the world of entertainment, wanted to hire "younger and more attractive" anchors and to jazz up newscasts with what they thought would be more entertaining programming. Eventually, *Inside Politics* was cut from an hour-long program to a half hour, and Woodruff was assigned to also appear regularly, as a coanchor, on an afternoon newscast named *Live From . . .* (a few months later, *Inside Politics* went back to an hour and Woodruff was no longer on *Live From . . .*).

On July 1, 2003, this hard-news journalist who had made her reputation grilling elected officials was assigned to interview Sally Field during the *Live From . . .* program. Why? Field was playing a congresswoman in the recently released movie *Legally Blonde 2,* with Reese Witherspoon. It pained me to watch this accomplished political journalist interview an actress about what it was like to *play* a congresswoman.

> Woodruff: "Sally Field, thank you for talking with us. You are playing in *Legally Blonde 2* a congresswoman. . . ."
> Field: ". . .[M]y character is not necessarily a good guy, and my character has got to play the game a certain way in Washington to stay in Washington, you know? She has to raise money and she has to appease certain people. And it's something we've heard about, and so basically, she trades off everything she believes in just to stay there."
> Woodruff: "Well, a lot of that—a lot of that sounds realistic, not all of it but a lot of it . . ."

Woodruff then asks what the movie's message is for women in this country.

Field: ". . . Reese felt really strongly about sending a message to young women and little girls, even, and ones that are a long ways from voting to close to voting, to say start getting involved, start reading, start knowing what your government is about. And participate, and participate now, and vote, read up and vote . . ."

Was this entertaining for viewers? Yes, most likely it was. Was this news? No. And to schedule one of the nation's top political journalists to interview an actress about a movie was simply irresponsible. Who else could Woodruff have interviewed that day to help explain what Congress or the president planned for Iraq? For the record deficit? For social security? For rising health care coverage? What news and information did viewers *not* get as a result of this interview? This was infotainment in its most obvious form. Sally Field's name would attract viewers. More viewers mean higher ratings. Higher ratings mean more advertising dollars.

The Field interview, though, wasn't the end of the silliness. Noting the incredible success that Oprah Winfrey was having with her book club, CNN decided to launch a regular feature called *Judy's Page Turners*. Again, this is on *Live From . . .*, the new program intended to lure younger and more affluent viewers, precisely what advertisers are willing to pay more for. Most of the people Woodruff interviewed had some connection with the world of politics, although some of those ties were a bit questionable. Among the authors she has interviewed and publicized is Walter Isaacson, CNN's recently departed chairman. He wrote a book about Benjamin Franklin, which was the tenuous link to political coverage for Woodruff. Isaacson is also a former editor of *Time* magazine, which ran a cover story about Isaacson's book when it was published. *Time* and CNN, it so happens, are both owned by Time Warner. Another choice for *Judy's Page Turners* was a book by Margaret Carlson. Carlson was not only *Time* magazine's first woman columnist, she is also a frequent panelist on *Inside Politics*.

Infotainment. Corporate cross promotion. And it is all disguised as news. Surely there is real news somewhere in the country, or in the world, that viewers should know about. Instead, producers and programming executives apparently believe that interviewing actresses and reviewing books is putting that airtime to better use. With the networks driven by the bottom line, programmers are interested in just one thing: attracting as many viewers as possible. So when they are deciding on which new entertainment shows to put on next fall, the decisions are based on what these media executives think the public wants to see. If that means hooking an audience with technical magic or smoke and mirrors, that's fine. I have little quarrel with this strategy when it is applied solely to sitcoms, dramas, or anything that is clearly meant to be entertainment. In that context, it is relatively harmless to give viewers what they want. But over the past decade or so, the same decision-making process has been increasingly applied to newscasts and news networks. That's where the problems lie. The responsibility of a free press in a democracy is not only to give people what they want, but also to give them what they need to know. It won't always be popular, but it is vital that people know what is happening in the world around them.

HOCUS POCUS, FOCUS GROUPS, AND CONSULTANTS

The downward spiral into infotainment has been one result of the battle for viewers, particularly at a time when Americans have so many news choices. Ignoring the crucial role an honest and professional media have in a democracy is another. "In a very real sense, virtually everything is driven by ratings, and ratings by money," said Joe Angotti, a former NBC senior vice president. "I don't think there are many instances anymore where at a television editorial meeting someone would stand up and say 'this may lose us viewers, this may turn people off, but it's an important story and we've got to do it.' I don't think that is happening anymore. The impact is that the public suffers. The impact is that we're giving people what they want and not what they need. Television news is not as interested as it once was in making a difference in people's lives."

Instead, television news is about making money in any way possible. And to do so, networks and local television stations have increasingly turned to the so-called expertise of consultants, who use polls and focus groups to identify what the majority of the public supposedly will or will not tune in to see. One company of nationally known and often-used viewer consultants, for example, tells news programmers that Asian men are a huge turn-off to the majority of the viewing public. Hence, there are no Asian men in prominent anchor positions nationally. "Think of how much more of a contribution we could make to this great society if we weren't so dependent on what I call those hocus-pocus-focus awful groups who tell us what people are not interested in," CNN correspondent Christiane Amanpour said, as an appeal, to a large group of news executives. "They tell us that Americans don't care about serious news, Americans don't care about this presidential election, Americans don't care about foreign news, Americans don't care about anything except contemplating their own navels. That's what they tell us." And that should have nothing to do with the role of good journalism in a democracy. "No matter what the hocus-pocus focus groups tell you," Amanpour added, "time has proven that all the gimmicks and all the cheap journalism can only carry us so far."

One result of the "gimmicks" and the "cheap journalism" designed to infotain viewers rather than inform them is the dumbing down of the viewing public. One thing viewers in this country weren't informed about—because it was deemed to be news they didn't want to hear— was news that might have better prepared them to predict and understand the events of 9/11. "Instead of informing the public more on international issues, the media let down the public," said Robert Wiener, a veteran network news producer with extensive experience in the Middle East. "The media did not serve the public well leading up to 9/11, which is why 9/11 came as such a shock to the American public. They really had no idea of the animosity that existed in much of the Islamic world toward the United States and, consequently, Americans tend to view themselves as the good guys. There was this feeling of why do people hate us? To some extent, if there hadn't been a cutback because of budgetary reasons and those polls that say Americans don't give a damn about international news, I think Americans would have been able to put 9/11 into a different context and would not necessarily accept at face value the buckets of bullshit the White House and Pentagon continue to spew out to this day."

Angotti, who once produced *NBC Nightly News,* says U.S. history would have been very different if the media had listened to consultants rather than follow their professional consciences forty years ago. "I shudder to think about what would have happened if there were consultants back during the civil rights coverage, when we got calls saying NBC News are 'nigger lovers' and 'we'll never watch this network again.' Consultants would have said ease off, you're making people uncomfortable, don't do these stories. And that's the unfortunate thing happening in all news media, because [news]people are avoiding stories that make people uncomfortable because they don't want to lose viewers and readers. That's not good for democracy."

TECHNOLOGY AS AN INFOTAINMENT TOOL

There is little question that new technology has given journalists the ability to inform the public in a faster, better, and more thorough way. But that ability also means that technology can be abused and misused in ways that clearly have negative consequences for the viewer. The obsession with electronic gimmicks goes far beyond CNN and other networks aping Fox, with its swooshes of sound and fast, snappy graphics. Making news more compelling to watch by using these techniques isn't necessarily a bad thing. The point is to inform the public. And if people tune in as a result of such gimmicks, then producers have done their jobs—as long as these techniques don't take away from the substance of the news or the time used to report it.

But some, perhaps many, news organizations and the journalists who work for them can be blinded by the technology and the access it provides to the public. They can turn around videotape—which means feeding the material from the camera to the satellite to the network—in seconds, not hours. They have the capability of going live from just about anywhere at any time. That must be a positive development, no? It depends. In some stories, the live pictures virtually speak for themselves, and the reporter should shut up and let viewers hear the sounds that go along with the pictures. (All too often, reporters simply narrate the obvious: "There is smoke billowing from the building.") But many other stories require more context and perspective, additional information or facts that are not readily or quickly obtainable. So all too often, the live report is superficial, lacking the depth needed to truly inform and make it relevant to viewers. Yes, we can show you this one battle, this one tiny slice of the story, but we can't tell you what it means for the overall war. During the 2003 war in Iraq, for example, the American public was overwhelmed by network and local TV live shots from the war zone. But what did these reports say? What did they mean? Few reporters knew, and as a result, few viewers were enlightened. Technology does not guarantee content and substance.

"One cannot fault Brokaw, Jennings, Rather or the others for at times tossing to the embedded reporters in desperation to hear anything new, but they should (and do) know better than to expect any truly astounding news," Peter Shaplen, a television news veteran and one-time Walter Cronkite desk assistant, wrote in an Internet blog. "They can look sincere, concerned, puzzled and reflective until their crows feet grow deeper and become more embedded on their own faces, but the handoffs to the satellite-phone equipped field reporter is likely to garner very little that is 'news.'"

The gratuitous use of technology is particularly endemic with twenty-four-hour news outlets. During a major breaking news story, the correspondent is literally tethered to a live microphone and camera nonstop in order to satisfy the news appetite of the programs that follow one after the other. As a result, the reporter has no time or way to report, to interview people on the scene, to make phone calls, to gather information, to even get close to the action. So are they serving the public—and democracy—by simply repeating the same information in different ways? No. But what matters to newscast producers is that they have a live report from the scene in *their* newscast. And few willingly give that up to cut the correspondent loose to do some actual reporting. "The press has abrogated its responsibility to be editors, rather preferring to become facilitators," wrote

Shaplen. "Unable or unwilling to edit and shape the reporting, they are content to use technology to let it flow into our living room."

Technology, in a very real sense, is overwhelming journalists' ability to do the job correctly. Quite often there's no time for thought, for weighing the information, for confirming it or finding balance to the issues before having to go on the air. Add the heated competition among networks to this reality and it's a recipe for disaster, for major mistakes. The Florida fiasco the night of the 2000 presidential election is a case in point. When Voter News Service (jointly funded by the Associated Press and the major broadcast and cable news networks as a cost-saving measure) provided erroneous exit poll information that Al Gore had taken the state, all of the anchors rushed to air trying to be the first with the news. No one took the time to evaluate or analyze the information, to confirm it or debunk it. No one took into account that polls were still open in the Florida panhandle, or that VNS could not reliably estimate absentee ballots. There were live reports from campaign headquarters and conclusions drawn by analysts. The networks further compounded the debacle by retracting the projection, later calling George W. Bush the winner, and finally retracting that projection, too, when it became evident the race was too close to call. It was not until about 4 AM the next day that these television news organizations actually took that step back and acknowledged that they truly didn't know who had won. Both the information fed into the computer system and the computer system itself were faulty. It was not just lousy, embarrassing, knee-jerk-reaction television journalism, it was irresponsible reporting from beginning to end. And hanging chads aside, there are some who believe that reporting a winner before citizens had finished voting in the state might have affected the outcome. Democracy was not well served.

As Edward R. Murrow, one of the CBS News pioneers, once reportedly said, technology should be used, not abused. But given the predicted "improvements" in technology, it appears his advice will continue to be ignored. David Westin, the president of ABC News, told a convention of journalists in 2003 that digital technology is leading to "fundamental transformations" in news gathering and reporting. "If it works well and we do it smart then it will enable editorial people to be able to get their reporting to the air more efficiently without as many people touching it and changing it and editing it along the way," Weston said. "And it will allow them to express themselves and do better work faster. And get it to air. I think it can be freeing, in a sense, for many editorial people." It could also have the absolute reverse impact and deny reporters the ability to think, consider, and weigh information before airing it. At a 2003 convention of television news directors, a company began touting software it was writing that would allow reporters to produce, edit, encode, and transmit video from just about any laptop computer. Now the reporter will be able to be producer, editor, and television engineer—while still—supposedly—carrying out his or her own editorial duties. Viewers will be wowed. But will they be truly informed? Unless professional behavior changes, it is not likely.

KEYS TO SUCCESSFUL (INFOTAINING) STORY SELECTION

Few people would deny that the death of John F. Kennedy Jr. was big news. Yes, he was a president's son and a so-called "American prince" whose picture appeared often in the tabloids. But the comprehensive, nonstop, play-by-play coverage of the search and rescue operation after his plane crash, the recovery of the plane's occupants, the church services, and the mourning—with live shots from every conceivable angle and site (including reaction from around the world), was more than just excessive. It was obscene. It was morbid infotainment that played on the emotions of viewers. And people watched in large numbers, which is why network executives continued to fuel the viewing fire. Newsmagazines such as *Dateline, 20/20,* and *60 Minutes* each spent nearly eight hours on the topic.

The cable networks went even more overboard. At CNN, for example, this was the biggest hike in ratings the network had seen in many months, and they weren't about to let sensitive, reasonable journalism get in the way. As the *Washington Post's* television critic Howard Kurtz wrote, "No sooner had the shock of last weekend's plane crash worn off [then]

the public was inundated by hype, blunders, death music and all manner
of blabbermouths—few of whom knew Kennedy well—filling the great
gaping maw of airtime on CNN, MSNBC, and Fox News Channel. With
ratings up six- and seven-fold, there was no penalty for being maudlin.
Over blurry, long-range shots of a Navy destroyer, correspondents mused
about the 'ocean's embrace,' and how Kennedy and his wife 'are now
together for eternity,' and 'how much can this family take?' But how
much can viewers take? Are we entering a new era of celebrity deaths?"

Yes, apparently we are. All of the networks were giving the public what
it wanted. In fact, 80 percent of the people polled by the Pew Research
Center for the People and the Press acknowledged that they had paid
attention to the coverage, with 54 percent saying they followed it "very
closely." The level of interest in this story was similar to that in the death
of Princess Diana. "It ranks as one of the most closely followed news stories of recent years, and only second in 1999 to interest in news about
the school shootings in Littleton, Colorado, which was followed very
closely by 68 percent of the public," the center concluded. At the same
time, though, a majority of viewers said the importance of the story didn't
justify the amount of coverage. "By a 55 percent-29 percent majority,
people say the news media covered it as much as they did because it was
an interesting story that would attract big audiences, rather than because
it was big news that people needed to know," according to the Pew report.

But they still tuned in, and that's what matters to the bottom line.
Extensive coverage of the death of a famous person—whether the death is
accidental or not—is always a winner. So is the death of young, pretty
women—especially if they're Caucasian and spend time with famous people. If not, being pregnant at the time one is murdered is enough reason
for exhaustive nationwide coverage. The final clincher is if these events happen at a slow news time. To many people, this might sound cold and calculating. It is. How else can we explain the over-the-top television coverage
of the O. J. Simpson trial, the murder of Laci Peterson, and the cases involving Chandra Levy, Kobe Bryant, and Michael Jackson? "We're operating in
a world where entertainment is so popular, and in television news, uniquely,
you're competing against entertainment shows," said Barbara Cochran, the

president of the Radio-Television News Directors Association, the largest organization of broadcasters in the country. "So I think the struggle to keep from applying entertainment values to news is always ongoing. There are some wins and there are some misses." Among the misses? "The big story or the trivial story that gets wall-to-wall coverage. The sensational story that doesn't have a lot of relevance to people, but there's a celebrity involved. What you have to hope is that even though there might be a lot of public interest in stories like that, that journalists are still doing the meat and potatoes, the investigative work, that they're still being the watchdogs."

In 2003, *Larry King Live,* one of CNN's top programs in the ratings, alone devoted much, and in many cases all, of at least forty-seven one-hour shows to the Laci Peterson murder and the prosecution of her husband, Scott. After Kobe Bryant was arrested on rape charges in July 2003, there were eight shows about him. There were also eight *Larry King Live* programs about Michael Jackson's arrest, and that story didn't break until November 18, 2003. And this program has not been alone. There is no telling how many hundreds of hours, or more, have been dedicated to these stories on other CNN shows and at other television news organizations. I don't for a moment suggest that Peterson's murder was not horrible, that the rape charges against Bryant and the molestation charges against Jackson don't merit coverage. But I do question why these stories have received so much attention in all the media. Neither Laci nor Scott was famous before. And there were certainly many, many other ghastly murders committed during 2003 that deserved some coverage. But for ratings-hungry networks and programs, this story was different: Laci Peterson was young, pretty, and pregnant. And at the *Larry King Live* show, for one, well-placed sources there say the decision to dedicate so many hours to the story has been easy: Laci Peterson programs routinely get higher ratings than even most of the celebrity interviews. Infotainment leads to higher ratings, which leads to higher advertising rates, which adds to the bottom line.

Just imagine how hundreds of hours of responsible, thorough reporting could have helped inform viewers about issues that affect them directly, allowing them—in many cases—to make wise decisions about how to vote, how to prepare for retirement, how to care for their family's health, how to survive financially during an economic downturn. And let's remember one other point that might offer some context to how irresponsible it is to devote so much time to such stories: In 2001, the United States went to war in Afghanistan and in 2003 in Iraq. And American troops continued to be killed throughout the rest of the year and well into 2004 in Iraq on a near-daily basis. Where are the news priorities?

NEWS ACTORS, BIMBOS, AND BUNNIES

As with the chicken and the egg, I'm not sure which came first: infotainment programmed as news, or the people who get into the profession to report or anchor infotainment "news." I can't in good conscience call them journalists. Instead, I use the words "news actors," because their conduct suggests they're utterly indifferent to the responsibilities journalists have in a democracy—and most couldn't care less. In general, news actors are not motivated by the public's right to know. Their reasons are more personal. As anchor Aaron Altman (who was played by Albert Brooks) said wryly about journalists in the remarkably realistic 1987 movie *Broadcast News*, "Let's never forget, we're the real story, not them."

In 2000, I strongly suggested to a journalism student at a university I was visiting that she seek another profession, such as acting, instead. I was at the school to speak to a few journalism classes and, as CNN's recruiter, to interview candidates for the network's entry-level positions. Aside from the fact that this young woman came to the interview looking and smelling like someone who'd do well employed professionally at a men's late night club, she made a fatal mistake when I asked her why she wanted to become a journalist.

"Well, I like being the center of attention," she purred. "I want to be a celebrity and make a lot of money."

I took a deep breath and tried to impress upon her the more important reasons. The right reasons include wanting to inform people in a fair and balanced manner so that they can make up their own minds on any and all issues. The right reasons embrace a deep-seated belief in the First Amendment and the commitment to the ideal that all people, everywhere, deserve and need a free press, and that without it, free and open debate—the cornerstone of representative government—is impossible. The right reasons include the fact that what we do is not about us, it is about the news—the people and the events we document and report about. I told her that our mission was to shine light on darkness, to focus international attention on a myriad of issues and problems. As a result of well-done journalism, people the world over have enjoyed freedoms and civil rights and, on occasion, have been educated enough to make major changes in governments.

I can't honestly say I saw her eyes light up with understanding. In fact, I'm quite certain that what I said either went over her head or through it, leaving little residual knowledge behind. "So does this mean I don't have a chance at CNN?" she asked. Yes, that's what it meant. (For then, at least.) Journalism, especially television news, is in dire need of professionals dedicated to gathering and delivering news to the public for less narcissistic reasons.

Over the past few years we've seen another trend develop that is dangerous both to democracy and to people's lives. It is TV news stations and networks dispatching pretty or handsome inexperienced young things to war zones with no training whatsoever. This practice is dangerous to them and to the people they are working with because one mistake, one bad call made innocently but in ignorance can mean death. The appeal of war reporting is obvious: it is now seen as a shortcut to earning one's stripes, to respect from the pubic, to celebrity and financial success. "Reputations are made in war zones," said Robert Wiener, who has more experience covering wars on more continents than most soldiers. "A lot of us made our bones in war zones, in Vietnam, in conflicts around the world." True, but most true veteran war journalists eased into this type of coverage, learning weaponry and tactics—guerrilla and conventional—from books and research, and from more-experienced war journalists, before actually putting themselves and their crews in the line of fire. "Now we send people willy-nilly on a plane to cover an event when they don't know the difference between a tank and an armored personnel carrier, couldn't tell the difference between a major and a colonel. They haven't done their homework, they haven't studied. They are TV bunnies."

TV bunnies who are forevermore known, thanks to their week or two in the Persian Gulf region, as brave, tested "war correspondents," regardless of whether they actually asked any tough questions or reported anything of value. They were in fatigues and looked good. Unfortunately, these are the so-called journalists the public is becoming accustomed to when they turn on their television sets to watch a newscast. These imposters not only ridicule the profession and weaken its credibility, they also dilute the importance a serious free media has in a democracy. The television reporters and anchors are not onscreen to entertain or to look good; they are there to serve the public in a vital, important manner.

POLITICAL CORRECTNESS EQUALS VIEWERS

The TV war bunnies, though, may be responsible in part for an increasing number of Americans who believe the media is patriotic, and that being patriotic means protecting democracy by supporting the current administration. A majority (51 percent) of people surveyed in 2003 by the Pew Research Center for the People and the Press say the media "stand up for America," compared with a third (33 percent) who believe news organizations are "too critical." Four years earlier, another survey conducted by the same center showed these numbers to be almost even: 42 percent said the media stood up for America while 41 percent felt the media was overly critical. The number of people surveyed in 2003 who believe news organizations "protect democracy" (52 percent) closely mirror the "stand up for America" statistics. Only 28 percent said the media "hurt democracy." In 1999, the numbers were 45 percent (protect) and 38 (hurt.) To nonjournalists, these changes in public opinion might seem to be developments that should please members of the news media. Instead, they concern many of us. Our responsibility is not to "stand up for America" if that means towing an administration's line. My idea of "protecting democracy," which is shared by scores of my professional colleagues, is to be the watchdog of government and elected officials, to ask

the tough questions regardless of whether the answers might reveal mistakes or improprieties, or might otherwise embarrass the political leadership. We are not cheerleaders for any party, group, or ideology. When the
numbers shift so radically in such a short period of time, when they are
less even, there is reason for concern. The efforts by some television news
organizations to go after the Fox News Channel's viewers by copying that
network's "U.S.A. right or wrong" coverage slant are, no doubt, also
responsible for some of this shifting of public perception. "It wasn't just
the conservatives who wanted it. It was the country," said Angotti.
"Support our troops. Don't ask questions, tough questions of the administration, don't ask how long it's going to take. When the other networks
saw the success Fox was having, they started imitating Fox and started
asking fewer tough questions. It was a bad trend happening in television
journalism because ratings were driving the editorial direction of coverage. It was not what the public needed, but it was what they wanted."

COMING UP AT ELEVEN, THE SAME THING—ON ALL STATIONS

As discussed in Chapter One, the effort by the Federal Communications
Commission (FCC) to allow megacorporations to own even more news
outlets in the same market clears the way to further consolidation
among fewer owners. And that means fewer choices for news consumers. But equally troubling is the concern that if these corporations
are already using infotainment to attract viewers to the outlets they now
own, they most likely would employ this same strategy to any additional
news companies they take over. "It's best for news when there's a diversity of voices in the marketplace," said veteran NBC News correspondent George Lewis. "And when you get fewer and fewer players, that
undermines the quality of the news, of the product. The product suffers." Having fewer independent watchdogs and fewer voices does not
bode well for the democratic concept of an informed public. When we
all start hearing the same entertaining information from what is ultimately the same handful of corporations, the reliability of that "news"

must be questioned. The companies clearly have a financial motive behind offering infotainment to the public, but are they also driven by ideological or political considerations? Without multiple news outlets, how is the public to know?

Infotainment may attract viewers for the short term. But it does not provide them with fair, balanced, and responsible information. It is not beneficial for democracy, and, as the next chapter shows, it is also a short-sighted business strategy that could threaten the corporations' bottom lines in the long run.

THIS IS GOOD BUSINESS?

Consider the following:

- Through the 1990s to the present, the percentage of minorities in on-air television news roles—as anchors, correspondents, experts, and even as subjects of news stories—has remained virtually the same. Given the tight competition for viewers, why are television news outlets ignoring demographic realities in this country and failing to serve more than seventy-five million people?

- According to media analysts, the broadcast news divisions can earn up to $100 million in profit in a good year and far less in a bad one. Given the series of cutbacks over the past decade, does paying just *four* of the big names at ABC News a combined total of more than $35 million make good business sense?

- To bring down costs, CNN laid off more than four hundred news employees in early 2001. But by mid-year, the network was spending $15 to $20 million to build a street-side studio on the ground floor of the corporate headquarters, the Time-Life building in midtown Manhattan. Why? Because every other morning show had a street-side studio in New York. Has this enormous expenditure paid off in higher ratings, higher revenue? No. Not yet.

Here's one of the sad ironies in today's news business: many of the steps news organizations are taking to cut costs, boost profits, and target and attract larger audiences are likely to backfire, causing even greater financial difficulties in the future. To produce profits, corporate executives are demanding cutbacks in news-gathering and news-programming costs. At the same time, they're insisting that news divisions and networks do whatever they can to attract a larger audience, even if that means using entertainment values and lower standards to hook viewers. The aim is to make news or infotainment cheaper to produce while targeting the largest chunk of potential viewers.

Still, the three broadcast news divisions have seen drastic drops in ratings for the early evening newscasts over the past ten years: ABC News, from 13 million viewers to 9.7 million; CBS News, from 11.6 million to 8.1; NBC News, from 11.6 million to 10.4 million. For cable news networks such as Fox and CNN, the strategy has increased ratings; CNN has come out of its ratings gutter, although it is still a long way from where it once was and is still being soundly beaten by Fox. But even at the cable networks, these so-called solutions do not ensure a growing audience in the long run; instead, they will drive news viewers away while threatening the integrity of television journalism. And equally as important, the corporate approach to cost-cutting and viewer targeting ignores important demographic realities by failing to serve large segments of the population. The interests and concerns of minorities are rarely reflected in coverage, in part because minorities are barely represented on news staffs. In short, these strategies are not only bad for journalism, they're also bad for diversity and bad for business.

"H. L. Mencken once said that no one would ever go broke underestimating the American people, but that's not true. It's in fact just the opposite," said CNN correspondent Christiane Amanpour. "What Americans don't care much about is the piffle we put on TV these days. What they don't care about is boring, irrelevant, badly told stories. And what they really hate is the presumption that they're too stupid to know the difference. And that's why, I think, they are voting with their off switch, which means that not only are we not giving them quality, because we think it costs too much and they don't want it and all the rest of it, but pandering to what we think they want is simply bad business. And not only that, we alienate our core constituency, too."

CUTTING COSTS—AND CREDIBILITY

Over the past two decades and even more so recently, every network news division and cable news network has closed down news bureaus in the United States and around the globe. While they steadfastly maintain that they still have the resources to cover news anywhere in the world, what they're not saying is *which* stories, *how* they're covered, and *who* is actually covering them. As for the *which,* most television news organizations are indeed airing reports about major news events around the world. But when it comes to international news, that's about it. How often do we see stories from the Middle East that aren't about bombings, deaths, destruction, wars, or the like? What about from Africa? Yes, these horrendous stories should be covered, but these aren't the only things going on in these regions. Not by a long shot. Such narrowly focused reporting lacks context and does not provide accurate portrayals of the lives of people in many, many countries.

Who is covering the stories and *how* they're covered, however, is even more disturbing. Increasingly, news organizations are going to outside sources for their news material, information, and video. It is far cheaper, because the networks don't have to pay travel costs, huge salaries, or benefits of any kind. Although the information obtained this way is less reliable, money rules. The two most common practices are to use stringers or television news agencies. Stringers are freelance reporters and photographers who generally live in the region where news is happening. For example, when CNN en Español was launched in 1997, this Spanish-language network seen in Latin America had only eight or nine staff correspondents, and that number has dipped to as low as six on occasion. To cover the world, more than one hundred stringers are routinely used, resulting in huge cost savings for the network. The stringers get paid by the story and, given that, it is in their interest to hype the importance of a particular story. While some stringers are exceptionally reliable and professional, most do not operate under the same professional or ethical guidelines as do staff journalists.

The other frequently used outside sources for material are the television news agencies—the video equivalent of companies such as the Associated Press. Clients, such as CNN or the broadcast news divisions, contract for their services and have the option of using any of the material that is sent daily either as a complete, fully edited story or in "raw" form. Raw material is generally two to four minutes of roughly edited video, with some soundbites (audio quotes) added. The news organizations buying this material have no control over what was shot, who was interviewed, or even whether the different sides to the story are truly reflected in the tape fed by satellite. The people responsible for shooting the material may send some written data via a wire service, but often the client has to rely on the print counterpart of the news agency for the latest information, as collected by that person on the ground. The raw material is handed over to a staff reporter or correspondent for him or her to put together an "in-house" package, a taped story done from what would be thousands of miles away.

In 1992, CBS News correspondent Martha Teichner, based in the network's London bureau, was already lamenting the beginning of this cost-cutting trend. "I was asked to do [the] Somalia [story] for the weekend news and I've never been to Somalia and I'm thinking, 'Oh my God, what am I gonna do?' I get every bit of research I can find, but even if I'm correct and accurate, I'm superficial. And I don't want to be superficial." When correspondents are simply voicing over material shot and reported by someone else somewhere else, superficiality is inevitable. The reporting part of the process, the actual news gathering, is critical if the final product is to be thorough, fair, and balanced. Oftentimes, correspondents will conduct numerous interviews on and off camera for one story but only use a couple of soundbites in the report. That, however, doesn't mean the other interviews were worthless or a waste of time. Quite the contrary. They often serve to confirm facts and positions on an issue, as well as provide background information and context. When a correspondent is denied the benefit of this process, he or she is on very shaky ground. The reporter is ethically and professionally responsible for all facets of a news story that ends with the reporter's name, the "sig out" (for example, "Jane Doe, NBC News, Kuwait"). Yet with news agency material, the correspondent can't independently confirm the veracity of the information or whether the video is fair and representative of the issue. "You can't say you believe in the importance of reporters—people who can go out and find a story and understand it—and then say, 'Look, it doesn't matter that you're not out there.' It matters," said Paul Friedman, then–executive producer of ABC's *World News Tonight*. But with news organizations trying to stretch their budgets, the use of video agencies and stringers is more common today than ever before. And that threatens journalism and the business of journalism. "I am concerned, on a very basic level, about news departments closing down, news gathering being turned into news packaging, and that the really basic function of journalists to go out and gather information and go out and write a story based on your original research is being compromised," said Barbara Cochran, president of the Radio-Television News Directors Association.

In a way, by outsourcing services news organizations are merely following a trend seen in other businesses. But unlike a company that sells widgets, news organizations should be held to a much higher standard of excellence. Unfortunately, quality control is virtually impossible when news organizations accept and then air independently reported news stories by people who may not be subject to the same rigorous fact-checking that staff correspondents go through as a matter of course. "When you do that [outsource], it lends itself to manipulation and error," said Tom

Wolzien, a former network executive and currently a senior media analyst for Sanford C. Bernstein & Co., a Wall Street research and investment
management firm. "There are far fewer cases now where the companies
have their own people on the scene. There's a giant river of video running
around the world, and news organizations take a ladle and dip out of the
news river instead of sending their own people. So did what you're seeing really happen? Or perhaps was it skewed? There's no telling."

At the network level, particularly among the cable news outlets, cutbacks have also resulted in traditional newscasts being ignored in favor of
talk shows such as CNN's *Crossfire* and many of the programs on
MSNBC. "Talk is by far the cheapest thing to do," said Wolzien. "So it's
easy to have people with polarized points of view yelling back and forth,
and you develop an artificial sense of excitement, which some people find
interesting. This isn't anything that resembles journalism. It becomes a
continual op-ed page. It's a very cheap format. So you wind up going to
pontificators and secondary sources rather than doing the work yourself,
because that costs money."

"In terms of immediate breaking news, talk gives you the appearance
of being live, and you can be responsive and you don't have to repeat the
story over and over. That makes talk a commodity that seems to be able
to hold an audience," said Cochran. "I think the most dangerous thing
about talk is to see it as a substitute for news, and that people might con-
fuse what they hear on a talk show with news reporting. That's bad." That
confusion leads to even more blurring of the lines between news and talk
and infotainment, which in the end can cause viewers searching for news
to tune out.

At local television news stations, cutbacks in news coverage are even
more dangerous to the bottom line. "What a good local TV station has
to offer is news and local sports. That's where its local audience comes
from and its claim to fame," said Wolzien, who estimates that local stations earn 40 percent of their profit from news. "So if you start cutting
there, it becomes short-sighted."

Barbara Cochran agrees, although she estimates that local newscasts
bring in 50 percent of a station's profit. "That's why a station needs to

protect the integrity of the product. The profits will not come if the news product suffers." And there will be no local news if a station goes under.

In the early 1990s, when some local television stations began emphasizing crime, sex, and violence, they did see success in the ratings and, as a result, in earnings. Their profits spurred other stations to follow suit, to toss out solid, measured newscasts and replace them with urgent, fast-paced programs that used close-ups of victims and shaky, off-the-shoulder photography to give viewers the illusion of being on the scene. But over time that approach to news has worn thin. Even some of the daytime talk shows that captured the nation's attention when they first began concentrating on sex and violence have seen a steep drop-off in the ratings. According to a Pew Research Center survey, the percentage of the American public that watched programs such as *The Ricki Lake Show* or *The Jerry Springer Show* went from 10 percent in April of 1996 to 5 percent in June of 2002.

It may take a while, but people who want solid, informative, and balanced news coverage eventually differentiate between empty talk and newscasts, and between superficial taped stories and solid on-the-ground reporting. And when they do, the companies that cut corners while cutting costs are the losers.

"Good journalism, good television, can make our world a better place," Amanpour echoes. "And I really believe good journalism is good business."

DOWN WITH SUBSTANCE, UP WITH SALARIES AND SUCH

It used to be that news was the star, the driving force behind any news machine. Most of the budget went to news gathering, not to the news gatherers. Sure, it was nice to have a snazzy studio, but priorities were priorities. However, news priorities—and how budgets are spent—have changed dramatically. Over the years, the broadcast news divisions and the cable news networks have spent more and more money on anchor and correspondent salaries. At CNN, for example, executives in 2001 began paying a couple of news stars salaries higher than any that had ever before been paid at that network. Ted Turner's dream of personalities never eclipsing the news died.

Like anyone else, I sure like making a big salary. And yes, I do understand how many viewers tune in specifically to see certain news anchors they believe and trust. And if more people watch, ratings go up along with advertising revenue. This is simple television economics. But at what point does this become bad business? And more important, at what point does it result in worse journalism? I believe we passed both points a long, long time ago.

Given the severe cutbacks in network and local news gathering, how can the salaries of some of the news stars be justified from a journalistic or good business point of view? According to numerous published reports and several private sources, here are the approximate annual salaries of some well-known news people:

ABC News

Peter Jennings:	$10–11 million
Barbara Walters:	$9–10 million
Diane Sawyer:	$8 million
Sam Donaldson:	$8 million

CBS News

Dan Rather:	$7 million
Mike Wallace:	$9 million

CNN

Lou Dobbs:	$4 million
Aaron Brown:	$2 million
Paula Zahn:	$2 million

NBC News

Tom Brokaw:	$7–8 million
Katie Couric:	$12–15 million
Brian Williams:	$5 million
Stone Phillips:	$6 million

Compare these salaries with the highest salaries paid to on-air people in the twenty-five largest local television markets in the United States, according to a 2003 survey conducted by the Radio-Television News Directors Association. (Some of the largest stations refused to complete the survey, so these numbers are most likely low.)

News anchor: $262,000

News reporter: $214,000

Weather anchor: $200,000

Sports anchor: $160,000

Even if these salaries were doubled to adjust for large markets that didn't complete the survey, the difference between the high network salaries and the high local television salaries is clear. What is also evident is that paying network stars so much more at the expense of news gathering is not only bad business, it's also threatening good journalism. As salaries go up, there is less independent, on-the-ground reporting being done in this country and internationally.

IF THE MAJORITY OF VIEWERS ARE WHITE . . .

In 1995, Nan Robertson—a Pulitzer Prize–winning former reporter for the *New York Times*—wrote these words referring to the history of the newspaper business: "Journalism was overwhelmingly male, overwhelmingly macho, overwhelmingly drinkers, smokers, f———s, all of these things. Women lost by it, blacks lost by it, gays lost by it, everybody lost by it, because it did not reflect the diversity of this country." There is no question these words also apply to the television news business. But not only do women and minorities lose when the country's diversity is not reflected in the on-air talent, in the executive suites, and when it comes to story selection and what is presented to the public, the business of television news loses, too. While a diverse staff that reflects the consumers that are served is, in theory, considered a smart business strategy, the national news companies and local television stations—much like many other corporations—are run primarily by white men, some of whom have no clue

about minority newsmakers and, in some cases, news reporters. But unlike
the business of other corporations, news is a public trust, a responsibility
to serve all people in this country. Maintaining the integrity of this institution, ensuring that it is responsive to and reflective of the citizenry, is
paramount. The news organizations keep going after one another's slices
of the news viewership pie, sometimes the more conservative part, sometimes the younger portion, and sometimes the wealthier segment. But it
is still the same narrow-demographic pie. With more and more news operations in existence, this is not a long-term strategy that promises financial
success. A lot of lip service has been paid to the concept of diversity in
the news business, and there have been some very misguided—and sometimes potentially illegal—attempts to accomplish it. But overall, its imple-
mentation has failed miserably. And ignoring demographic realities in
this country is simply bad business that could lead to financial doom.

At work here is the fundamental belief that any good reporter can
cover any story no matter what. A good reporter will get the facts right,
will understand the issues on at least a basic level, and will inform the
public in a responsible manner. But diversity among news gatherers also
brings greater depth and nuance to the story being covered. If I have been
assigned a story concerning a topic I'm not very familiar with, I'm going
to seek information and context from people who are. I'll speak with our
on-staff Hindu reporter about Hindu burial rituals or with our Mexican
executive producer for a story about Cinco de Mayo (and learn it is not
a holiday in Mexico). My colleagues will share names and numbers of fascinating people with different points of view whom I can interview, people I may not have thought of before, as my Rolodex contained the names
of only one or two people who are always interviewed on the subject. I'll
learn about and be more sensitive to these issues, and I'll have more
sources who can speak on more topics. Viewers will see a greater variety of
perspectives on air, not just that of the reporter but also those of the people the reporter now can choose to interview. The stories will be more relevant to all. It is a win-win situation.

Also important, though, is that viewers will see people who look like
them reporting about all sorts of issues, not just pigeonholed into cover-

ing their own "kind." (This is a potential hazard, especially when the story involves specific knowledge such as language skills. For example, my first big job was at the *Miami Herald*'s Spanish-language newspaper, *El Miami Herald.* When editors on the English side recognized my abilities, they then assigned me to cover Hialeah, which had the largest population of Cuban-Americans in South Florida at the time. From there I was hired to cover Latin America for NBC News. I'm still grateful for these opportunities, but I know all of these jobs were offered to me because of my background and because I speak Spanish. To ensure I wasn't being pigeon-holed, I then volunteered for war duty in the Middle East.)

The bottom line is that diversity is smart. Still, various surveys show no appreciable difference in the percentage of minorities in on-air television news jobs over the past ten years. Diversity is not simply a question of quotas, but numbers and percentages are a way to keep track of progress or lack of it. If, for example, a minority group made up 12 percent of the population but only 6 percent of the on-air (or executive) positions at the news company, and this was a pattern that had seen little upward fluctuation over years, then it would be clear that that group was underrepresented. That possibility might explain why the network news divisions and cable companies refuse to release such information to the public. When questioned directly by minority journalists, the presidents of the broadcast news networks offered these explanations to justify keeping the numbers secret: "To make it just about the numbers can be deceiving," said Neil Shapiro, president of NBC News. Andrew Heyward, the president of CBS News, said, "I do think that the numbers game can be problematic in that it suggests that by hitting a certain quota somehow things are all right. And to me, notions of diversity both in the workplace, also what you have on the screen, are so much more complex than that." The president of ABC News, David Westin, acknowledged he does pay attention to the numbers of minorities on staff, but that this information is for internal use. "It just makes sense to me that we're going to be more effective in finding the right stories, covering them the right way, and presenting them in the most effective way, if we generally reflect the population of the United States because we're national."

Those are words that minority journalists associations like to hear, but so far the words have not translated into any noticeable change in staff diversity at the network level. In fact, the situation may actually be worse than a few years ago. While a 2002 analysis of network and cable news operations showed that 46 percent of the people on air were women, there are currently no full-time women or minorities anchoring evening newscasts, even on weekends, at the main three broadcast networks. (At CNN and Fox News, there are two at this writing.) ABC News, which made history in 1978 by hiring Max Robinson as the first black anchor (on a team of three anchors) for *World News Tonight,* demoted its only remaining black prime-time anchor in October 2003. Carole Simpson had anchored *Sunday World News Tonight* since 1988. She is now an "ambassador" from ABC News to public schools. With her removal there is no prime-time anchor of color. "It makes you wonder what ABC News stand for. Anything But Color?" said Barbara Ciara, the vice president of broadcasting for the National Association of Black Journalists. "And when I look at the landscape of network news today, I find there are fewer faces of color covering the big stories. Ten years ago I saw more faces of color. So we're losing ground."

Kweisi Mfume, the president and CEO of the NAACP, agrees TV news organizations are far behind where they should be. During an October 2003 speech at the National Press Club to publicize an NAACP report on minorities in the media, he said, "None of Fox News, CNN, or MSNBC are doing well with diversity or equal opportunity. On the cable side, I think it's just horrendous." During a separate press conference releasing the report, Mfume added, "Sadly, when it comes to news, news specials, television newsmagazines, and the Sunday talking head shows, none of the broadcast networks or the cable news operations are doing exceedingly well with diversity or equal opportunity in front of or behind the camera. In fact this area has showed the least amount of progress or change."

This lack of progress is especially obvious when compared with population statistics. According to the U.S. census in 2000, 75.1 percent of the people in the United States are Caucasian, 12.3 percent are

African American, 3.6 percent are Asian American, and .9 percent are Native American; 12.5 percent are Hispanic (Hispanics can be white, black, or Asian). Although, as noted earlier, the networks don't release such figures, a July-August 2003 report on women and minorities in local television news—on and off air—revealed the following breakdown: 81.9 percent Caucasian, 8.4 percent African American, 6.5 percent Hispanic, 2.7 percent Asian American, and .5 percent Native American. "Part of [the reason for this imbalance] is short-term thinking versus long-term," said Randall Yip, the vice president for broadcasting for the Asian-American Journalists Association. "A news director is given eighteen or nineteen months, and if there's no improvement in the bottom line, they're out. Say if I invest time and money in diversity, it may not be reflected in the bottom line in that short period of time. The entire culture of broadcast [news] has to change and start thinking more in long term." Another issue, said Yip, is that many white hiring managers may, even subconsciously, reject minorities simply because they are different. "People hire who they're comfortable with, and white managers feel more comfortable hiring white people. It's not something apparent on the surface, and they may not even be aware of it. But I really think a lot of managers don't get it. When they look at minorities they just don't understand the culture."

Staff diversity cannot be achieved without diversity in management. "I think that has everything to do with it," said Ciara. "If you don't have a diverse managerial staff, diversity among your CEOs and your owners, it's not top of mind. It is a bad business strategy, but it's very difficult to get people to wake up and smell the cappuccino when you realize that diversity is not a priority." Art Rascon, the vice president of broadcasting for the National Association of Hispanic Journalists, agrees: "The demographics of this country have changed dramatically over the years. But that change is not being recognized in the newsrooms in America. Latinos are growing in strength and numbers, but on the TV screens you don't have those numbers. The reporters and anchors do not reflect the audience. In management the picture is even worse." Among news directors, the managers who run news departments and hire the on-air staff, the numbers of minorities are even less reflective of the general population: 93.4 percent are Caucasian, .9 percent are African American, 4.4 percent are Hispanic, .9 percent are Asian American, and .4 percent are Native American. As for station general managers, the top bosses, 96.4 percent are Caucasian and a total of 3.6 percent are minorities (mostly Hispanics at Spanish-language stations). The report found no Asian American or Native American general managers at local television stations. At stations in the twenty-five largest cities, the station managers are 100 percent Caucasian.

These statistics may be the most troubling of all, and the most indicative of discrimination in the news business. To be politically correct, most local television stations have hired a few minorities for on-camera positions because that is what the public sees. But while having a diverse reporting staff is essential, it is equally if not more crucial to have a diverse managerial staff. The news managers are the ones who decide what is covered and how, who should cover it and why. The news managers are responsible for crafting news coverage that is relevant to all of the viewers. The local news business is also the feeder system for national networks, broadcast or cable. The vast majority of network executives first got their experience in local news. If there are only a few local minority news directors or general managers, there will be even fewer minority news executives at the network level. Therefore, it is immensely important to have a diverse off-camera staff at local stations.

When I met with journalism students at universities as CNN's vice president of recruiting, easily 95 percent of them, whether minorities, women, or not, were aiming at on-air positions, even though fewer than 25 percent would be successful. My message to them was this: sure, you can be a reporter and that is a very rewarding and important job. But staying behind the scenes and working toward management is even more important. Aim high—set your goals on being a news director, a general manager, or a network executive. Or all three. The most powerful positions in news are not on camera, despite the celebrity that goes along with those jobs. If *all* beginning journalists are equally encouraged to pursue a management track and are allowed to compete on a level playing field,

I'm convinced more women and minorities will earn management positions, which will then lead to diversity across the board.

What the NAACP's Mfume calls "systematic and institutional racism" also extends to the "so-called 'experts on the subject' (who) continue to be overwhelmingly white." These are guests on news programs, not employees (although some are on retainer), who are sought out for their expertise. During the war in Iraq, for example, every network had a military "expert." These experts are also overwhelmingly male, despite census numbers that confirm there are more women than men in this country. A more telling statistic, though, is this: although males outnumber females up to age thirty-four, women outnumber men from age thirty-five on. So, there are more women than men at ages where experience, knowledge, and education should count when it comes to positions of authority. Is it reflected in actual jobs? No.

The White House Project is an organization dedicated to increasing the number of women in positions of power and influence. The group examined the guests that appeared on the following weekend talk shows: *This Week* (ABC), *Face the Nation* (CBS), *Late Edition with Wolf Blitzer* (CNN), *Fox News Sunday* (Fox), and *Meet the Press* (NBC). "Television, our culture's most powerful medium, has the ability to confer authority, to set the agenda for national debate, and to establish the profiles and visibility of leaders," according to the report. "The Sunday shows have the potential to allow women to be seen in intimate settings as trustworthy authority figures, debaters, leaders, communicators and experts. Conversely, they have the potential to maintain traditional gender roles and to perpetuate existing notions that women lack the credibility, expertise and authority to address our nation's most significant problems." And the latter is precisely what the report concludes is happening. Only 10 to 11 percent of the guests on these Sunday shows are women. And of repeat guests, those who are invited back, only 7 percent were women. One clear example cited by the report was the fact that male senators made 245 repeat guest appearances on the shows, while female senators were only invited back eight times.

Most critically, the *content* of the coverage suffers when news organizations' management teams and staff don't reflect the diversity of the

American population. In 2002, the National Association of Hispanic Journalists released a report called *Network Brownout: The Portrayal of Latinos in Network Television News.* The results showed a stunning disregard for a huge portion of the population. The authors of the report looked at the sixteen thousand or so news stories that aired on ABC, CBS, NBC, and CNN in 2001 and determined that only ninety-nine of them were about Latinos. This is a little over half of one percent of the total, or just under 4 hours of news stories out of 728 total hours. The main topics covered included the controversy over Navy bombings on the Puerto Rican island of Vieques, the nomination of Linda Chavez as U.S. Labor Secretary, immigration, sports, food, and music. "We must conclude that the nation's 35.3 million Latinos are still being relegated to the margins of U.S. news consciousness by ABC, CBS, NBC and CNN. The networks' dismal record of covering the nation's fastest-growing minority group undermines the information needs of all U.S. residents and distorts the public discourse so necessary for any democratic society," the report concluded.

In the mid-1990s, while I was still a national correspondent for CNN, I wrote a long memo to senior executives about the same concern. When I became an executive myself, I resurrected it, updated it, and sent it around once again. My points were clear: CNN routinely ignored Hispanics and other minorities when covering everyday events such as medical issues, housing starts, family stories, and so on. When correspondents personalized their stories using "real" people, they rarely used Hispanics or other minorities. This, I wrote my colleagues, was ignoring a huge demographic reality that not only hurt us with viewers but also hurt us journalistically. Our coverage was weaker because we excluded this segment of the population. What little response I received to my e-mail was either lukewarm or defensive. One note suggested that CNN was doing well because the week before we'd even aired a whole story about a female Cuban-American physician who made house calls.

From a business point of view, ignoring this demographic is financially irresponsible. Published reports peg the current Hispanic buying power and financial clout in this country at between $531 billion and

$580 billion. By 2007, that buying power is projected to rise to $926 billion; by 2020, to $2.3 trillion. But Hispanics are just one demographic group badly served by these foolhardy diversity-blind practices. Virtually all minorities are treated the same, and some even worse. When you consider that the joint buying power of Hispanics, Asian Americans, African Americans, and Native Americans in this country was estimated at $1.3 trillion in 2001, ignoring or underserving this population isn't just negligent, it's financially suicidal.

Not only do all of these reports, these studies, and these statistics reveal practices that are obviously immoral and potentially illegal, they also highlight decades of lousy business decisions that don't make sense. If networks such as CNN and Fox are able to make healthy profits with between 500,000 and 700,000 viewers daily, how can it be smart business to ignore or underserve more than 75 to 80 million other potential viewers? It simply isn't. So why are minorities so underrepresented on and off camera? It is hard to come to any conclusion other than Mfume's charge of institutional discrimination. Television news networks, cable networks, television stations, and even the print media cannot defend their diversity records or pretend they weren't aware of the issues. The Kerner Commission report, responding to President Lyndon Johnson's order in the 1960s to analyze the racial divide in this country, concluded that the media helped create that divide. "The press has been basking in a white world, looking out of it, if at all, with a white man's eyes and a white perspective." As a result of that report, the American Society of Newspaper Editors vowed that newsrooms in this country would reflect the population by the year 2000. When that pledge failed to be kept, the date was reset—to the year 2025.

EXPERIENCE VERSUS "TOO OLD FOR NEWS"

The past ten to twenty years has also seen the birth of a new type of discrimination in television news staffs, this one based on age. A mere glance at TV screens quickly reveals that younger news reporters, anchors, and correspondents are replacing more experienced veterans.

In an interview CBS anchor Dan Rather did with *Brill's Content,* he admitted that age discrimination is an ingrained part of network television news. But he added that if he were to be taken off the anchor set because CBS News executives thought that a thirty-five-year-old anchor would attract a younger generation, "I don't think it would be wrong." That this noted newsman would not only go along with but support such illegal hiring and firing practices helps explain how the networks have gotten away with it for so long. Why the networks do it is also plain to see. Advertisers want to target viewers between the ages of twenty and about forty, so television news organizations believe younger, hipper on-camera talent will attract a younger audience—although there is little if any empirical data to back that up. "Older people face discrimination in the newsroom," said George Lewis, a long-time NBC News correspondent. "This is a business looking for the younger demographic. This seems to be one of those businesses where experience is viewed as a liability rather than an asset."

Ageism in the news has serious consequences. Less experienced journalists are less likely to have a broad array of trustworthy sources with access to information or knowledge about newsworthy topics. And they will lack perspective on some stories. When the first bombing of the World Trade Center occurred, only a handful of veteran journalists were able to speak intelligently off the top of their heads about previous car and truck bombs aimed at U.S. targets. They knew this was the first attack of its kind within the borders of this country, but also that a U.S. marine base was blown up in Beirut on Oct. 23, 1983, killing over 240 servicemen, and that two U.S. embassy buildings there were also destroyed in the same manner. In a breaking news situation, being able to offer this sort of insight and factual detail is very valuable information for viewers.

Investing in employees for the long term also makes good business sense. Training and turnover are very expensive and threaten any type of continuity in coverage. Replacing a veteran correspondent who over decades has become an expert on campaign finance reform simply because the network bosses want younger and more attractive people on the air is, at the very least, foolhardy. But it is also a trend that can only lead to bad journalism. And that can certainly lead to embarrassing on-air moments for a news organization. For example, in the early 1990s, a CNN executive known for having an eye for pretty women hired a young and very attractive female anchor who looked fabulous on the studio set. She was the definition of eye candy. But what she had in looks, she lacked in experience, basic knowledge, and brains. There are many stories about things she actually said on air, and, like other people who were at CNN at the time, I have my favorites. While reading a story on the TelePrompTer about New Mexico, this anchor actually pronounced Albuquerque as Al-bah-cue-cue. And while reporting on one of the national dog shows, she mispronounced the Chihuahua breed as Chi-hoo-a-hoo-a.

While having people of different ages and levels of experience on air is good business, so is having that combination of ages behind the camera, particularly in management. A mix of experience provides decision makers with a diversity of perspectives that is crucial to properly serving all viewers. But just as most news executives are male and white, they also are increasingly becoming younger and younger, replacing veteran journalists in their late forties and older. Hands-on experience is being swapped for youthful exuberance. And that shows on air, as the CNN case study that follows will demonstrate. This is not good, smart journalism. If older viewers, such as the large baby boomer generation, are turned off by superficial news reporting, it also promises to be bad for business.

CNN AS A CASE STUDY

I can report the statistics and quote the studies that have analyzed all of the broadcast news divisions and cable news networks, and the results are plain to see by any reader. But how are staffing decisions made behind the scenes at a network? Having been an executive at CNN for five years and involved in recruiting on- and off-air personnel, I can share some of the background, some of the context, and true vignettes that will shed light on this network's issues with diversity. And while the broadcast news divisions and the other cable networks no doubt have behind-the-scenes diversity stories of their own, the on-air results—or lack of—are clearly similar.

Making Up for the Past

From CNN's birth in 1980, it has been primarily a network of white people putting together news for white viewers. With some brief exceptions, it can also be said that people in nearly all top news executive positions have been men. In 1999, then–CNN chairman Tom Johnson made it clear he wanted minorities hired for virtually every on-camera opening. One example of his not-too-subtle pressure was an e-mail to then–Headline News head Bob Furnad, strongly suggesting that an anchor opening at that network be filled by a male or female African American, or a female Hispanic. (The first question that came to mind when I read the e-mail was "And do you want fries with that?" This was the hiring equivalent of going through a fast-food drive-through.) Between Headline News and CNN/USA there were a handful of minority anchors, including journalists such as Bernard Shaw, Sachi Koto, Joie Chen, and Leon Harris. But their numbers were small. And neither network had ever had a Hispanic anchor.

While diversifying the CNN News Group was clearly the moral, ethical, and sound business thing to do, when applied in this fill-as-many-openings-as-possible-with-minorities manner it was also illegal. I was copied on Johnson's e-mail to Furnad, and later during a private conversation with Johnson I told him that although his intent was no doubt to do good, I believed this was a dangerous way to implement diversity. As a vice president assigned by him to oversee CNN's first full-time office of recruiting and talent development, my aim was also to bring greater diversity to CNN. But from the start I maintained it should never be at the expense of nonminorities. Diversity takes care of itself if the best candidates for any position are actively sought out and then considered without regard to race, age, gender, or ethnic background. The network's affirmative action policy—which said that if two candidates for a position are equally qualified but one is a minority, that minority should get the job—would also assist in addressing past imbalances over time. Achieving diversity is not a short-term project.

Over the next two years, however, the CNN News Group practiced obvious quota-filling based, in part, on Johnson's orders and what was considered to be smart programming. There had never been an Asian or Hispanic correspondent at CNN's Los Angeles bureau, so only Asians and Hispanics were considered for the two openings there and one of each was hired. There had never been a Hispanic in the Dallas office, so an opening there was filled by a Hispanic. CNN's medical unit was all white, so only minorities were considered for the next two openings. In fact, most of the on-air openings in the correspondent ranks were filled by minorities. Often, nonminorities that I had included in the recruiting pool were not given any consideration by network heads. At Headline News, whites *were* hired mainly for primary news anchor positions while a large percentage of secondary anchor jobs often went to minorities. With only two or three exceptions, CNN en Español only hires Hispanics, the vast majority born in Latin America. There have been no blacks or Asians in on-camera staff positions. At CNN International, a reverse type of discrimination has been the rule for the past several years. Only non-Americans or nonwhite Americans are considered and hired for anchor positions. Although I shared my concerns with many of the network heads and other hiring managers, to a one they all felt the ends justified the means.

During this time, Jesse Jackson—who had organized boycotts against some of the broadcast networks—was also taking aim at CNN and had warned executives that he would draw attention to the appalling lack of diversity on and off air. But because the News Group had made so much "progress" in on-air hiring in the previous year or so, Jackson was appeased. (I was one of the executives called on to provide information on recent minority hiring so that then-news-gathering-chief Eason Jordan could defend the network.) The next step, ordered by then–President of Domestic Networks Jim Walton (currently president of the CNN News Group), was for me to assemble files on the top twenty-five or so African American television journalists in the country. Walton was creating a new vice president position specifically for an African American. At the time there were no blacks in senior news executive positions at the domestic network. This person would be number three in the hierarchy at CNN/USA. When I pointed out that there were also two very qualified female executive producers who had—through exceptional work at the network—proven themselves also worthy of consideration, he reiterated that he wanted a minority, an African American. These two women are white. I did as I was ordered, but I also included some of the top Hispanic and Asian journalists in the country as well and continued to let Walton and other senior executives know when other qualified candidates of any race or gender became available.

In the end, Walton and the top two people at CNN/USA chose to interview four African Americans and hired one of them, Kim Bondy, a superior journalist who had been executive producer of the *Weekend Today Show* at NBC News. She became the only black news vice president at CNN's headquarters. The irony is that Bondy still would have been the top candidate if Walton had considered all people regardless of race, ethnic background, or gender.

"We Have Enough!"

In 2001 CNN did a complete turnaround. The top positions at Turner Broadcasting had been handed over to men whose entire careers were in the world of entertainment. This included Jamie Kellner and Garth Ancier, who had launched the Fox entertainment network and spent years in Hollywood. Ancier had also been president of NBC Entertainment. Both men were brought to Turner Broadcasting with one mission: to increase ratings at any cost. And they made it clear they intended to instill the values of the entertainment world—in terms of programming and hiring (or "casting" as Ancier called it)—into the news networks at CNN. If it worked for the entertainment divisions at other networks, they said, they believed it would work with news too. At my first meeting with Ancier, when I was showing him tapes of anchor candidates chosen by Headline News and CNN/USA chiefs out of the pool of candidates I'd shown them, he said, "Why are all these tapes you're showing me of minorities? We don't need any more of those people! We have enough! Bring me others!"

Ancier scoffed in a very belittling sort of way, pointed to the television monitors in his office, and said, "We have enough minorities." When I looked at the screens, two of the handful of the News Group's black anchors were on the air—one at CNN and one at CNNfn. I pointed out that this was an anomaly, that minorities were still horribly underrepresented at CNN, on camera and off, and that we needed to continue including all minorities in our hiring pool. What was also going through my head was that CNN was going from hiring only minorities or primarily minorities to no minorities. Both strategies were flawed. "That's enough," he said.

Age (Out the Door) Before Beauty

The same day Ancier decreed he did not want to hire any more minorities, he also sent me an e-mail ordering me to hire "younger and more attractive anchors." As given by the person who now had to approve all on-air hires, Ancier's orders echoed throughout CNN Center and were followed by network heads. If one reviews even a partial list of on-air people who were let go (and paid severance if they agreed to "retire" or "resign" and to sign a document saying they'd never sue CNN or publicly say anything negative about the company) in 2001 and 2002, and compares it with a list of people hired during or just after this time, the age difference is striking. While this is not a complete list, nor scientific in its research, here are some of the on-air people who left the CNN News Group during this time for whatever publicly stated reason: Natalie Allen, Bobbie Battista, Ralph Begleiter, Charles Bierbauer, Chris Black, Richard Blystone, Nick Charles, Joie Chen, Tony Clark, Roger Cossack, Bill Delaney, Pat Ethridge, Bruce Francis, Allen Dodds Frank, Ed Garsten, Tony Guida, Andria Hall, James Hattori, Jim Hill, Peter Humi, Brooks Jackson, Donna Kelley, Patricia Kelly, Elsa Klensch, Don Knapp, Greg LaMotte, Greg Lefevre, Mark Leff, Karen Maginnis, Anne McDermott, Eileen O'Connor, Linda Patillo, Perri Peltz, Mark Potter, Gene Randall, Jacque Reid, Carl Rochelle, Ceci Rogers, Dan Ronan, Sonia Ruseler, Lynne Russell, Patricia Sabga, Beverly Schuch, Frank Sesno, Bernard Shaw, Flip Spiceland, Laurin Sydney, Kalin Thomas-

Samuel, Bill Tucker, Garrick Utley, Lou Waters, Ralph Wenge, Larry Woods, and Charles Zewe. The vast majority of these journalists are over the age of forty, with many in their fifties and older. Some are "CNN Originals," the people who risked their careers in the early 1980s to join Ted Turner in a crazy scheme to provide twenty-four-hour news on a cable station.

Among the on-air people hired during the same time, or afterward, were the following: Dana Bash, Andrew Bond, Kat Carney, Whitney Casey, Matthew Chance, Marcia Cohen, Jamie Colby, Anderson Cooper, Carol Costello, Alisha Davis, Thelma Gutierrez, Erica Hill, Ed Lavandera, Carrie Lee, Suzanne Malveaux, Miguel Marquez, Robin Meade, Chris Osborne, Christi Paul, Thomas Roberts, Kevin Sites, Bob Van Dillen, and Fredricka Whitfield. Most of these journalists are in their twenties and thirties. That does not mean they are not good. When I was ordered to find younger on-air people, I brought in the best available young journalists for the managers to consider (along with qualified candidates of different ages). I'm very proud of many of them—they are extremely talented and knowledgeable, for their age. And they have the potential to become exceptional journalists—if they don't lose their jobs, like many of their predecessors did, because they simply get "too old"—that is, if they reach their forties and fifties and beyond. As George Lewis said earlier in this chapter, news organizations can best serve the public by having correspondents and staff who represent all factions of the public, from the young to the older, of all ethnic backgrounds, of all races. And I'll add gender and religion to that comment.

At the same time much of this concern about "younger and more attractive anchors" was going on, management was also worried that CNN had been hiring too many women. "We need men!" I was told time and time again in 2000 and 2001. After decades of anchors being overwhelmingly men, which didn't seem to perturb anyone, CNN's male leadership could not brook the idea of actually having anything approaching a fifty-fifty split of men and women on camera. As a result, some of the good female anchors I found who were available were not given much consideration.

I knew then and know now the legal implications of this. I did my best to discourage these types of hiring practices, but in the end, I was ordered to find what the top executives wanted.

"The Caucasian News Network"

Despite the contradictory orders to hire either all minorities for on-air jobs or, later, no minorities, a few trends have remained firm over the years. First, from launch in 1980 until 2003, there had never been a Hispanic anchor at CNN/USA. Soledad O'Brien, whose mother is Cuban, is the closest CNN's domestic network has come to having a Hispanic anchor in twenty-four years (as of early 2004). Second, while Bernard Shaw—an excellent journalist by all accounts—was the main male anchor for much of CNN's history, he was replaced by a white man when he was urged to retire. The only other African American male anchor at CNN, Leon Harris, left the network in frustration in late 2003 after being told he would be assigned to a less visible program that he had already anchored years earlier. (The day the network president went to the studio to try to convince Harris that it would be in his best interest to leave his daytime slot and begin anchoring a 5 or 6 AM show, Harris was overheard by several people saying, "What are you trying to create? the Caucasian News Network?") When Joie Chen, a very accomplished long-time CNN anchor was fired, CNN then hired Connie Chung, who executives eventually got rid of, too. So as of the end of 2003, there are no minorities anchoring prime-time programs at CNN/USA. None.

Throughout CNN's history, white non-Hispanic men have primarily had the final word on hiring and promotions. They have hired people they are comfortable seeing on camera and working next to—people who look and act like them. And most of them haven't been smart enough to see the pattern of discrimination. I was asked by Sid Bedingfield, the head of CNN's domestic network at the time, to help create during part of 2000 and 2001 a new morning show with high-visibility anchors. When I heard that Antonio Mora's contract was coming up at ABC News, where he had anchored the news on *Good Morning America* for three years, I thought he'd be a strong contender. I had never met him, but Mora was clearly a major player. So on June 22, 2001, I e-mailed the senior executives to let them know.

The e-mail back from Walton was short and to the point. "What does he do?" This, from the man who was in charge of CNN/USA, CNN Headline News, CNNfn, CNN/SI, and the Airport Channel (and is now the president of the CNN News Group). I had to wonder whether minorities simply didn't register on Walton's talent meter—and whether he didn't bother to watch other networks, CNN's competitors. Most of the other executives didn't seem to know who Mora was, either, or, worse, they weren't interested in someone with a "Spanish" name. While I was given the go-ahead to bring him to Atlanta and scheduled six or seven of the executives to meet him, all but one—Kim Bondy, our new vice president hired away from NBC News, who clearly knew the competitive field—dropped off the schedule by the day Mora arrived. I managed to talk another of them into meeting him out of simple courtesy. Mora, of course, was not hired. What didn't seem to matter is that Mora had higher Q scores than all on-air people at CNN. Q scores are research numbers that measure a reporter or anchor's familiarity, impact, and favorability. While some executives pretend they don't care about these numbers, especially if their on-air people rank low, these numbers do come into play when networks are choosing main anchors. Mora's numbers were higher than all of CNN's stars, higher than Bernard Shaw's, higher than legal eagle Greta Van Susteren's, higher than Headline News anchor Lynne Russell's. How could hiring Mora not increase CNN's ratings?

Ignorance also contributed to CNN blowing another major opportunity: the chance to hire one of the nation's top television talk-show hosts, who also happens to be black. "We already have Jesse Jackson on our air," they pointed out to me. The implication was clear: we have *one* and don't need another. The day it was announced that Tavis Smiley was leaving Black Entertainment Network (BET), where he had a hugely successful talk show with ratings that beat CNN in the same time slot, I immediately e-mailed the top executives to let them know. "Who is he?" was the standard response. Not one of the white male executives I e-mailed knew. He wasn't on their white radar. I explained that he was *the* draw at BET, arguably one of the top, if not *the* top, black talk-show hosts in the country. He could get any guest he wanted. In terms of successful talk-show hosts for CNN, he'd be right up there with Larry King—if not giving King a run for his money. (And King had one of the two top-rated programs on CNN.) Smiley's firing from BET over a squabble was huge news, and if we hired him, we'd not only serve our viewers better, we'd also get phenomenal press out of it. And CNN desperately needed good press at the time.

In addition, I wrote, "He's a regular guest on *The Tom Joyner Show,* a very popular syndicated radio show, primarily among African Americans. He was selected by *Time* magazine as one of the fifty most promising young leaders in the country. And *Newsweek* called him one of the 'twenty people changing how Americans get their news.' We've had him on as a guest on *Talkback* several times. . . . He is an extremely articulate, compelling man who has an edge. He'd be an interesting addition to our lineup. . . . both for television and radio." Hiring Smiley was the proverbial slam dunk, the most obvious move for CNN to make. He was smart and would provide informative programming for the network. Research showed that Smiley's following was affluent, which is a good thing for advertisers. And he had published five books very successfully.

The reaction from network executives? Lukewarm, at best. But because Smiley was being courted by other entities, they reluctantly agreed to meet him. When he arrived at CNN Center, I escorted him around from executive to executive, as I did for all visiting applicants. When I brought Smiley in to meet Phil Kent, then the number two person at CNN (and now the head of Turner Broadcasting), Phil invited him to sit down and then quickly followed me out into the hallway. "Who is this guy?" he asked. I had to fill him in again.

The consensus? They liked him, but for reasons they had a hard time articulating, they didn't think Smiley would "fit in" at CNN. I implored Sid Bedingfield, the head of CNN/USA, to reconsider. In the end, Bedingfield negotiated an agreement for Smiley to appear on CNN a certain number of times a year. That is all he would go for. Smiley began his appearances and did a spectacular job from the get-go. A short while later,

Bedingfield called me into his office to find out if we could get him full time. It was a bittersweet moment. The answer was no. Smiley had signed an agreement with another company that had a year to develop a show around him. If they didn't, he'd be free. But CNN had lost the opportunity and the momentum for now. It was too little, too late, once again.

Freedom of Religion (Unless You're *Too* Observant, That Is)

Ninety-six percent of Americans believe in God, with 54 percent attending religious services at least once a week, according to *U.S. News & World Report*. This places the United States ahead of all other industrialized nations in terms of religious observance. Still, religious diversity is virtually nonexistent at CNN and at many of the other news organizations. That explains why few correspondents can do more than a superficial job of reporting about religion and why most devout believers, whether Muslim, Christian, Jewish, or any other religion, are often labeled as "extremists" in news lingo. This lack of understanding is clearly reflected in news coverage and, as such, has an impact on the way American viewers see religions that are different from their own. (For many people, the words "Muslim" or "Arab" are nearly interchangeable with "terrorist." As soon as it was evident that a truck bomb was used to blow up the Murrah federal building in Oklahoma City, federal authorities and many people in the news media jumped to the conclusion that Arabs were behind the attack. CNN was one of many news organizations that had to retract their initial reportage.) It also explains why devout Christians and others in this country believe that CNN and some of the other networks are antireligion. For a couple of months while I was in charge of recruiting, those of us lobbying for a religion reporter actually convinced management to fund such a position. I interviewed several people and was very excited about one particular candidate who was in seminary and had what appeared to be an unbiased view of religions in general. He also had the ability to articulately explain a broad range of religious concepts in an unbiased manner. But just days before we were to offer him the job, the position was cut from the budget—for monetary reasons, we were told. CNN could afford war correspondents, medical correspondents, general assignment correspondents, financial correspondents, technology correspondents, ecology correspondents, sports correspondents, travel correspondents, and weather anchors—but the network could not afford one religion correspondent. One correspondent who could serve seven television networks, two radio networks, and CNN's Internet sites. Religion was not important enough to merit its own beat on CNN. This was not just bad journalism, it was a stupid business decision.

And why did it go nearly uncontested? Few, if any, of CNN's top management—or anyone else, for that matter—are devoutly religious. Company policy makes it very difficult for people to observe a day of rest, which is called for in many religions. In 2000, a recent college graduate applied to become a video journalist, the entry-level position at the News Group. (My office was in charge of recruiting these people, too.) These are the folks who run the TelePrompTers, stand by the cameras in the studios and cue anchors, make tape dubs, and handle a myriad of other critical—though not difficult—jobs. These positions, though, can lead to others. Jim Walton, who is now president of the CNN News Group, started at the network as a video journalist.

This VJ candidate was well qualified and would have been hired, but in her final interview she mentioned that she is a Seventh Day Adventist who observed a day of rest. As such, she would not be available to work from sundown Friday to sundown Saturday. Instead, she volunteered to work any other shift, including Sundays and overnights. She was not hired. CNN has a strict policy that—as a 24/7 network—it requires employees to be available to work at any hour on any day. I appealed this decision to her division head, Cindy Patrick, but was told there would be no exceptions.

This type of decision is not wise in any way. Diversity of all sorts is smart, good journalism *and* good business. If news organizations reflect the broad range and depth of the viewers they serve—on camera and in the off-camera decision-making positions—they will win more viewers. This is not pandering to viewers. It is offering them news that reflects a diversity of interests.

By March or so of 2001, some four-hundred-plus people had been let go. It was clear that many of the people who were laid off, pushed out, forced to retire early, terminated, fired—you name it—were women, minorities, and people over forty. These were staff members who took a lot of hard work to hire, train, teach, and promote—but who no longer held any value for CNN.

As for CNN/USA, the domestic network known as the "mothership," there are few women executives. At least fifteen female vice presidents left (fired, laid off, "retired," "resigned") CNN in 2001 and 2002, this at a time when the Annenberg Public Policy Center at the University of Pennsylvania had determined that AOL Time Warner—CNN's parent— had one of the worst records among media companies for women in top ranks. As for other minorities, there are as of this writing two at CNN/USA in senior management. One is Kim Bondy, the vice president I recruited who was hired for the job created specifically for an African American. Walton eventually made her, the only minority vice president at the domestic network, the lead person on diversity for CNN. Then Princell Hair was brought on board in late 2003 as her boss, to head CNN/USA, the domestic network.

But in a staff memo issued on Feb. 27, 2003, Walton wrote, "Many of you have heard me define success at CNN in the following four ways: Journalism, Shareholder Value, Audience Growth, and People . . ." At this point, under the "people" category—the last in the line of what is impor- tant (especially after "shareholder value")—the man who had never heard of Antonio Mora or Tavis Smiley then wrote about the importance of diver- sity. "Whether they (the diversity team led by Bondy) are developing ways to encourage greater diversity in the stories we cover, or how we cover them or in the recruitment and support of a more diverse staff, I am of the firm belief that this effort is good for business, good for ratings, good for journalism and, most of all, good for all of us who devote so much time and effort to the mission of CNN." I find this statement dismay- ing, given CNN's history. Actions always speak louder than words. And in that spirit, I want to disclose—so that readers can weigh my arguments in an informed manner—that I filed a lawsuit against CNN in 2003 alleging, among other things, the same facts that I describe here. I charged that CNN discriminated against me and also retaliated against me, in part, because I fought against what I believed to be discriminatory hiring and firing practices regarding others.

❏   ❏   ❏

Although I used CNN as a case study, it is critical to acknowledge that the problems are industry wide. The lack of diversity—race, gender, age, ethnic background, religion, and so on—is still an issue at *every* network, *every* local television station. And at the same time that jobs and news-gathering budgets are being cut, a select few on-air "stars" are banking millions of dollars a year. Meanwhile, parent corporations feeling pressure to please shareholders are diluting and contaminating a very precious resource with infotainment and other values that do nothing but hurt journalism. That, alone, is cause for alarm. But the fact that these knee-jerk, short-term strategies make lousy long-term business plans should be a true eye-opener for followers of the bottom line. "Flash may get you a momentary bump in the ratings, but in the long run, when people turn to your news program they expect to be informed," said Barbara Cochran. "They don't want to have their time wasted. If they see you doing stories that are sensational or titillating, that's not what they're looking for. The most successful stations and station groups, and the ones that are doing the best financially, are the ones doing excellent news."

In short: solid, responsible news can be profitable.

THE GOOD

I N BOISE, IDAHO, the work of journalists at television station KBCI defined the concept of public service in 2002 and 2003. By simply following up on a lead that the mayor and his chief of staff had spent city funds to go to a Broadway play while attending a conference in New York, reporters eventually exposed a string of illegal practices that resulted in the mayor's resignation, indictment, and, finally, guilty plea on two felony charges of misuse of public money. Boise now has a new mayor and city council that are taking charge. "That illustrates that in a community where the local station is the most powerful voice and most powerful watchdog, it's very important for them not to be afraid to investigate powerful elements in the community," said Barbara Cochran, the president of the Radio-Television News Directors Association, the largest organization of broadcasters in the country. "It was important to give the reporters the time to do the investigations and sustain their [viewer's] interest in the story. If not for this television station, Boise would have had no idea about what was going on."

This is a classic example of why a free press is so critical and so essential. This is good television journalism. And it was done by a small local station in a small city on what was most likely a very modest news budget. Journalistic excellence and public service can be achieved anywhere.

Good television journalism is arguably the key component of a free press, a free media, in this country today. Without good television journalism, without people having open access to information, a democracy would crumble. Some good TV news reports, such as fair coverage of a presidential campaign or election, play a very direct and obvious role in the practice of representative government. When it's done right, voters are provided with solid information about the candidates and where they stand on a number of issues. Their access to quality information affects how they will vote and sometimes even whether they will vote. That sort of public service can hardly be questioned.

But for television journalism or any sort of journalism to be good, it does not necessarily have to help viewers make such critical decisions. Journalism will be good simply if it informs the people in an honest, unbiased, fair, and balanced manner. Letting people know what is happening in their world, their country, their state, or their city—whether or not it leads to direct action by them—is an important function of a free media in a democracy. It provides information and context to lives, to governments, to issues, to virtually anything and everything that is going on around the world. That knowledge—the *access* to it—is priceless, even if that viewer in Springfield, Illinois, never again thinks about that airplane crash in Argentina or the nuclear power plant scare in Russia. He or she was able to *choose* to watch the reports and learn about the accidents, something citizens who live in countries with totalitarian-style governments do not enjoy.

In such countries—for example, Iraq under Saddam Hussein—all media is government controlled and is simply a propaganda tool, which explains why throughout the Iran-Iraq war and the Gulf war, Iraqi citizens truly believed they had won. Their government news people told them so and they had no other access to information. In fact, for the whole of the Iran-Iraq conflict, which I covered, I marveled at how every newspaper and newscast for years reported that all Iraqi air force jets that had taken part in sorties that day had returned safely to base. They never lost one. I always wondered whether the Iraqi people really believed that garbage, but without alternative sources of unbiased information, who knows? In the 2003 war with Iraq, the world got a glimpse of this same sort of disinformation when Mohammed Saeed al-Sahhaf, the Minister of Information and Hussein's spokesman, continued to tell the world that Iraq was winning the war. "The infidels are committing suicide by the hundreds at the gates of Baghdad," he said one day, while the rest of the world saw live pictures of American troops taking over the city. To the western media, he became known as "Baghdad Bob," or the "Minister of Disinformation." Still, the people who lived in the capital believed what their government was saying until they saw uniformed American soldiers on their streets.

In the old Soviet Union, very few people knew about the Chernobyl nuclear plant accident in 1986 until word-of-mouth stories began spreading about people dying from radiation exposure. It was the world's worst nuclear disaster—that also affected agriculture and farming in several countries in Europe—but the government sought to keep it quiet. (I was assigned to cover the impact on crops, vineyards, and livestock in Europe. The camera crew I was to work with was a husband-and-wife team. She was pregnant. We knew enough to send her away from the radiation, back to the United States, for the duration. But Soviet Union citizens in the vicinity of the nuclear plant didn't have this information, and many are still dying from their government's decision to keep it quiet.)

Even in the new Russia, officials have lied outright to their citizens and to the world to save face. When the submarine *Kursk* sank in the Barents Sea within the Arctic Circle in August of 2000, the Russian navy kept the accident a secret for at least two days. Officials then said they had the situation under control; they were hearing knocking on the side of the sub and could handle the rescue themselves. In the end, 118 people died, and many of the official comments about the disaster—including the knocking—

turned out to be lies aimed at saving face. The Russian press flexed its muscle for the first time and took Vladimir Putin and his government to task, reporting on the false statements made, openly criticizing the government for its delayed response to the accident, and informing the Russian public that the government's effort at propaganda had failed miserably. It was a new day in Russia. What happened on the floor of the Barents Sea had a direct impact for the submariner's families, but not for most other Russian news viewers. Yet they all deserved to know the truth as it was happening. In this country, we call it the people's right to know, and it is a sacred public trust.

That said, though, how else is good television news coverage distinguished from bad? What are the necessary elements? How is good television news reporting measured against bad coverage? Is it judged by how the stories are produced and whether there are snazzy graphics? Is it the writing? The reporting? The collection of information? The video or the sound? Is it the ability to take viewers where they've never been before? The actual news event? The format, whether it is breaking news or a newsmagazine? Is good television news defined by whether one station or network scoops the others? The answer to these questions is yes, sometimes. And no, sometimes, depending on the situation and the news event.

Some of the most extraordinary moments of television news—the first televised presidential debate between John F. Kennedy and Richard Nixon in 1960, Martin Luther King Jr.'s dream speech, the assassination of JFK, the first step on the moon, coverage of the war in Vietnam, the Watergate hearings in 1973, to name just a few—weren't especially well-produced or exceptionally well-written stories for the most part. But they showed viewers historic moments that would change many lives forever. They gave the public important information that allowed many citizens to make informed decisions. These stories were extraordinary because they showed the unvarnished truth of breaking news events as they unfolded in living rooms throughout the United States. They had an impact despite the fact that sometimes the coverage was not very popular.

Joe Angotti, a former senior vice president of NBC News and the current chair of the broadcasting program at Northwestern University's

Medill School of Journalism, vividly remembers the onslaught of phone calls and mail the network received as a result of its coverage of the anti-Vietnam War movement. "We were hated by both sides. The hippies thought we were establishment and the police thought we were pro-hippies and pro-revolution and so both sides were dumping on us," Angotti said. "But there was a determination that that story had to be told. And talk about patriotism, we were being called unpatriotic Communist sympathizers because we were covering this growing opposition to the war and people didn't like that." That coverage, however, played a large role in the ending of the war—an important lesson, says Angotti. "Sticking with coverage that isn't popular . . . I think those are some of the finest moments for television news."

TECHNOLOGY'S ROLE IN GOOD TV JOURNALISM

CNN's breaking coverage of the *Challenger* shuttle disaster was one of a kind, literally. The network was the only one that showed the disaster live. By the time this shuttle was launching into space, the other networks no longer carried the liftoffs; it was old hat. CNN's policy was, and is to this day, to show all launches and all landings live. It was a decision that paid off on January 28, 1986. Viewers around the world gasped as equally stunned NASA officials and CNN reporters at the Kennedy Space Center struggled to explain what was happening before our eyes. The coverage wasn't flawless—there were some small technical errors—but in the whole scheme of things that was irrelevant. Viewers could see the explosion, the plumes of white smoke streaking through the sky, the pieces of the space shuttle falling into the ocean and the crowds at the space center crying as they looked skyward. No other news medium could have delivered the story with that impact, that level of intensity and involvement. This was live television using satellite communication at its best.

The United States lost nine astronauts including a teacher, who had become a role model in classrooms everywhere, but the country and the world also lost the benefit of the experiments and other work the crew was slated to complete. The shuttle program would be halted until a full investigation was completed and during that time, satellites used for telecommunications and other functions that were usually delivered to space by a shuttle would remain grounded, too. Did the coverage of this disaster affect the lives of viewers in Los Angeles or Cairo, Egypt in a direct, tangible way? Probably not. But it did inform the world as it was happening, and there was mourning in the global village. In a way, people on all continents were touched by U.S.-style television reporting. They enjoyed the power, the responsibility and the truth enabled by the First Amendment.

Important live coverage that was far smoother from a technological point of view was that of President Bill Clinton's impeachment hearings. No matter how one felt personally about Clinton, his extracurricular activities, or his political party, one could watch monumental government work in progress. Coverage was bipartisan and unedited. For the most part, the news was not being filtered through reporters; it was live, with elected officials and lawyers asking the tough questions. The bottom line, though, was that the outcome showed the fallacy of the Republican position that this was an impeachable offense. Americans saw their government at work, whether they liked the outcome or not.

Videophones are one of the latest technological advancements in television news gathering. During the wars in Afghanistan and Iraq, they were used by dozens of networks and television stations. Due to its small size, no larger than two medium suitcases, the videophone is very portable. It also costs only about $7,000. Given the price and portability of the device, in comparison with the $1 million price tag of satellite trucks, it's easy to understand why television news organizations are willing to accept its lower-grade picture quality. Voices come through clearly, but images often look like an episode of the old Max Headroom program—jumpy, jerky, and robotic. Still, the videophone has earned its place in television news history. Make no mistake, technology alone will never determine whether news coverage is excellent or not. But if used wisely in combination with smart, thorough, balanced, and fair reporting, it can be magnificent.

In April, 2001, twenty-four U.S. Navy crewmen from an EP-3E surveillance aircraft full of the latest eavesdropping equipment had to make an emergency landing on Hainan Island, China, after a collision with a Chinese fighter jet. This emergency instantly became a major story. The United States immediately requested that the crew and their plane be returned, but the Chinese refused, demanding a public apology while delaying any real resolution to the crisis to give them time to nearly dismantle the aircraft for military intelligence purposes. The standoff lasted eleven days.

China is among the hardest countries in which to practice U.S.-style journalism. Journalists report that they can rarely go out by themselves without escorts and that they must request permission to shoot video of just about anything. At CNN, which helped invent the videophone and was the only network with them at this time, the story was considered worth breaking the Chinese government's rules. When it was learned that the American crew members would finally be permitted to leave, CNN producer Lisa Rose Weaver and a camera crew armed with a videophone clandestinely stationed themselves at the far side of the airport. From this vantage point they could see—albeit at a distance—where the Americans would board another plane that would take them out of China. They set up their equipment and went to work.

In the CNN newsroom, all eyes were on the monitors, all fingers were crossed, and a rare hush fell across the room. When the jumpy images appeared on the screens and Weaver began answering a question from the anchors, the usually unflappable and impossible-to-impress journalists in the newsroom were awed. They exchanged high fives, with smiles on every face. What a news coup. But seeing live pictures of the airfield and the bus that took the crew members to the airport, and, finally, watching them board their homebound aircraft were just the beginning. CNN International was being monitored by Chinese officials, who immediately set out to stop the illegal, unauthorized transmission. While those of us in the newsroom and viewers around the globe watched, vehicles pulled up to where the CNN crew was set up. The photographer trained his camera on them while Weaver narrated what was happening. We all saw the officials waving angrily at the camera and yelling, the universal signal for "turn it off!" But she continued talking live and explained that they were being detained. The last image was of a Chinese official's hand covering up the camera lens.

While colleagues in the Atlanta newsroom were concerned for their arrested staffers, that didn't diminish the cheering that exploded seconds later. This was truly a phenomenal moment in television news history. Why? For a couple of reasons. First, viewers saw the resolution of what had been a very tense standoff between two well-armed countries. They saw the U.S. servicemen and women heading back home. But second, they saw—live and in living color—an example of the media repression in China. It is one thing to simply report about the strict rules under which the few international journalists who are allowed to live there operate. It's quite another to hear it and see it in action. The outrage and anger on the faces of the Chinese officials who arrested the CNN crew spoke volumes. This live report reinforced the lessons from the Tiananmen Square coverage: if you step out of line, you're in deep trouble. As Weaver herself reported on a cell phone while being driven to the police department for hours of questioning, "Simply the fact that we were out collecting information is enough to initiate action on their part," she said. "This is not a country where journalists, international or otherwise, roaming around collecting news and gathering information is tolerated."

TV JOURNALISM DOESN'T HAVE TO BE PERFECT TO BE GREAT

The best recent example of excellent television journalism across the board was the spectacular breaking news coverage of the 9/11 attacks. The cable networks and news divisions of all the broadcast networks provided textbook examples of how well-done television journalism is an important public service, particularly in a democracy under attack. Within moments of the first explosion at the World Trade Center, viewers knew it was a plane. As the story continued to develop, the nation immediately saw and heard what was happening in New York, in Washington, D.C., and in Pennsylvania. We watched in horror as the towers collapsed, heard government officials urge caution in public areas, were promptly told of airport closings, and were kept informed second by second. It was not pretty television production, not at all. Every network experienced numerous technical glitches. Anchors tossed to reporters who weren't where they were supposed to be or, if they were, the satellite hookup wasn't ready. Color bars appeared on screens. There were audio problems in live reports and in taped ones. Anchors on camera were seen asking their control room producers what they should be doing next, who they should toss to, or what story they should read. They hemmed and hawed at times, shuffling through papers or reading from wire-service news reports on their set computers. Reporters in the field popped up on screens unexpectedly, dabbing on makeup and not knowing that their image was being beamed around the world.

No, this wasn't smooth television news. It wasn't textbook high-gloss, snazzy production. But it was amazing. Television journalists in front of and behind the cameras, as well as technicians and support personnel, scrambled and provided the best, up-to-date information to a frightened American public they could under very trying circumstances.

"Our 9/11 coverage was superb," said NBC News veteran correspondent George Lewis, speaking of all television coverage. "We showed on that day that we're still capable of performing an enormous public service and [of] knitting the nation together as we have throughout the years. I thought we really rose to that occasion in a magnificent way. All the networks did. We had a situation where the nation was under attack and, for awhile, we didn't know whether there would be more attacks to follow. The public was demanding information and we were able to pump it out and put it in its proper perspective. I think the anchors were superb that day in staying calm and in giving people the truth when the entire nation was demanding the truth in what was going on."

After a pause, this veteran journalist added, "I was proud to be in the business and proud to be part of pumping out that information that people were hanging on to." It is not a sentiment that Lewis or many other television journalists have expressed very often in recent years.

While the coverage over succeeding days also hit some lows with erroneous reports, rushes to judgment, and unethical flag-waving by some journalists and networks, TV reporters also led the way—often ahead of government investigators—in uncovering information on the hijackers, their backgrounds, how and where they were trained, where they lived while preparing this attack in the United States, and what their motives were. ABC News, for example, was the first to identify Mohammed Atta and how he and his fellow terrorists had obtained flight training at flight schools in the United States. ABC also was the only news outlet that had the audiotape of cockpit conversations of the hijacking of United Flight 93, which crashed in Pennsylvania. An editorial in the *Baltimore Sun* remarked, "It looked as though the FBI was playing catch-up with ABC News."

In November of 2002, when all of the broadcast news divisions and cable networks were being honored by the National Television Academy for their coverage of 9/11, NBC News executive Neil Shapiro spoke of a phone conversation he had had on 9/11 with the president of CBS. Andrew Heyward, he said, called to suggest that the networks share footage for a day and not compete for news. "There may be times in the future when once again the American public will be better served when we act together," Shapiro told the audience.

The 9/11 coverage was an example of textbook journalism. The classic who, what, where, when, and how questions that journalism students are taught in school were answered time and time again. The U.S. television news press corps delivered.

LONG-FORM JOURNALISM CAN HIT THE MARK

Now and then good TV news can also be seen in some of the television newsmagazine shows. *CNN Presents,* which is aired on a weekend day, often produces high-quality reports on topics that are extremely relevant to viewers. For example, documentaries on the world's population explosion and on the working poor in the United States, to name just two award-winning programs, educated, informed, and warned of dangerous trends. *CNN Presents* reports are generally well written, well researched, and well shot, which makes them compelling to watch. Some of the other network news magazines—such as NBC's *Dateline,* ABC's *20/20,* and CBS's *48 Hours*—also achieve greatness now and then. But all too frequently all of these magazine shows become bottom feeders offering celebrity profiles and other stories that have absolutely no weight on the news scale. Have J-Lo and Ben truly split up? And if so, why? I know these stories are of great interest to many viewers in this country, and they definitely have a place on television—but not in newscasts or newsmagazines.

Recent news specials that rate highly on the quality scale include the coverage of the millennium and the handover of Hong Kong to the Chinese. Overall, the major cable networks and broadcast news programs all provided compelling reports, live and taped. CNN's coverage of the twentieth anniversary of the Vietnam War provided context and depth to an important chapter in history that young Americans now only read about. "There was some superb writing and insightful reporting that led to a better understanding of relations between Vietnam and the United States," said producer Robert Wiener, who covered that war and later was CNN's executive producer and mastermind in Baghdad and who oversaw that network's groundbreaking coverage of the Gulf War. An older example of good, solid reporting was the Pierre Salinger special on ABC News in 1981 on how the Carter administration freed the American hostages in Iran. As colleague Tom Lubart, a former ABC employee, recalls, "Cameras recorded the critical meetings and were there until the end. The result was spectacular and an example of how things happen in the real world."

Indeed, U.S.-style television journalism done right has had tremendous impact in many other countries. "I'm proud of the work western journalists did in exposing genocide and mass murder around the world and spurring action, sometimes belatedly, nonetheless, spurring action in Bosnia, in Kosovo, in East Timor . . . and getting these people help and changing things," said CNN war correspondent Christiane Amanpour. To that list, add the coverage of Sarajevo and Somalia, to name just two more. In each story, television journalists shined bright lights on darkness and helped stop the murder of innocent people.

RESPONSIBLE JOURNALISM THAT IS NEVER SEEN

Still, some of the best, most ethical decisions made by television journalists do not result in news stories. The public rarely hears of these decisions due to the very nature of them. In a way, that's a shame, given the

poor opinion many people in this country have of all journalists, particularly the TV type. A very common criticism of the broadcast media
raises its ugly head every time U.S. troops are deployed somewhere in the
world. Americans condemn the media for reporting too much, for giving away secrets, for endangering the lives of U.S. service personnel. We
heard it during Vietnam, during all of the wars in Iraq, in Afghanistan,
in Somalia. We've heard it time and time again. But the reality, the truth,
is quite different. There is not a single case of a U.S. military person dying
as a result of a journalist's work. Not one.

And why? Because so far, the journalists involved in covering these
conflicts have exercised restraint and proven themselves to be responsible. Make no mistake, that does not mean that they are pro–American
troops. They have simply taken every precaution needed to ensure that
their reports—albeit accurate and informative—do not directly lead to
the death of anyone in the conflict. In a manner of speaking, it *is* self-
censorship. I have to acknowledge that as much as I detest the thought
of it. But it is deciding what should be reported and what should not. In
the end, it is also responsible journalism.

I wish I could provide several examples of such restraint by other journalists, but because *not* making such decisions public is the point, it is
hard to do. However, I will share an instance in which CNN senior executives and I made the decision to withhold information on a major
national story for a later date. CNN chairman Tom Johnson also forbade
us to air some specific video.

The story was the 1993 standoff in Waco, Texas, between the
Branch Davidians and federal authorities, including the Federal Bureau
of Investigations (FBI) and the Bureau of Alcohol, Tobacco and
Firearms (BATF). I was CNN's main live reporter from 6 AM to 8 PM
(EST) during the month-and-a-half-long standoff. During the first two
to three weeks of the story, I had befriended—over beers and during
games of pool—several of the tactical agents and commanders of the
FBI and BATF. They, no doubt, checked with colleagues who had
encountered me in other situations and, after awhile, began to trust
me and to share critical information with me. By the twentieth day of

the standoff, which lasted over fifty, I knew that tracked vehicles had been retrofitted to be able to deliver tear gas. I knew that the Cessna that flew above us several times a day contained infrared cameras that allowed the feds to pinpoint human activity in the compound. I knew that the reason the BATF had not knocked down the flagpole flying the Branch Davidian banner was because sharpshooters were using it to gauge wind direction and strength. They also told me about the listening devices that were hidden in milk containers delivered to the Branch Davidians and about the robot that was wheeled to the side of the building on many evenings. It, too, contained several cameras and listening devices. During the day and during the night, agents were also close to the building, lying on their bellies in the high grass, observing. For this reason alone, the FBI asked CNN chairman Tom Johnson not to permit the airing of live pictures or video from our thermal-cam, which turned muddy nighttime pictures into clear daytime ones. Johnson agreed.

But the decision to withhold the rest of what I knew was made by me and by CNN senior executives, without the knowledge or request of the federal officials. We determined that if the Branch Davidians had battery-powered television sets or radios, the lives of federal agents could be jeopardized by revealing this information. It was a risk we would not take. It was not until the final showdown, the day the compound went up in flames, that I revealed these facts. I had flown back to Atlanta the night before to anchor CNN's coverage of the assault the next day. It was information the public deserved to know and it was finally being reported at a time when it would no longer jeopardize the lives of the federal agents. Did viewers figure out that we had withheld information to protect lives? Probably not. And that's fine.

GOOD LUCK AND GOOD JOURNALISM

Sometimes news coups and top-notch coverage have nothing to do with advance planning, spending money, or having excellent sources in the know. Though we generally hate to admit it, sometimes being in the right place at the right time is just the result of plain dumb luck. *Then* it's up to the reporter's training, skill, and experience to take advantage of an opportunity to provide the public with information.

One such story came to ABC News on May 21, 1991, when Rajiv Gandhi was assassinated in India. Many national U.S. news organizations instantly dispatched crews from nearby countries and from the United States. To the dismay of the other networks, ABC had a senior correspondent on the scene almost immediately. Within hours of Gandhi's death, John Quinones was in India reporting the story and beating the hell out of all other U.S. television news organizations. How did it happen? Luck, pure and simple. He was already on his way to India to do a story for *20/20* when the assassination took place. He simply got off the plane, did his job of finding out the latest facts and getting the latest material, and bingo: major news coup. And American viewers were the recipients of up-to-date information.

When I was managing editor of the fledgling CNN en Español network, I experienced near nirvana with a similar episode. It was the evening of August 31, 1997, and I had just gotten home from a long day in the newsroom. Moments later, though, the phone rang. Princess Diana, I was told, had been in an accident in Paris. We immediately swung into action, and within a short time, CNN sources were saying that the princess had died. We were all concerned for our coverage, as our stringer in Paris was untried in circumstances like this, which would call for days and days of live broadcasts and information digging with no time off.

Then my phone rang again and I heard the best news possible. Our top Latin American correspondent, Harris Whitbeck, had just landed in Paris moments before to change planes on his way to a vacation. When he heard what had happened, he called us from the airport. I will never forget my reaction: "Harris is in Paris! Harris is in Paris!" Within minutes, Harris was on the air reporting by phone. Not long after that, he began what seemed to be a never-ending series of live broadcasts from Paris. I can still imagine our competitors at CBS Telenoticias watching Harris on a newsroom monitor and wondering how the hell CNN en Español pulled this one off. It was the combination of luck, a staff of experienced assignment editors and producers, and an excellent correspondent who knew how to responsibly take advantage of this opportunity.

SOMETIMES GOOD JOURNALISM IS ACHIEVED BY JUST DOING ONE'S JOB

In all of the reports I did in twenty years as a correspondent, I'm most proud of one particular series of stories because they truly had an important, measurable impact. It was 1984, and I was working as a foreign correspondent for NBC News based in Beirut, Lebanon, during the height of the civil war there. But I was also tasked with covering stories throughout the Middle East and Africa. It was in this capacity that I witnessed what remains for me the single most heartrending drama of my professional life. It started out as a natural disaster of huge proportions, but the tragedy was magnified many times over by man's inhumanity toward man. I believed then, and still do now, that if I never reported on another story, my career would have been complete.

The British Broadcasting Corporation (BBC) broke the story of the 1984–1985 African drought and ensuing famine. After years without rain, an entire swath of sub-Saharan Africa, from the Atlantic Ocean to the Indian Ocean, had become a lifeless desert. The images the BBC transmitted to the world were devastating: bone-thin men, women, and children, their huge frightened eyes looking out from their emaciated faces, their sunken chests heaving a final breath after months of starvation. The death toll was in the millions.

In London, NBC News bureau chief Joe Angotti saw the BBC reports, knew this was an important story, and immediately called the New York headquarters to confer with assignment editors and executives. "When I first talked to New York about the story, they said no one really cares about what happened in Africa. I remember someone saying we just did a study about what viewers want to see and Africa was at the bottom of the list. And they wouldn't let me send anybody." But Angotti persisted, first convincing *NBC Nightly News* to air some of the BBC reports from Ethiopia. He said he knew that the story, especially the video of such helpless reed-thin people, would touch the hearts of viewers and that that in turn might galvanize NBC News managers into action. Angotti was right. The American people responded with horror, compassion—and dollars. Aid agencies immediately pledged relief, and ships and planes loaded with food began streaming toward Addis Ababa, the Ethiopian capital. And Angotti, the London bureau chief, was given the go-ahead to send NBC News crews and correspondents to Ethiopia.

A day or two after the first reports hit the airwaves in the United States, I was contacted in Beirut by a small aid organization called Grassroots International, headquartered in Boston. Grassroots had been given my name by a source at the International Rescue Committee who—having seen my work in Latin America and beyond—felt that I had the guts to take on dangerous assignments and the heart to tell the world about human atrocities. I was told that the pictures we had seen of the drought and resulting famine were just the tip of the iceberg. And then I was told the most disturbing news of all: that the Ethiopian government was practicing genocide on its own people. The story seemed too awful to be true.

The two regions of Ethiopia hit hardest by the drought were the provinces of Tigray and Eritrea. But because these two areas had been fighting for independence from the Marxist central government in Addis Ababa, officials there came up with a convenient strategy to weaken and even wipe out the enemy: starve them to death. Although food was beginning to arrive from aid organizations and governments around the world, the central government wasn't distributing any of it in the rebel-held areas. The result was an exodus of starving refugees to neighboring Sudan and a human catastrophe of historic dimensions.

I knew immediately that I had to go to Tigray and Eritrea. I conferred with my bosses in New York, not knowing what Joe Angotti had gone through, and filled them in on what I had been told. Since there was no guarantee that my crew and I would be able to get into Tigray and Eritrea through Sudan, the foreign assignment editor weighed that fact and the cost of such a trip against what we might be able to uncover. Finally, I was given the green light.

Correspondents are encouraged to be enterprising with stories, to come up with good reports, investigations, and things of that nature on our own. But the vast majority of news stories on all of the cable and broadcast networks are not this type. They are assigned by producers and assignment editors at the network's main office. All too often, to our shame, they are stories that our bosses read in the *New York Times* that morning. Other stories that make it on the broadcast networks' newscasts are generally the other most obvious major stories of the day. These are stories producers believe must be done: the president's speech, the latest economic indicators, the high school shooting that day. (This explains why the story selection for the three broadcast networks is often identical.) Because *NBC Nightly News with Tom Brokaw, ABC World News Tonight with Peter Jennings,* and *CBS Evening News with Dan Rather* only use about twenty-two minutes of their half hour for news—the rest is commercials—this means an average of no more than five or six taped reports per day to cover domestic and international news. And that means that getting an enterprise story on the air, although the bosses profess to love them, is nearly impossible. So when the NBC assignment editor finally agreed to let me proceed, I didn't give him a chance to change his mind. My crew and I were on planes within hours heading to Khartoum, the capital of Sudan, which lies in the east-central part of the country at the confluence of the Blue Nile and the White Nile.

Numerous aid agencies had set up operations on the Sudanese border with Ethiopia, offering food and medical aid to those fleeing refugees who managed to get out alive. But most of the agencies wouldn't cross the border into Tigray and Eritrea, where the need was far greater. The awful truth was that organizations such as the International Committee of the Red Cross refused to go into Tigray and Eritrea because they knew that if they did the Marxist government would kick them out of the rest of the country, where they were also providing aid. And many countries, including the United States, had a policy of not distributing aid to rebel-controlled areas during civil wars. The policy was designed to appease ruling governments and to avoid becoming involved in other nations' internal conflicts.

Before leaving Khartoum to head to the border, we stopped by the United States embassy to let them know our plans. As in most totalitarian governments, the leaders of Ethiopia had no use for a free press and would think nothing of killing us should they discover our presence. Not only did the officials at the U.S. embassy discourage us from going, they ordered us not to go. And it was made very clear that if something happened to us, we would be on our own; the United States government would not intervene on our behalf. To underline the warning, I received a handwritten note the next day from First Secretary William A. Pierce. I found it telling that the note was written on a plain piece of white paper and not on embassy stationery. Depending on what happened, they could pull out a copy and say, "See? We warned them," or they could declare, with disingenuous honesty, "We have no official record of their trip."

The note read: "Ms. Anderson—After hearing of your plans, I would be remiss in not cautioning you on the dangers inherent in any travel you might make across the border. The areas in which you wish to travel constitute a zone of war and military action between the Ethiopian Government and the TPLF [Tigrayan People's Liberation Front], in which you could become unnecessarily exposed to danger. . . . We at the embassy suggest that you not proceed with these plans."

Fair enough, I thought, I've been warned. I shared the letter with my team so that everyone would be aware of the warning and given an opportunity to back out of the assignment. This is a journalistic practice called "road rules." If any member of a team, when informed that his or her life may be at risk, decides to withdraw, then the entire team withdraws— but no one outside the team is ever told who made the original call. There is no shame, no recrimination. This variation on "all for one, one for all" creates a deep bond on tough assignments and leads to the cohesive teamwork that is crucial to success—and survival. Everyone on my team read the embassy letter and we unanimously agreed to continue with our plan to go into Ethiopia.

While we waited to meet up with the guerrilla soldiers who would escort us into Ethiopia, we traveled around western Sudan. Vast stretches of former farmland had turned into desert. We saw farmers trying to sell their bony oxen and cattle because there was no grass to feed them and nothing but dust to hoe. Others from the countryside simply abandoned their homes and camped out in the dust and dirt of nearby villages. But the most desperate people we saw were the refugees from neighboring Chad, which was being devastated by the same drought, begging soldiers for a handful of cattle fodder. Then there were the children born with deformities or missing limbs as a result of their mothers' malnutrition. My heart was breaking, and we hadn't even crossed the border into the hardest hit areas.

Because the only stories on the famine so far had centered on Ethiopia, it was clear that we needed to get our report on the Chad refugees out immediately. Even though NBC News had a strict policy that every script had to be approved in advance, we had no access to phones. So I took a chance. I wrote from my heart and read the script on tape several times, with minor variations, to give the tape editor in London some options. I included editing instructions but knew that the moment my colleagues at NBC saw our footage, they'd carefully craft it into the best possible story. (Weeks later when I saw the pieces, they were even better than I had imagined. In a rush, a news story can be edited, "cut," in half an hour, but the best video often never sees the light of day. It was obvious to me that the tape editor who married my voice with the images took painstaking care to choose the absolutely best shots so that the pictures added to what I was reporting.) Then we found someone to courier the material to Khartoum, put it on a plane to London, and call NBC to give them a heads-up. Only after we were assured that our story was safely on its way did we travel to eastern Sudan to meet up with our Tigrayan guerrilla contacts in preparation for crossing into Ethiopia.

The Tigrayan People's Liberation Front was made up of men and women, professors and farmers and businessmen, who desperately wanted their freedom and were willing to risk their lives fighting for it. Once the famine began, however, they spent much of their time doing what they could to feed their countrymen. With just a handful of trucks, they'd load up food at the Sudanese border and drive into Tigray along dusty roads booby-trapped with land mines. Along the way they would distribute the food to the neediest. On the return trip they'd give rides to freedom—and life—to those they thought might actually survive the trip.

We began our trip just after dark, which is when the refugee roads really came to life. During the day the Marxist government's Russian-made MIG fighter planes strafed anyone and anything they came across. As it hadn't rained in years, the ground was covered by inches of fine dust and sand that billowed up around each truck. All we could see in our headlights was the faint outline of the vehicle ahead.

But no amount of dust and sand could obscure the human tragedy unfolding around us. Tens of thousands of refugees, skeletal men, women, and children, were walking toward the Sudanese border in a desperate effort to save their lives. Some had been marching for hundreds of miles, many of them even during daylight hours because they were so desperate. I watched in horror and sorrow as a weary, bone-thin old man slowed his measured walk to a halt, sank to his knees, and leaned his head against his walking stick. Moments later, he fell back against the dirt, placed his hands over his eyes, and died. Exhausted mothers who had given their last morsels of food and drops of water to their children openly wept as they realized that their trek, and their time upon this earth, was over. I sat with one woman who was cradling her two-day old infant, talking with her through an interpreter, when the baby suddenly sighed and became still. The woman simply bowed her head in knowing resignation, never uttering a sound.

It didn't matter which way we pointed our camera, there was material for our stories everywhere we turned. At first, the overwhelming numbers of victims made it hard to see them as individuals. But all it took was talking to one or two people, through our able Tigrayan interpreters, before we realized that every person's story was different and unique, and deserved to be told. This hardly made our job easier. We were planning a series of stories, at least half a dozen, and struggled to shape them as we filmed. Finally, we gave up on that approach, deciding instead to simply shoot everything and interview everyone we could. I'd sort it all out later. It worked. After a couple of days we knew that we had the material we needed. We could have stayed longer and gotten more of the same, but we felt a sense of urgency to get the story out to the world. We cut the trip short.

The stories—there ended up being about ten of them—were all aired on *NBC Nightly News with Tom Brokaw.* I reported not only about the lack of food, but also about the lack of good drinking water and medicine. We showed pictures of people digging deep into the desert floor until they found foul, brown, brackish water to drink. I interviewed a British doctor, one of the few who dared help the rebels, as he treated a young, emaciated baby boy named Mohammed Rukar. This boy could easily be saved with simple IV fluids, he told me. But Tigrayans had no access to IV fluids, and so Mohammed died the next morning. Each report was filled with several of these personal stories, which I knew would have an impact on parents and children and, frankly, anyone who watched them. There was an immediate public reaction across the United States. Newspapers picked up the story and it continued to spread like wildfire, with aid agencies being inundated with contributions from generous Americans.

Within a couple of days, I got a call from a "high" official at the State Department. NBC gave me permission to brief him, although I had to swear never to reveal his name. I agreed to speak with him as long as we discussed only what had been reported in my stories: food that was being sent to Addis Ababa, the capital, was not being distributed to Tigray and Eritrea because the Marxist government was trying to win the civil war with these regions by starving them out. The official asked how aid could be sent to the rebels, and I reminded him about the convoy of trucks that left from the Sudanese border. He thanked me in a businesslike manner and after ten minutes, the call was over.

About two days after this conversation, I got a call in London from the assignment editor at NBC's Foreign Desk in New York. He read me an AP story that had just crossed his desk: the State Department had issued a directive reversing American policy of not sending humanitarian aid to rebel-controlled areas of foreign countries. I was stunned. U.S. government policy had been changed as a result of the stories done by my crew and our producers and support people in London and New York. Food, water, and medicine were at that moment heading to Tigray and Eritrea. Even though my scripts weren't the most polished I'd ever written, this was the best, most responsible journalism I've ever done. Lives were saved in Ethiopia for one reason: because my colleagues and I simply did our job.

Whether it's a case of a local television reporter exposing corruption in a small town or a network correspondent revealing more global evil, the result is the same: good journalism. You know it when you see it. Unfortunately, as Chapter Five shows, bad journalism is sometimes difficult to identify because it is more subtle and often involves deals and actions taken behind the scenes. That's what makes it so dangerous.

THE BAD

ON JANUARY 12, 2000, at the height of the controversy surrounding whether young Elian Gonzalez should be permitted to stay in the United States with extended family or be returned to his father in Cuba, the Miami media ignited yet another firestorm. It centered on some ten seconds of videotape of the Cuban boy playing in the backyard with a friend, surrounded by Miami relatives and neighbors. As a plane flew overhead, Elian stopped his horseplay for an instant, looked up at the sky, and with his back partially toward the camera, said, "Avion! No quiero volver a Cuba!" Airplane, I *don't want* to return to Cuba!

Or did he? Instead, might he have said, "Avion! Yo quiero volver a Cuba!" Airplane, I *want* to return to Cuba?

Depending on which television station you watched, you got either answer. News stations and newspapers even hired linguists who swore the boy was saying he did not want to go back to Cuba. But then again, there were other experts who were absolutely positive the boy said he wanted to go home. And that is what they reported—as incontrovertible truth. The controversy became a story in itself, with the tape being played time and time again on the Spanish- and English-language TV stations.

Should these newscasts have concluded what the boy said one way or another when the tape was not clear? As soon as CNN got a copy of it, I was asked to review it for the national assignment desk. After all, they figured I was born in Cuba and would be able to tell what Elian said. I watched the tape numerous times and then listened to it with my eyes closed. The boy could have said either sentence; the quality of the recording was simply not good enough to tell conclusively. So the debate about what to do began. The discussion included senior management, the executive producer in charge of script approval who was also well respected in the field of ethics, assignment editors, the show producers, and literally everyone else who listened to the debate and wanted to weigh in. In the end, CNN took what I believe was the most ethical approach under the circumstances. The network reported on the controversy itself, played the tape, and explained how the two completely opposite interpretations of Elian's words had created such a brouhaha in Miami. CNN did not venture to guess which one was correct. Many of the Miami stations had. I would like to think that it was because they truly believed what they were reporting. If that is the case, then what they did was not an intentional ethical lapse. But, in retrospect, it wasn't responsible journalism, either.

There has never been a time when the line between what is ethical and what is not in television news was clear, recognizable, and unmistakable. In Vietnam, for example, was it ethical for journalists to travel with soldiers, hitching rides on U.S. helicopters and other modes of transportation? Did that align them too closely with one side of the war? After tremendous soul-searching by many news operations, most independently arrived at the same conclusion: no. Because the journalists could decide where to go and when to go, what to cover and what not to cover, what could be reported and what should not, they could maintain their independence. This is quite different from the "embedding" of journalists with U.S. troops during the 2003 war in Iraq, which will be discussed in greater detail in Chapter Nine.

In the same vein, other ethical debates have centered on whether reporters covering political campaigns should accept free transportation aboard the candidate's plane, and whether reporters should fly on Air Force One when the candidate is the sitting president. The same issue arises when it comes to traveling with the pope to cover his international visits. Then there's the matter of reporters who do travel and vacation stories. Should they accept trips to resorts so that they can report on them? Should entertainment reporters accept complimentary tickets to performances? Twenty-five or thirty years ago, these practices were often overlooked by news managers because they weren't very routine. But over time, more and more news organizations—particularly the larger, national ones—acknowledged the conflict of interest and began paying all travel expenses and picking up all costs. Today, for example, news organizations always reimburse the White House or the Vatican for the real costs of flying with these heads of state. But some still justify junkets if they deal with coverage of issues seen as less controversial or less important, such as show business or travel. Journalists, including network executives, still argue over whether any harm is really done when an entertainment reporter hitches a ride with a celebrity on his private plane.

What is clearly evident, though, is a general, across-the-board decay of ethics. There are more and more examples of bad journalism to point to as infotainment, and the lust for profits gnaws at professional standards. Practices that would have gotten any television journalist fired a decade or two ago are now commonly used by nearly all reporters in the business.

JUDGMENT CALLS: THE TOUGH AND THE TOUGHER

Should television newscasts include close-ups of the horrors of war? Can viewers grasp the horror of a bombing in a marketplace in Bosnia without seeing the decapitated body of a victim? When Islamic Jihad in

Lebanon released a videotape of American hostage Col. William R. Higgins showing him dead, hanging by the neck, was this something viewers in the United States should have seen so they could truly understand the animosity this extremist terrorist group had against this country? Or was it enough to show only a few seconds of his legs dangling in the air? Should news organizations air al-Qaida videotapes of Osama Bin Laden urging Muslims worldwide to wage war against the American infidels? These are all judgment calls, and they are difficult to make.

Even more difficult, though, are ethical questions that are less obvious. Even the *appearance* of impropriety, journalists are taught in school, should be enough to regulate what we do or don't do. So, was it OK for Rick Kaplan, then-president of CNN, to spend the night in the Clinton White House along with his daughter and confirm to the world his status as an FOB (Friend of Bill's) while he was heading the "most powerful news network" on Earth? Is it ethical for Fox News Network executive Roger Ailes to advise President Bush while simultaneously running a news organization that he claims is "fair and balanced"? Should executives from CNN and other networks display in their offices photos of themselves smiling with an arm around Fidel Castro, while at the same time saying their coverage of Cuba is unbiased and accurate?

In many television newsrooms across the nation, particularly those of the national networks, these kinds of ethical debates are waged almost daily among staff members. It is a healthy exercise that more often than not results in better journalism. But in many other newsrooms there are few such discussions, and very little scrutiny of standards and techniques takes place. The sole aim is to get the story on the air as soon as possible. Be first, not necessarily right. And if the video is shocking, that's even better. If it bleeds, it leads.

TRUST US, WE ONLY FAKE THE SMALL STUFF

Things that would never have been seen in newscasts even a decade or so ago are now seen daily. As William Hurt's character in the movie *Broadcast News* said about the line between what is ethical and what is not, "They keep moving the little sucker, don't they?" Not only that, but it is also as blurry as the boundary that now exists between news and entertainment. It is important to explore this gray area, which I call the Bad (sandwiched between the Good and the Ugly), because here is where once unethical practices are transformed into acceptable routines over time, sometimes openly, sometimes not.

In this category falls the common use these days of some shots that have been set up in advance, video of events that did not occur naturally. A cardinal rule of ethical television journalism has always been that the video should be honest, nothing faked. But over the years, a few practices have become standard operating procedure. When you see a reporter walking alongside the person they're interviewing, this wasn't just a lucky break for the photographer. He or she set up a camera and then cued the reporter and subject to walk by. I've participated in this same charade myself on both sides of the camera, as a reporter and as an interview subject. When *60 Minutes* did a story in 2001 about my father's murder in Cuba, I did "the walk" with my Mom. In retrospect, I'm uncomfortable with that.

In many news stories, you'll also see video of the interview subject sitting at a desk answering a phone or typing on a computer as you hear the reporter's voice introducing the person. This video, called b-roll, is generally set up by the reporter or the photographer saying, "Do what you would normally do if we weren't here" or, more directly, "Please sit down and type on your computer so that we can get some b-roll." Similarly, when you see a reporter asking a question during a sit-down interview, all too often—and especially in local television—that, too, is faked. Few stations have the resources to send two camera crews on one story. So once the interview is completed, where the camera has been focused solely on the interviewee, the photographer sets up behind where the subject was seated and the reporter asks the same questions again, this time on camera. Oftentimes the person who was interviewed is no longer even in the room, so the reporter is talking to an empty chair. You wouldn't know it when you see it on TV. That's the point.

Are these inexcusable, horrible ethical lapses? Well, at one time they were considered that. But not anymore. The assumption is that viewers are smart enough to know that these shots are set up. And in CNN's ethics policy handbook, for example, these shots are permissible, as are so-called "re-ask" questions, under certain circumstances. But are these practices, at the end of the day, all bad? While they might make the lives of reporters and photographers easier, they deceive viewers. If we're not honest about something so basic, how can we expect the public to believe us on more major issues? If viewers know or suspect that we're cutting these interview-related corners to save time, money, and effort, it would not be unreasonable for them to also believe that television journalists routinely engage in more serious unethical practices. And that leads to further erosion of credibility. The truth is that all of these situations could be avoided by using additional camera crews and dedicating more time (which means more money) to the story. Network programs such as CBS's *60 Minutes,* NBC's *Dateline,* or *CNN Presents* all have the resources to do the stories properly, and they generally do. But to cover daily news, networks don't and neither do the local stations. So this is a sleight of hand now considered acceptable for economic reasons. News, after all, has become a race against time and competitors, and managers will not "waste" precious news-gathering dollars to prevent what is now considered a minor peccadillo.

JUST BECAUSE WE CAN, SHOULD WE?

As technology improves how we're able to communicate news, new situations arise that create whole new and different ethical dilemmas. For example, we're now able to videotape people's voices and pictures in more clandestine ways than ever before. But is it the right thing to do? We have the capability to show executions live, but should we? Does it serve the public?

Technology has revolutionized television news time and time again. And that has surely had an impact on ethics. When it is used properly to better collect information or help transmit it faster, it is a very valuable tool. In just over three decades, cameras have gone from using film to using tape, which eliminated the time and effort needed in processing. This is a case of good news/bad news. The good news is that stations and networks can get images on the air faster, in a more timely fashion. The bad news is that stations and networks get images on the air faster—before reporters and producers have the chance to evaluate the material, to investigate, to obtain context and balance. If you wonder why the news you're seeing seems to be shallower and less informative than in years past, realize that you've traded depth for immediacy. Is it a good thing?

The technology for doing *live* television has changed the way news is delivered even more—again, for better and for worse. Live television has allowed viewers to experience major news events around the globe, from war zones to natural disasters to momentous assemblies of the United Nations Security Council. And it has helped citizens keep an eye on local government in real time with live reports from city council meetings, from election campaign headquarters, or from police departments. This technology, though, has become so commonplace that it is now used all too often simply for effect, to jazz up a newscast regardless of news value. It is the modern version of using smoke and mirrors to make viewers believe stories are far more important, or far more immediate, than they really are. And that is not only stupid, it's deceptive.

In 2002, I was watching an 11 PM newscast on an Atlanta local station when I saw three live shots that made absolutely no sense to me. In the first place, it was raining so hard the reporters were barely able to hold on to their umbrellas. From experience, I figured the camera crews were getting even more wet. Second, it was pitch black outside—so viewers could not see anything behind the reporters. But what was even more ridiculous was that there was no reason to have these live reports originating from a courthouse and other such places. The news that was being reported had taken place many hours earlier. The stories could have been told very well, even better, in taped form.

Seeing three such live shots in one broadcast prompted me to pick up the phone and call the station. When I got the night assignment editor on the line, I identified myself as a network journalist in town and asked why the station felt compelled to do something so foolish. "We're under orders from our news director," I was told. "We have to have three live shots in our 11 PM newscast no matter what."

Live for live's sake. It is using technology for reasons that have nothing to do with news or journalism in an attempt to impress viewers with the "we're taking you there live" ability. I suspect viewers couldn't care less. And consider that although local television live shots are most often done with microwave trucks, which don't entail buying expensive satellite time, they do run up bills for staff overtime and equipment maintenance and repair. The cost for transmission of a satellite live shot, depending on where it originates, can run as much as $5,000 to $15,000 for a fifteen-minute window, not to mention possible truck rental and crew costs. So doing live shots for no real justifiable news reason wastes money that could be spent on pursuing other news.

Around 1990, when I was reporting for WTVJ, the NBC-owned station in Miami, I was ordered to do something similar by a young, inexperienced news director who wanted to hype the weather department's new set and fancy radar equipment. It was called the Storm Center, and it had cost millions of dollars to build. The station had been promoting its enhanced storm-forecasting ability for weeks, and the news director wanted to "own" weather coverage in South Florida. So the first day that the morning weather person suggested there might be a thunderstorm that afternoon—as if a thunderstorm in Miami during the summer is news—I was dispatched with a crew and our satellite truck to be in position to lead the 6 PM newscast with storm coverage.

There was only one problem. It wasn't storming. It wasn't even raining. In fact, the skies were clear blue and very sunny. When I called the news director to inform her about what we hadn't found, I was told to stop being difficult and to prepare for the live shot. The station had promoted the Storm Center, and it would have its debut that evening no matter what. The camera crew, the satellite truck engineer, and I continued to drive around South Miami looking for rain until the very last minute. At about 5:40 PM, we pulled off the side of U.S. 1 and set up for a live shot. I again called the newsroom to report that we were, unfortunately, experiencing a very nice, sunny day—but was told the newscast producer wanted the damn live shot so we had better deliver.

I know I have done some silly things in my professional life, but this ranks up there with the best of the worst. The newscast opened with music and graphics and then dissolved to the anchors on the set, who informed our viewers that the Storm Center had forecast a huge thunderstorm for South Florida. And to bring us the latest, they were going to me—live on U.S. 1.

Squinting, as the sun was in my eyes, I faced the camera and said in a very serious voice, "So far, the weather seems to be holding up, although in the far distance there—" and I turned, pointing over my shoulder, "we can see a cloud over what is probably Homestead." My cameraman zoomed in to the whitish cloud, the only one on the horizon, as I continued. "We'll keep a close eye on this and get back to you should the weather turn foul." I then tossed it back to the anchors. I later timed a taped copy of the live shot; it lasted under fifteen seconds, the shortest I had ever done and probably a contender for the shortest live shot on record. I looked stupid, the station looked stupid, and viewers were not served. This was not just live for live's sake, it was live for the sake of promoting a Storm Center. This had nothing to do with journalism or informing the public. The news director never asked me to do anything like this again, but I was also not high on her list of favorite reporters because I was so contrary.

"EXCLUSIVE" COVERAGE OF THE END OF THE WORLD!

Another disturbing trend in television journalism is the overuse and false use of the word "exclusive" when local stations or networks tout that they are the only ones with a particular story. The aim is to entice viewers to watch only your newscast because you offer the most comprehensive and innovative coverage. More often than not these days, it's simply not true. The next time you see or hear the word "exclusive" during a newscast, flip around to the other stations on at the same time. Quite often you'll see the same so-called "exclusive" stories elsewhere. How is this rationalized? Well, sometimes by splitting hairs. If a producer believes her or his station has even one shot that other stations didn't get, or one piece of information no one else knows, that justifies branding the entire report as exclusive. But few viewers actually watch multiple newscasts at once, so they don't realize this is another form of subterfuge.

Robert Wiener is one of the top field producers in the network news world and author of *Live From Baghdad,* the story of how CNN managed to be the only network reporting from Iraq's capital city during the Gulf War. On 9/11, he was dispatched to Pakistan to help report reaction from that part of the world. "What really disturbed me was what happened with the first news conference held by a high Pakistani official," he recalled. "I said this press conference is important, so we'll drop a [satellite] cable from the roof [where the dish was located] and we'll cover it. Suddenly I look up and see 'exclusive' on the [CNN] screen. Now what the hell is exclusive about a news conference?" To the CNN producers in charge, the fact that CNN may have been the only U.S. network taking the press conference live was enough to justify the "exclusive" banner. It didn't matter that other U.S. networks were there, and that the press conference was also seen live in dozens of other countries. And it apparently didn't matter that viewers seeing some of the same video on another network later in the day might conclude CNN had been dishonest. A news organization's greatest asset is its reputation. This sort of "little white lie" is not only unethical, it's irresponsible and it's bad business.

CONTENT CAN'T BE MORE IMPORTANT THAN HOW THE NEWSCAST LOOKS, CAN IT?

The truth is that many newscast producers, especially in local television, worry more about how their shows *look* and *flow* than about content. Believing that younger viewers used to multitasking are drawn to newscasts with snazzy graphics and bottom-of-the-screen crawls that offer another stream of information, producers are often putting news snippets on the screen as fast as they can. As a consequence, they're all too often sidestepping normal script approval and fact-checking procedures that the video stories go through. Equally worrisome is that much of the information thrown into the crawls along the bottom of the screen is simply lifted from wire stories reported by other news organizations. This, along with professional laziness or sloppiness, has resulted in errors of all sorts. When I was a CNN executive with several TV monitors in my office tuned to different CNN networks, rarely would a week go by without me calling a control room to correct a fact or a misspelled word on screen. One week I called three times: to let them know Morocco was not spelled "Morroco" and to have them correct what I hoped were typos, "Amercan" and "Untied States." NBC correspondent George Lewis agrees that these types of errors have unfortunately become routine. "On banners or crawls I see a lot of information plastered on the screens every day that is just plain wrong. When I got to NBC the rule was that we won't necessarily be first but we do want to get it right," said Lewis. "Now that has been flip-flopped, getting it first seems to be first . . . so as a result a lot of inaccurate things get on the air first." Now and then such inaccuracies are corrected, but viewers who saw the wrong information the first time will probably not be tuned in to see the correction.

When producers "stack" their newscast, which means organize the elements in a certain order, the aim is to ensure good "flow" so that no one segment is bogged down with too much information that might, they believe, prompt viewers to pick up their remote control. To help achieve this fast-paced show, producers order reporters to keep their taped stories short, often under a minute and a half each. (I acknowledge that this is a broad generalization, but it is not intended to be mean-spirited. I simply have yet to meet a newscast producer who, (A) doesn't ask, beg, or demand that stories be shorter or (B) has ever asked a reporter to actually lengthen a report!) Somewhere they were taught that the public really notices and cares about the flow of a newscast, and if that means cutting out important content, so be it. At the same time, though, most newscast producers believe that some stories must be repeated every year. There is no evil intent in this foolishness; it is simply ingrained behavior for many news people, from news directors to producers to reporters. This explains why, every year, every station will air stories about the shopping rush the day after Thanksgiving, stories about the first day of summer (and fall, and winter), the White House's Easter egg hunt and the pardon of the Thanksgiving turkey, and the pope's blessing in many languages at the end of the year. These stories are covered because they are there—and because, quite often, producers believe there is nothing else going on that merits coverage. In the news biz, that's called "filler." And all too often, it's just stupid.

Steve Safran, an executive producer for NECN in New England, hits the nail on the head with his list called *Things Viewers Never, Ever Say*. Here are a few examples:

- "The police want *my* help in solving this crime? Cool!"

- "Good thing they ran that VO [video] of people putting on seat-belts during that seatbelt law story. I had no idea what seatbelts looked like."

- "I'm glad they referred to him as 'the Pontiff' on the second reference and "John Paul the Second' on the third reference. I would have been bored if they just said 'The Pope.'"

- "It's gonna snow/be hot/be very cold? I sure hope they'll tell me what to do with my pets and the elderly. I have no idea."

- "Remind me: 'Can Halloween be dangerous for my kids?' 'Should I wear sunscreen when I go out this summer?' 'Are there benefits to drinking wine?' 'Can I get an update on this crap tonight at eleven only on your station?'

- "Sadly, the station that I am watching presented this story to me fifteen seconds after its competitor did. I know this, for I watch four televisions at once."

- "You mean there were *previous* stumbling blocks on the road to peace in the Middle East?"

- "I know it's going to be 70 degrees and sunny today. Please, for the love of God, tell me about the barometric pressure!"

- "It really helped my understanding of that story that they asked a couple of random idiots on the street what *they* thought of it."

I agree that these examples are very funny, but, sadly, they are all too true and very commonplace, especially (but not exclusively) in local television. And what it boils down to is that airtime that could be used to truly inform the public, to educate viewers about important topics relevant to their lives, is wasted on this sort of fluff. And it becomes self-perpetuating.

"You wouldn't believe how many people in newsrooms that I know have a hard time even recognizing news anymore," said CNN's chief international correspondent Christiane Amanpour. As a result, she added, it has become harder and harder to get serious, solid news stories on the air. "I'm no longer sure that when I go out there and do my job it'll even see the light of air, if the experience of my network colleagues is anything to go by. More times than I care to remember I have sympathized with too many of them assigned, like myself, to some of the world's bad places. They would go through hell to do their pieces, only to frequently find them killed back in New York because of some fascinating new twist on 'killer Twinkies' or Fergie getting fatter, or something."

Some of the producers making these decisions are obviously not driven by any sense of journalistic responsibility to the public. Others may simply be using the wrong criteria when defining what makes a newscast good. Joe Angotti, the chair of the broadcast department at Northwestern University's Medill School of Journalism, says journalists today who value infotainment and glitz over content have abandoned, to the detriment of society, the principles that motivate truly dedicated and committed journalists. "When you think back about great editors and great producers, if you ask them why they wanted to be a journalist, they would say in one way or another, 'because we think we can make a difference in people's lives, a positive difference,' and we can. Journalists can," said Angotti. "There's no other profession where so few people can make a difference in the lives of so many people. And that's the way people used to think."

BLOOD AND GUTS, SELF PROMOTION, AND REPORTER INVOLVEMENT

Gratuitous violence in news has also become an alarming trend. More and more newscasts, particularly in local television, lead with stories about everyday crime in the belief the video will compel people to watch. But this has also hyped fear of violent crime across the nation, which in turn led to the election of politicians who made good on their promises to pass two- and three-strikes-you're-out legislation—all of this at a time when violent crime rates have actually declined. It is not responsible reporting. It is aimed at alarming and titillating viewers in hopes they'll stay tuned for the next crime-wave update.

A station in Pennsylvania used a version of the shocking-video technique when it aired a prerecorded tape of the suicide of the state treasurer. R. Budd Dwyer had been convicted of racketeering and mail fraud and had called a press conference. The assumption was that he was going to announce his resignation. Instead, he pulled out a pistol, waved it around, and finally shot himself. In later newscasts, most of the television news producers edited out the shooting part. But one ran the whole horrible incident the way it happened. According to an article by Stephen G. Gottlieb in *ERIC Digest* (Indiana University), "Interestingly, a survey of more than 800 viewers showed that members of the public were fairly evenly divided between those who supported the decision to carry the shooting in its entirety (46 percent) and those who opposed the choice (54 percent)." Does the fact that many viewers want to see such carnage justify putting it on air? Absolutely not.

And just what journalistic function was served by having MSNBC anchor Ashleigh Banfield, who had made a name for herself anchoring during the U.S. invasion of Afghanistan, immediately afterward travel around the United States on a tour bus that had her picture plastered on both sides, reporting stories about the country? At a time when the networks were crying poor and taking news-gathering shortcuts, NBC spent a lot of money on this publicity stunt that flopped. What else could have been covered instead?

"Reporter involvement" is a concept that has increased tenfold over the past two decades and something that old-school journalists deem to be idiotic, at the very least. But there are different degrees of involvement. When I see, or have done myself under news director orders, a reporter pumping gasoline into a tank for a story about fuel prices, I think that's just plain stupid. Unethical? No. Just dumb. Our viewers know how gasoline gets from the pump into the gas tank. But reporter involvement can, and does, get very close to crossing the line. Again, this is a very gray area.

During the 2003 war in Iraq, veteran CNN correspondent Walt Rodgers did a live report about how he and his crew helped treat a wounded Iraqi. His live television conversations with anchor Anderson Cooper were later posted on cnn.com on April 4, 2003, as a major coup.

> The Army's 7th Cavalry was in a standing position a few miles from Baghdad's main airport Friday, and continued to encounter determined pockets of resistance. Traveling with the 7th Cavalry, CNN correspondent Walter Rodgers and his crew discovered that an Iraqi soldier thought to be killed in a skirmish was actually alive. CNN crew members helped to treat the soldier as the Army summoned a medic. Rodgers spoke to CNN anchor Anderson Cooper:
>
>> Cooper: It is remarkable just to observe this, Walter, and to know that even under fire they would send people out to aid a wounded Iraqi soldier.
>>
>> Rodgers: Well, that's standard operating procedure. That wouldn't come as a surprise to U.S. soldiers. This is what the U.S. military has been noted for doing. Our crew is working on him. One of our crew members, Paul Jordan, an Australian former SAS (Special Air Service) soldier, is very good with first aid. He appears to be administering first aid. I can't leave the tether of the microphone to find out how badly injured the soldier is, but he has been lying beside the road wounded for some five hours.
>
> (Several minutes later.)
>
>> Rodgers: What you're looking at is a Pvt. Waterman, Jeff Barwise, our satellite engineer; and Paul Jordan, our security officer. They discovered an alive Iraqi in the ditch, 110 to 120 yards from where I'm hunkering down in the road . . . As you can see, our unit's giving him water at this point, even as we remain under fire from other Iraqis. But that Iraqi soldier,

according to the CNN people who are now administering
first aid to him, appears to have a badly injured leg but otherwise will probably survive. We need to tell you that the
Army has radioed for a medic to come up and take care of
the Iraqi soldier. The problem, of course, is the Iraqis are pin-
ning down everyone in the rear, so the medic's armored personnel carrier cannot come forward at this time. The medics
are under fire. The Iraqis are shooting on everyone of the rear
contingents, both ahead of us and behind us.

This exchange revealed a couple of worrisome issues. The first was
that Rodgers, like so many other embedded reporters, referred to the U.S.
unit as "ours" and the entire conversation was a rah-rah-U.S.A. chant.
For supposedly unbiased journalists not taking sides, that was a huge signal. Yes, he and his crew are traveling with these American troops, but
that is precisely how he should have referred to them. By saying "our"
unit, he—inadvertently, at the very least—took sides.

As for helping U.S. soldiers treat the wounded, there is no question
that these are tough ethical calls. We are supposed to be observers, not
participants. But I, too, have aided wounded during a war, though they
were always civilians, innocent bystanders. I was never in a position to
have to decide whether or not to help a government soldier or a guerrilla
fighter engaged in the battle. There were always medics close by who
could handle first aid while I did my job. Still, it's important for journalists to have some guidelines, some ethical rules about what we should
or should not do, even if, when push comes to shove, the journalist makes
the decision to help. I know this is hard for most nonjournalists to understand, but if reporters and photographers and the like begin to help the
wounded on any side of any conflict they, in essence, have taken sides and
are fair game for the opposition. When journalists remain observers only,
they preserve their right and ability to report independently and do not,
under usual circumstances, become targets themselves. The fact that we
are unarmed and have no alliance helps keep us alive and able to report
news around the world.

But there will always be exceptions. If you asked ten different journalists what they would have done in Walt Rodger's position, you'd get ten different answers. These are spur-of-the-moment decisions made under extreme stress. Since I haven't had to make mine under those circumstances, I would like to believe that I would help the wounded person if no one else were available. And it wouldn't matter whether the wounded person was aligned with U.S. forces or not. But I would not have reported on it. The point isn't to let viewers know what a good person you are, it is to inform them about what really matters, what is happening in the conflict. That is where I would have drawn the line. Did it matter in the overall reportage of the day's war in Iraq that one Iraqi had been helped by an American television crew? Of course not. So the motive behind that report is suspect.

By the same token, I had a different opinion about another, similar episode. Dr. Sanjay Gupta, CNN's medical correspondent and a neurosurgeon who specializes in brain surgery, was traveling with Army physicians—the Devil Docs, they called themselves—at the front. He was reporting about the portable surgery suites, and how the doctors with them saved lives under very difficult circumstances. While Sanjay was there with his crew, a young Iraqi boy was brought in with a bullet wound to his head. The Army surgeons had many areas of expertise, but neurosurgery was not one of them. Sanjay later said that he considered the ethical implications of him, as a journalist, performing the operation. But he felt his primary duty was to his Hippocratic oath to help people in need. He operated on the young boy. After the operation, Sanjay stood in front of the camera and explained what he had done, and why. He mentioned the ethical dilemma and his conclusion. And he reported that the young boy died anyway. He was not patting himself on the back for having helped out. He did his best to serve two masters.

When I saw Sanjay's taped on-camera piece, I immediately e-mailed him. I had recruited and trained him for CNN and knew he had a very fine-tuned sense of ethics. I congratulated him for how he handled himself with this difficult decision, including his choice to put everything on the table for viewers to know. Let them decide how to weigh the story.

A few days later, though, I heard that Sanjay had performed surgery at least one more time, if not more. While he faced the same ethical dilemma as he had the first time, the situation had changed in my mind. To operate once, in an emergency, was one thing. To continue to work alongside Army surgeons was another. If neurosurgeons were needed on the front line, which Sanjay's first operation proved to be true, the Army should have immediately assigned them to the Devil Docs group. To start relying on Sanjay for these types of surgeries was to virtually enlist him. And for Sanjay to go along with it, well, that crossed the line in my book.

IF THEY'RE WATCHING, WHO CARES IF THERE'S NO NEW NEWS?

Another common practice of television news is to keep a story going as long as we can, as long as it "has legs," as we say in the business. Quite often, though, we keep it going much longer than that because the networks are still getting the ratings. It becomes repetitive news for the sake of the bottom line, not because it is updating the public on important news.

One of the most famous cases to date was the O. J. Simpson trial. When one analyzes this story, how many people did it truly affect? Maybe twenty, and that's it. But because the defendant was a celebrity, CNN and other networks dedicated an inordinate amount of airtime to this story. "Certainly the O. J. Simpson trial had all the ingredients of a great news story, but we went over the top in covering it because we thought it had great entertainment value," said George Lewis, who is based in Los Angeles. "As a story that has lasting impact and importance to society it was overrated. But we covered it beginning to end in great detail. We devoted hundreds of hours to that story." And that was just NBC. CNN dedicated eight to ten hours a day for months.

At CNN and elsewhere, the gavel-to-gavel coverage was rationalized by the ratings; they zoomed up and stayed high. There were more viewers watching CNN's coverage of the O. J. Simpson trial than had watched

CNN's daily coverage in years. In the minds of the bean counters who control the news executives, that made it right.

If a network dedicates eight or nine hours a day to one story, it only follows that news coverage of the rest of the world will suffer. I was just one of over a hundred CNN correspondents covering the other news of the day anyway, though knowing it would never see air. Frustrating doesn't begin to describe what we experienced. Did the public lose? Absolutely.

The same phenomenon occurred with the murder of Laci Peterson and the coverage of Chandra Levy and Gary Condit. These occurred in slow news periods, so they received more attention than they deserved. "The need to latch onto a soap opera, to keep people tuned in, turns into nonstop coverage," Lewis said. "And while we were covering those stories nonstop, al-Qaida was getting ready to attack the World Trade Center. I'm wondering if we should have been spending more time on international terrorism during those months leading up to that than we did [on] Gary Condit. We, as an industry, may have been a little remiss. The hints were there, we had the threatened attack on the millennium, the guy who was captured in Port Washington who was going to take out LAX. Looking at this in hindsight makes me think we should have paid more attention to that."

Joe Angotti adds, "We didn't do a good job with the Chandra Levy story. In fact, I think that television news was just real close to irresponsible on that story. Going on the air every single day without anything new to report. Keeping the story alive when it should not have been kept alive."

The impact of this sort of mindless, newsless coverage is even more detrimental when one considers what didn't get on the air as a result. Angotti, who once produced NBC's *Nightly News* program, says he used to look forward to the days when there was not a lot of breaking news to report. Why? Because that gave him the time to air other stories of importance that would not be considered breaking news. "You used to be able to pull off a wonderful in-depth story off the shelf, something that was exceptionally well-reported and produced, stories that viewers needed to know about. But now they hype stories that shouldn't be hyped and bring prominence to stories without having information to justify the coverage." And after a pause, he continued, "And then these stories go away and no one bothers with them anymore."

Robert Wiener recalls a story that was never done because executives in Atlanta deemed it too expensive and not important enough. "While CNN made a much larger commitment to coverage in Africa than the other nets, the majority of stories you see out of Africa are related to famine, corruption, fucked-up UN (United Nations) programs, and stories that are basically negative. And it's only occasionally that we see positive stories about progress," Wiener said. "Admittedly, progress is slow in Africa, but it does exist."

Wiener learned of a United Nations program in Brazzaville, Congo, that was actually working well and pitched the story idea to producers and managers in Atlanta. "For whatever reason, we, CNN at the time, were not prepared to spend the money. But I guarantee you that if some five hundred people had been massacred in the Congo, no expense would have been spared to send someone to cover it."

Both the progress piece and a massacre piece should be considered important stories that could shed light on the good and the bad developments in a country that is often ignored by the Western media. A massacre story, though, has violence and horror in it. The story about a social program that is helping the people of the country does not. In many newsrooms, that makes it less newsworthy.

Besides, who cares about a country in Africa when our newscast has the latest photos and gossip about Prince William?

AND THE UGLY

E VERY PROFESSION has its hall of shame: the biggest screwups, the
most serious ethical lapses, or, worse yet, the most extreme examples
of intentional disregard for professional standards. Television journalism
is no different. Sure, there's checkbook journalism, but there have also
been disgraceful episodes of personal bias driving what is covered or not.
Video is faked, news scoops by other news agencies are not properly
attributed, newscasts become company cross-promotion outlets, executives refuse to be accountable when a story they pushed goes sour—those
are just a few of the reprehensible things that have occurred in the news
world. Some are happening more often now than ever before. Still, it is
comforting that there have been few truly grave incidents of journalistic
irresponsibility. While a couple of the episodes described in this chapter
occurred years ago, much of what was going on behind the scenes or
behind the story has not been told before now. Here, then, are some of

television journalism's most unethical practices and a few of the profession's most appalling moments.

MONEY, MONEY, MONEY

At the height of the President Bill Clinton-Monica Lewinsky scandal, it seemed that every news organization, every talk show and every media person was trying to get the first interview with the former White House intern. And most were. Well-known media celebrities wrote personal letters to Lewinsky hoping to lure her to their networks, to their shows. This would be the biggest "get" in many years.

Then word came in the news community that Oprah Winfrey had succeeded in landing this very controversial interview. A short while later, however, Winfrey publicly turned down the opportunity, saying Lewinsky wanted to be paid. The talk show chose to operate under the same ethical guidelines embraced by most journalists: we do not pay for interviews. Winfrey did not have to play by the rules that govern newspeople. She's a talk-show host, a person in the world of entertainment. It is not unusual for entertainment programs to pay folks they interview. In fact, it's often unusual if they don't. While Winfrey was turning down the interview, Roseanne Barr was unsuccessfully offering as much as $2 million to Lewinsky to come on her new show.

The high-stakes competition among news organizations, then, was back. After all, the show and the network that nabbed this prize would garner huge ratings and, as a result, could demand enormous amounts of money from advertisers. As a profit earner, this interview could be the Super Bowl of news.

Barbara Walters of ABC News was the eventual winner of the Monica sweepstakes. She conducted the interview at the end of 1998, and it ran on *20/20* in early 1999. "She (Lewinsky) will get no money from ABC News," Walters said at the time. "No movie on Disney. No movie on Lifetime. No *Barbara Walters Special.* No money under the table." That Walters's reputation and cachet had won Lewinsky over was not hard for competing journalists to understand. It was a big loss, but this was Barbara Walters, after all.

On August 9, 2000, however, the *Washington Post* reported startling information. "ABC paid $25,000 to Washington attorney Theodore Olson after Olson—who was hired by Lewinsky's book agent and adviser—helped persuade [special prosecutor Kenneth] Starr's deputies to allow Lewinsky to go on the air with ABC's Barbara Walters." In other words, because Lewinsky's immunity-from-prosecution deal forbade her from speaking to the media about her relationship with the president, ABC paid her attorney to lobby the office of the special prosecutor. The *Post*'s article also connects a few other important dots. The day after the two-hour special edition of *20/20* aired, Lewinsky's book was released, making the timing of the program appear, at the very least, to be part of a coordinated advertising campaign. The *Post* also reported that "In another unusual arrangement, ABC gave up international broadcast rights and allowed Lewinsky to sell interviews overseas, netting her about $1 million." What did ABC get in return? More than $20 million in advertising revenue, as more than 49 million people tuned in, the *Post* reported.

Money did not go directly into Lewinsky's hands, but it did pay one of her attorneys and she benefited from it. This was checkbook journalism no matter how it is spun. (I have no evidence one way or another, but I believe Walters would not have been involved in this unethical trade.) Reputable news organizations do not—under any circumstance or through second or third parties—exchange money for interviews. But if it is unethical to pay someone for an interview, is it all right to pay for video shot by someone else? This is done all the time. For example, it is how CNN obtained its footage of the Olympic Park bombing: by buying the tape shot by a tourist in the park that evening. It's also how the world got to see the beating of Rodney King by Los Angeles Police Department officers. So is there a difference between that and the fact that in 2002 CNN paid $30,000 for sixty-four al-Qaida videotapes that showed members training and Osama Bin Laden calling for death to Americans? Well, at first CNN gave the impression that the network had not exchanged money for the material. Later, a spokeswoman explained that the misunderstanding was due to CNN trying to protect its people in Afghanistan. CNN went to great lengths to explain that the tapes were not obtained directly from the terrorist group but from a middleman who got them from a place where Bin

Laden had spent some time. Given that, spokeswoman Christa Robinson said network executives were "convinced that the money did not go to anyone connected to Osama Bin Laden or al-Qaida."

This is where the logic fails me. How could CNN executives truly know that the money didn't go to anyone connected with Bin Laden? Bin Laden, like many other sought-after terrorists, has spent years setting up networks of safe houses, places where he can stay at a moment's notice. This fact is common knowledge in the antiterrorism world and has been confirmed by U.S. officials. So it strains credibility that someone not connected to Bin Laden would simply stumble over an apartment of his and find tapes. In addition, shortly after 9/11, CNN news executives— including President of News Gathering Eason Jordan—compiled a list of questions for Bin Laden that was (they hoped) to be delivered to him through a web of sources—people who knew people who knew people. CNN did not have a direct connection with Al-Qaida, and to the best of my knowledge there was no money connected with this attempt to get answers from Bin Laden. Did CNN's first effort to get Bin Laden to answer questions have anything to do with the tapes CNN eventually bought? I don't know, but it certainly doesn't look good.

Another extremely worrisome practice has received even less attention: when companies who want their executives to be used as on-air experts provide their own studio, camera, and crew to make it easier— and less expensive—for the television station or network. This procedure often happens with Wall Street financial organizations. "Five years ago, when CNN or CNBC or whoever wanted to do an interview with me, a crew would show up with a reporter," said Tom Wolzien, the senior media analyst for Sanford C. Bernstein & Co, a Wall Street research and investment management firm. "Three years ago a crew would show up without a reporter or producer, and we'd dial up and have questions over a speakerphone. But over the past year or so, the financial organizations have started putting in cameras, having their own studios, and so the crew costs have been shoved off onto those financial organizations that want to be available. So now the initial tendency for the assignment editor or producer is to go with places that have a camera."

The interview subject simply sits down in front of the camera, his company logo behind him, without the need for a reporter or camera crew. So rather than choosing a guest or an expert based on qualifications, knowledge of the topic, balance, or other factors that should be considered when making editorial decisions, producers now often choose based on ease and lower cost. "This is the meeting of journalistic need and economic imperatives," Wolzien continued. "As a producer, I need to fill my show, but I will go to places that will provide me with video and put on someone who is applicable or at least tangentially interesting."

By providing the camera and studio, the financial organizations are—in essence—buying their way on air and receiving massive amounts of free, positive publicity. But don't blame them; they're smartly advancing their own cause. The news organizations are completely at fault for selling out, for ignoring their editorial responsibilities in favor of the bottom line. The losers are the viewers who will only hear what a small number of potential guests with ulterior motives (publicity) have to offer on the topic instead of benefiting from a broad range of expert knowledge. So far, this in-house studio trend has been spotted primarily within financial institutions in New York. But with news organizations eagerly taking advantage of the free studio-camera-expert combo, it will surely spread to other areas of expertise. Watch and see: anytime someone is being interviewed at a location different from the anchor's studio, check whether the expert's company logo is behind him or her. If it is, this is a company studio and the news organization just got a freebie.

As for the anchors themselves, all the airtime they get plays a big part in the amount of money they can take home. Brokaw, Rather, Jennings, Walters, Couric, Lauer, and many, many other news stars pull down salaries between $2 million and more than $12 million a year. While these are obscene salaries by any definition, these news "personalities" do attract viewers and, as a result, bring in revenue. Still, the regular paycheck is just one way of cashing in on one's name recognition and celebrity. There's also a lot of extra pocket money being earned by the people who host or regularly appear on shows such as PBS's *The McLaughlin Group,* or CNN's *Crossfire* when the shows go on the road. Author James Fallows, who has written extensively about television news, reports that *The McLaughlin Group* guests earn $20,000 or more for these appearances. In addition, many of the hosts and frequent guests on these shows parlay their new-found celebrity into huge paychecks from speaking engagements.

Even if the program host or guest isn't a journalist, accepting money for a speaking engagement can still create conflicts of interest. Take, for example, someone who is a frequent guest expert on any of the talk shows that concentrate heavily on politics and Washington. If this person accepts $25,000 to speak at a banquet hosted by a well-known national accounting firm, should this expert comment on the firm's investigation by the federal government on the next show? The answer is no, but it happens all the time. And there's no question large amounts of money can compromise a person's willingness to investigate or criticize the source of that income. Even as important, though, is the appearance of a conflict of interest. No matter what the guest later says about the company in question, people who know about the big paycheck will always doubt the sincerity or honesty of the guest's comments. Perhaps that explains why so many on-air people, journalists and experts, are reluctant to divulge information regarding their speaking fees. For a lot of them, participating in these programs that are supposed to be grounded in news and journalism is simply the track to a gravy train.

PERSONAL BIAS

One of the most fundamental tenets of journalism is that a reporter should strive to keep his or her personal feelings or opinions out of news stories. It is part of our training in journalism school and early on in our professional careers. That doesn't mean it is easy, though. There isn't a journalist who hasn't experienced an internal struggle when covering controversial topics such as abortion, the Palestinian-Israeli issue, the death penalty, gay rights, gun control, or race relations, to name just a few. For the most part, though, journalists have reported responsibly on these issues day in and day out. Credit should also be given to all types of producers, to script approvers, and to management—people part of a news organization's vetting system who have the right and responsibility to address and correct potential imbalances in coverage. This process of checking and double-checking helps ensure fair coverage. Sometimes, though, this system breaks down. When the process is sidestepped, say by a network star who believes he or she is above the ethical and professional "law," appalling examples of personal bias can get on the air.

In 1984, I was temporarily assigned by NBC News to work with a new magazine show, *American Almanac*. This was NBC's umpteenth attempt at creating a magazine show that would last, but in the end it, too, failed. But it was here that I experienced the most egregious example of unethical behavior—an anchor's personal bias skewing what would be reported and what would not—that I have ever witnessed.

The show's anchors were Connie Chung and Roger Mudd. I was very excited about the prospect of doing some in-depth television journalism working with the best, most-experienced anchors, correspondents, and producers the company had. And I was also very interested in the story I was assigned. From extensive research conducted by a producer, we learned that AIDS—up until then considered only a gay disease—was being transmitted in other manners to people who weren't homosexual. While this is common knowledge now, it wasn't then. The story was going to break big ground by informing viewers that even if they were heterosexual, they could get this potentially fatal illness. It would be a huge public service. Many people didn't seem to care that gays were suffering and dying from this disease. Others applauded it, saying it was God's curse on the sinful. Regardless of the political ramifications, if we had scientific and medical evidence that anyone could become infected, it needed to be reported.

We worked on the long-form story for a couple of months, profiling three heterosexual people who had AIDS or had died of it. Among them was a young woman from Washington, D.C., named Sunny, who got it through heterosexual sex. Her partner, though, was bisexual and had had homosexual sex before meeting her. Another person we profiled was Sammy Kushnick. This three-year-old boy died in October of 1983, before I could meet him, but his parents and his twin sister told his story eloquently.

Sammy and his twin, Sara Rose, were born prematurely, and both had very low birth weights. Sammy, though, needed a teaspoon or two of blood, a transfusion, to survive. The blood was tainted, and the boy eventually died of AIDS. Though devastated by Sammy's death, the Kushnicks became fighters and helped change the way blood banks operate to this day. Primarily as a result of these parents' efforts, some blood banks began testing donated blood for the disease. Eventually, laws were changed to force all of them to do so.

We also traveled to a San Francisco hospital, where the most AIDS patients had been treated, and to the Centers for Disease Control in Atlanta for interviews with the top experts who had been dealing with AIDS—even the fellow who coidentified it. And we interviewed important researchers at the National Institutes of Health in Washington, D.C. Everyone stated without a doubt that AIDS did not discriminate. It was an equal opportunity disease for all.

Our story was very compelling. It showed very real, heterosexual people coping with life *with* AIDS and death *from* AIDS. I was very pleased with the script. And the tape editor, Terry Verna, had done a potentially award-winning effort assembling the material. On top of this, we had heard through a source that Rock Hudson had AIDS. After several conversations with his spokesperson, we were given the exclusive right to break that story when we aired ours. In theory, the anchor would start off on camera saying that NBC News had confirmed that Rock Hudson had AIDS and was admitting he contracted it through homosexual sex. The anchor would go on and give some statistics on deaths and cases at the time. But then he or she would state that there was now proof it was not solely a disease affecting gays. Then they'd roll our story.

Well, that's the way it was supposed to go.

We were slated for the premier show of *American Almanac,* a show that was supposed to be about real people, real problems, real issues that affect us all.

But then Roger Mudd stepped in.

Roger demanded to see the segment before it aired. We cued it up in a large editing room and waited for him. When he arrived, he sat down, took off his glasses, and turned to a blank wall ninety degrees away from the television screen. Although I was still young enough to be impressed by this famous person, I was stunned at this. I figured, though, that once we rolled tape, he'd watch. He didn't. Throughout the entire story, which ran about ten minutes, he never once looked at the television monitor. When it was done, he stormed out.

We learned a short while later that Roger had killed the story. Why? Because it did not categorically state that AIDS *was* a gay disease. He made it clear to the executive producer that his personal religious beliefs would not permit him to believe otherwise. We had been warned by several people who worked closely with Roger that he was homophobic, so we made a point of not showing a lot of gay men. In fact, the most risqué shot we had in the story was of two men holding hands and walking away from the camera. Still, Roger didn't care. Despite our research, despite what we had learned from the nation's top experts, Roger did not want this story on "his" air.

Within two weeks, the topic of our story made the cover of two national news magazines and many, many others. The fact that Rock Hudson had AIDS was broken by another news organization. We had it first, but we were forced to sit on it. I hate to think of the thousands of people who got AIDS through blood transfusions, dirty needles, or sexual activity because they had not been informed sooner about the dangers we knew about—but didn't report.

WE'RE LIVE! (SORT OF . . .)

Many mornings on *The Today Show*, viewers see news reader Ann Curry turn to a screen and supposedly toss to Tom Brokaw "for a look at what's coming up this evening on *NBC Nightly News*." Tom thanks Ann, and launches into a thirty-second monologue about stories that will appear that evening. When he's done, he tosses back to the *Today Show* anchor, "Ann?" "Thank you, Tom," she replies. Dan Rather and Peter Jennings do the same thing now and then, thanking the morning anchor by name and tossing back to him or her when the news commercial is over. On occasion, ABC News anchor Peter Jennings also tosses to anchor Ted Koppel to find out what will be coming up on *Nightline*. When Paula Zahn anchored CNN's morning show, she, too, would toss to the evening anchor, Aaron Brown, for his recitation of stories that would be on his newscast that night.

It looks live. It gives the impression the evening anchors—the network stars—are always on duty to bring viewers the latest news. But it's generally faked. When the morning show news anchors supposedly "toss" to the evening news anchors to find out what's on tap for that evening's newscast, the control rooms—more often than not—simply roll clips taped the evening before of the anchors teasing nonbreaking news stories that have been preprepared. This subterfuge even has a couple of names: "live on tape" or "look live." (How can "live on tape" even be part of the vocabulary of television? It can't be live if it's on tape.) It is simply using smoke and mirrors to cut expenses and still impress viewers.

"Do you think the public knows the difference? I really don't think so," said Joe Angotti, a former NBC News senior vice president and the current chair of the broadcasting program at Northwestern University. "But it is deception. I think they think it is innocent deception; no one is being hurt by it. But it's a step in the wrong direction."

"When I see a morning anchor talking to a piece of videotape that the evening anchor sent down the night before, I wonder if these people go home and talk to their VCR. I think it's stupid," said longtime NBC News correspondent George Lewis. But more important, he adds, this practice is dishonest. "Broadcasters should not be in the business of trying to mislead their audience, and doing so-called "look lives" are a misleading practice and I try to avoid it. But I'm asked to do it, particularly on MSNBC. I try to talk them out of it as much as possible. But it's convenient, and sometimes economics dictates it. They don't want to stay up on the satellite, which costs more money, so they do this and have the thing (the so-called "live" report) in the can." Lewis acknowledges producers wouldn't have even dared ask him to participate in this sort of news fraud fifteen or twenty years ago. "No, I would not have been asked. There used to be a rule on the books on the FCC (Federal Communications

Commission) that you had to state what was live and what was recorded, and it was a violation of the FCC rule to pass off recorded material as live. Those rules either don't exist anymore or, if they do, no one is paying attention to them."

As Lewis touched on, the main reason for resorting to the fake live shots is purely economic. Not only do the networks and stations not have to pay for additional satellite time, they also don't have to pay overtime to camera crews and live truck engineers, or assign a new shift to do this one story. Once again, the incessant drive for greater profits has led to unethical practices that affect the news viewers see virtually every day.

There are many variations on this theme. In mid-2001, CNN's Headline News network was relaunched with a new, live, fast-paced format that included a screen with various streams of information and at least two anchors at all times. For two years prior to this, though, virtually everything that aired on the network was prerecorded in order to cut staff and save money. Although CNN executives never overtly claimed Headline News was live, the newscasts and promotions were carefully crafted to give viewers that strong impression. What was happening behind the scenes reveals the extent to which producers went to convey that their newscasts were live.

Anchors would sit on the set and tape several different versions of the same story or the lead-in to the same story. Over the course of the day, or that shift, the producers simply alternated the taped versions so that it appeared to be a new, different, and live newscast. ESPN still practices this sort of fakery on a daily basis.

At ABC News, correspondent and anchor Cokie Roberts participated in another variety of live reporting deception. While covering a political story in Washington, D.C., one day, she put on a coat and stood in front of a chromakey blue wall, the sort that is used for weather broadcasts. The control room then projected a shot of Capitol Hill behind her, so that it appeared that she was reporting live from the Capitol rather than from the warm studio. After the broadcast, someone at ABC who clearly thought she had crossed the line blew the whistle on her.

A far more accepted and far more common practice is the use of so-called "generic" live shots. If you've ever watched a local newscast and wondered how that network correspondent covering the big story had the time to do a live shot for the tiny station you're watching in the middle of nowhere, chances are it was a "generic" live shot. The broadcast news divisions and the cable networks all provide material to their affiliates several times a day as part of their service. When there's major breaking news, they will also provide live shots and taped stories. For the stations, it's a win-win situation. They save a ton of money by not having to send staff to the breaking news story, and they get network-quality material. In addition, to the untrained viewers' eyes, the live reports appear to be done specifically for the station they're watching.

Here's how it's done: a story has broken in the early evening, so the networks let affiliates know (either by mass e-mail or a direct-voice connection into all of the newsrooms) that the first generic live shot will be for the 11 PM local newscast. If it is undeniably a top story, then the time chosen is usually 11:01:00 PM or 11:01:30 PM. The affiliates know that if they want the live story in their newscasts, all they have to do is downlink the live signal with the correspondent and then have their anchors supposedly "toss" to him or her at the precise moment. Producers have written the introduction to the story and have timed it so that their anchor can seamlessly toss to the live shot: "And joining us with that breaking story is Fred Jones." Fred, the reporter, meanwhile, has had a producer counting down the seconds in his ear until he is finally cued to start speaking. By this time, stations across the country have Fred on screen. He talks for twenty seconds or so and then says a predetermined roll cue, such as "I spoke with investigators earlier today." At that point, the stations roll the taped story that fed in earlier. When Fred is again cued to speak, he then wraps up his live shot and often ends with something like, "Now back to you in the studio" as though his live shot is only being seen in one place. Across the country, though, anchors are nodding and thanking Fred for his great report even though they and Fred were never directly in contact. The whole process is deceptive. But there's more.

The stations can then customize Fred's taped story for later broadcasts. Correspondents who routinely do the generic live shots read all the possible station "sig-outs" on tape, such as "Bonnie Anderson, Channel 4 eyewitness news," "For the WFWQ's night team, I'm Bonnie Anderson," or whatever. These are then transmitted on a satellite so that affiliates can record them and edit their appropriate sig-out to the end of the correspondent's taped report. The customized news report lends further credence to the subterfuge. These practices are so common now that few consider them questionable. But even these lines can be crossed.

Then–ABC News employee Tom Lubart recalls the coverage the network's affiliate division did of a tornado that touched down in Nashville one late afternoon in 1997. In this case, there weren't many injuries or much damage, he said, "but we had very good video of things flying through the air and we, since this was the 'news,' had to do an 11:01:00 live shot." Lubart prepared a backup taped story narrated by an affiliate reporter just in case the ABC correspondent didn't arrive on time. Just after 10:35 PM, though, correspondent Jim Sciutto landed in Nashville and read the same script of the story over the phone to New York producers who crashed the story, meaning they edited it in record time. "He then did the live shot and signed off, '. . . Jim Sciutto, ABC News, live in Nashville.' But where was he? Well, all you could see was a tree behind him and it was dark. He was on the ramp of the airport terminal. He knew less about the tornado than I did, and maybe less about Nashville than I did," said Lubart. "I went home feeling bad. 'Live from Nashville?' What we had done that night was close to fraud, and I began reassessing TV news from that point on."

If the news media is to be effective, not only in informing the public but also in protecting and preserving the public trust, it must *have* the trust of the public. Faking live shots is dishonest and leads to the further disintegration or evaporation of the media's credibility. And if reporters, anchors, or networks can justify bending or breaking these professional rules, what will be next? It is a slippery slope that only leads to further ethical transgressions.

"STAGING" NEWS

In the early 1980s, when news in Central America was about civil wars, coups, and U.S.-backed and financed counterrevolutions, the correspondents of the two other television networks and several print reporters and

I saw something that convinced us that we had to start policing our own. We were in a northern province of El Salvador—a rebel stronghold—getting ready to witness a historic meeting between guerrilla leaders and top Army brass. They had been fighting a horribly bloody war for several years. Thousands of civilians had died by this time, and so had several journalists, including one just a few weeks before this meeting. As we waited for the top general to arrive by helicopter, we watched a film crew from PBS rehearsing a group of old women and children. The idea was that as soon as the general got off the chopper, they were to run up to him, surround him with smiles, and welcome him. We couldn't believe what we were seeing. This was guerrilla country; these people would not normally be so welcoming to the Army that had been killing its men, women, and children. But beyond that, we'd never seen anything staged like this before. My colleagues and I first had our cameramen capture this unethical behavior on tape, so we had proof. Then we approached the film crew (they were using film versus videotape.) What the hell where they doing? We were told it was a "docudrama," part truth, part drama, and that we should "fuck off." This didn't sit well with us. You don't do "docudramas" while the story is still continuing. Hell, it took many years after the Vietnam War before anyone had enough perspective to do a movie about it. My colleagues and I sent a letter and the tape to then–PBS president Larry Grossman, telling him about what we had seen and why we thought it was inappropriate as well as unethical. Grossman responded quickly, telling us that the program had been cancelled. That was the right thing to do, the only way to address such an ugly ethical lapse. (A short time later, Grossman was named president of NBC News, but he didn't hold this against me.)

Robert Wiener, an executive producer responsible in great part for CNN's huge coups in its coverage of the first war with Iraq, says unethical behavior is not as uncommon as we'd like to believe. "All of us in the field have seen examples of networks staging coverage, asking people to say certain things that basically violate any standard practice." While Wiener would not identify the correspondent involved, he added, "I've seen it with a very respected reporter in Iraq in '98 who works for [a popular magazine-style network program]. He was basically doing an interview with an Iraqi, and when the Iraqi did not respond to the question in a clear-cut soundbite, he said, 'I'd like you to say this.' He [the Iraqi] then repeated it in soundbite fashion."

The most infamous case of news staging known to the public in recent years was seen on NBC's program *Dateline* on November 17, 1992. The story was about how certain General Motors pickup trucks would allegedly burst into flames during side-impact crashes. And to prove the point, the program showed impressive video of a truck blowing up. It wasn't until later, however, that the public learned that the truck explosion had been staged by NBC employees and experts hired by the network. GM had hired detectives and spent a great deal of time and effort to prove that the accident had been faked. After an internal investigation, NBC apologized. "That was a gross violation of every ethic in journalism and it caused all of us a great deal of mortification," said NBC's George Lewis. "It led to the firing or resignation of everyone concerned with that, including the president of the news division."

While *Dateline* producers and correspondents no doubt try to make sure something of that nature never happens again, it is disturbing that this same program was one of the first to use re-creations in its news stories. Viewers may be so used to seeing them that they don't care, but this is still a very deceptive practice. The video in news stories should be real, should be actual footage of actual events. *Dateline,* however, will dramatize certain events, such as the path a murderer took or the view of a fleeing vehicle. They dramatize because they don't have the actual video of what happened. There's no question such practices do add flair to the report, but even if the story alerts viewers by having the word "dramatization" on the screen, this still crosses the line into infotainment. At what point do viewers start confusing what is real and what is not? And even more troubling is that many local stations now use dramatizations and re-creations on a daily basis. If it's OK for *Dateline,* a premier network magazine program, why not them, they reason. So what was once unethical becomes common, acceptable practice—especially with a new generation of journalists who don't know better and certainly aren't seeing any better behavior to emulate.

"SOURCES (THE LOCAL NEWSPAPER WE DON'T WANT TO GIVE CREDIT TO) SAY . . ."

Re-creations and their sort of dishonesty, unfortunately, often lead to the bending or breaking of rules in other ways. In attempts to hype their investigative skills, networks and local television stations all too often boldly rip off someone else's work without giving proper credit. Some news reporters are no different; they hate being beaten by competitors on their same beat, and they're loath to admit when a colleague gets the story first. Journalists who may abide by all of the other ethical rules often feel compelled to use uncredited material so that viewers don't know they're getting the story an hour or a day late. As a result, the phrases "We have learned" or "Channel x has learned" no longer indicate that the reporter or the station has independently dug up the information through good old-fashioned news-gathering techniques. Substitute "we read it in the newspaper or saw it on another station" for those phrases. "One of the things that drives me crazy is when they say 'NBC News (or CBS, or Channel whatever) has learned . . .' and the implication is that that correspondent got that story on his or her own," said Angotti, of the Medill School of Journalism. "Meanwhile, I've just read the fucking story in the *New York Times* that morning. It's out there. There's nothing exclusive about it at all. But people do it all the time. And it's wrong. It gives an impression that they've uncovered something when they really are just stealing it from someone else."

The phrase "sources say" is also often misused. Ethical journalists turn to those words rarely and very sparingly, and only when there is no other on-the-record way to attribute important information the public must know. The Watergate break-in coverage by the *Washington Post* was a prime example of a news organization using unnamed sources with great and historically important effect. It was clear to readers why "Deep Throat" and other sources who provided information to the newspaper could not be publicly identified. Reporters Carl Bernstein and Bob Woodward, with the guidance of very astute editors, cross-checked information to ensure its veracity and never used just a single unnamed source for anything. If the sources are to remain unnamed, one source does not meet the standard of proof required by most respectable news organizations. This news story was so fundamentally important to democracy in this country that the news-gathering process had to be intensely vetted, and more than once.

But unfortunately, when reporters use "sources say" these days they all too often mean "one source said." In an age where news can be delivered instantly and the public expects it, reporters rarely have more than a day to gather information for air. Standards and ethics suffer, but the integrity of the news-gathering process and the quality of the news delivered to the public suffer most. At the end of the day, the information reported as truth is unreliable. And that is the antithesis of journalism's mission. The news media loses even more credibility, and when that happens, the public may eventually turn to other, even less credible, sources of information.

DISGUISING SELF-PROMOTION AS NEWS

In news organizations, the sales and marketing departments have historically been kept very separate from news operations so that journalists do not feel pressured or influenced in any way by advertisers or in-house sales people. Reporters need to be free to investigate and report about all companies, including their own, without being concerned about whether the news stories will result in lost advertising revenue. By the same token, reporters have never been expected to hawk products the parent company makes. You may see an NBC News correspondent covering a news story involving General Electric, but in virtually all cases the correspondent will also make the company connection crystal clear so that viewers have the full story. What you probably will never see, however, is that same NBC News correspondent promoting the efficiency and durability of jet engines made by General Electric in an effort to increase sales. The idea, again, is for the journalist to remain independent and not be seen as a spokesperson for other goods and services offered by the parent company. That's what ads and promos are for. Or at least that's the way these issues are supposed to be handled.

Times, however, are changing. Anchors and hosts now routinely and openly promote programs running on their same network. Whole program segments are even devoted to this shameless self-promotion. On November 3, 2003, the day NBC was premiering its first installment of *Average Joe*, Matt Lauer interviewed three contestants and the program host on *The Today Show*. When he asked one of the men if he had been insulted by being called an "average Joe," program host Kathy Griffin jumped in, "Matt, what's with all the heavy-handed questions? We're trying to cross promote!"

"This is the continual blurring of entertainment and news," said George Lewis. "When a news division is promoting a show on that networks' prime-time schedule, I tend to worry about the ethical problems of that. I see a lot of Disney-related stories on our local ABC outlet. Every now and then *The Today Show* is running interviews with prime-time stars on NBC, and I wonder what the pressures are for that to get on the air."

Perhaps it is primarily a reality-TV disease, but it is evidently very contagious. On *CBS This Morning*, anchor Bryant Gumbel began a segment by saying, "Who gets kicked off today?" He then spoke with an expert about the wild animals that live where *Survivor II* was staged, another fluff piece in a long line of stories promoting the *Survivor* programs on CBS. In his *Los Angeles Times* column, critic Howard Rosenberg charged that CBS was "using all its resources to publicize its colossal new cash kangaroo." Those resources, Rosenberg wrote, also include KCBS, the network-owned local television station in Los Angeles, where the news set was decorated a la *Survivor*. "We've all got palm leaves in our hair around here and are eatin' outta coconut shells," anchor Ann Martin said. Months later, a KCBS evening newscast devoted six minutes of its "news hole" (which is generally twenty-two minutes out of a half hour) to "a manufactured *Survivor II* story and tie-in, while failing to mention the $1.6 trillion tax cut proposal President Bush had sent to Congress that day."

Then there is the issue of having news people do stories that directly or indirectly hype products sold by the parent corporation. In October of 2003, CNN widely promoted a special report that anchor Paula Zahn had put together about President George H. W. Bush's experiences in the

U.S. Air Force during World War II. The show was titled, "A Flyboy's Story." At the same time, Barnes and Noble was featuring a new book called *Flyboys*. The publisher, Little, Brown, is a subsidiary of Time Warner, the parent company also of CNN and Barnes and Noble. This isn't quite the same as endorsing a parent company's jet engine, but it's on the same slippery slope. "When you start doing news that is really a promotion in disguise for something that is going on with the organization that owns you, that's dangerous," said Joe Angotti.

A similar shady practice is doing so-called news reports that tie in to entertainment shows on the station's same network. For example, the night the Jessica Lynch television movie was scheduled to air, local news teams scrambled to interview current or former soldiers who had been held captive, or knew someone who was. The idea was to air the interviews and then plug the movie. If a movie topic is spousal abuse, then there might be a story on the local women's shelter—and a reminder to "be sure to watch the movie tonight at 9 PM."

Such interrelated stories are clearly advertising during a newscast. "That's bad, for the business, for the people who do it, for journalism. The public loses trust when it sees things like that," said Angotti. "If the public isn't wise to this trickery now, it's going to get wise very quickly. And when it does, the trust factor is going to go away. And that's a thing that has really declined. People just don't trust the new newscasters of today the way they trusted Huntley, Brinkley, and Cronkite."

IF THEY SAY HE'S GUILTY, HE MUST BE

Heated competition for viewers, for ratings, and for profits can lead to rushes to judgment and shortcuts through or around standard news practices. All too often, the result is inaccurate reporting. Sometimes, the erroneous information comes from federal, state, or local officials who cut off media access to a story, or at least try to, in order to sway public opinion by force-feeding their version of events to the media and, therefore, the public. When this happens, news organizations with very little else to report end up airing the only information they have. Such stories are not just one-sided, they are most definitely slanted, because there is no information to balance the report. And most of the time, news organizations don't let viewers know that what they're hearing is only one side of the story.

The increasing frequency and seriousness of this kind of slanting is dismaying. Chapter Nine, on the Bush administration and the media, goes into greater detail on the unprecedented lack of information coming from the government regarding major public issues, but one example is the detention of hundreds of foreigners held without formal charges. Justice and immigration officials have been ordered by the attorney general to withhold as much information as possible about them. As a result, we don't know names, ages, citizenship, or why any individual in particular is being held. In fact, we don't really even know exactly how many of them have been detained. Journalists are hamstrung, unable to independently investigate many cases, and are instead forced to simply report the only information they have, which is, of course, provided by the administration. The stories for the most part are very clearly one-sided. Journalists covering this beat and many others that are affected by the shroud of secrecy surrounding federal government now need to remind viewers consistently that the whole story is not being told, that the administration is denying access to documents and information that were public record under every other president. Without that reminder as a counterbalance, viewers can't put the information they receive into proper context.

It doesn't have to be this way. But withholding information so that only one side of the story, the government's side, is told is not new. On August 21, 1991, about 120 Cuban detainees held in a federal prison in Talladega, Alabama, gained control of one wing of the facility and took nine hostages. They had been told they'd never be released from behind bars, even though their sentences for criminal offenses committed in the United States had been completed months and, in some cases, years earlier. The U.S. government intended to deport them back to Cuba, a process provided for in American immigration law. The Cuban refugees, however, faced further imprisonment or even death if they returned to Cuba. When the media learned of the prison takeover, federal officials immediately cut off electricity and phone access to the cellblocks so that the prisoners could not speak with reporters. They then proceeded to release misleading information to the media about inmates' actions and motives, and how they were continuing to be fed and otherwise cared for. FBI and prison officials wanted the public to believe they had the situation under control and that all prisoners were being treated humanely. And that was the story many members of the media reported, particularly journalists working for local news outlets.

What officials didn't count on, however, were a couple of hard-nosed reporters who refused to go along. Using signs, they provided phone numbers to the inmates, a couple of whom had access to portable phones. The prisoners' stories were, of course, quite different. There was no way for these reporters to know what was actually occurring behind the fences and walls, but at least they were able to report what both sides had to say—until federal authorities jammed the phone signals. The inmates then went to the rooftops to flash messages written on bedsheets, something all the media could see and report about. But that activity stopped as soon as the authorities threatened to shoot anyone on the roof. There was no more direct contact between the media and the inmates. Federal officials stormed the facility and ended the standoff after nine days. Reporters were never able to independently confirm what went on behind the walls.

The media are the eyes and ears of the people in this country. If reporters allow themselves to be government mouthpieces without disclosing that officials have denied access to the other side of the story, that's shameful. If the authorities manipulate reporters, they are doing the very same thing to the American people. Neither serves the public interest. And they both can lead to erroneous information being reported as fact.

That is precisely what happened to several U.S. news organizations that reported on security guard Richard Jewell. On July 27, 1996, a bomb exploded in Atlanta's Centennial Olympic Park during the games. One woman died of her wounds from the bomb and several other people were wounded. I was CNN's national correspondent based in this city, and was the first news person on the air for the network after the bomb exploded. I, and many of my colleagues, spent the next forty-eight hours on duty without rest, and the next two weeks on the air with little respite. This was a very competitive news story, and with its international headquarters based in Atlanta, CNN wanted to own it. When the FBI told the media that a security guard named Richard Jewell was a suspect, we all jumped through hoops to get as much information about him as possible. Jewell had been on CNN a short time after the bombing and seemed to be a hero since he had originally spotted the suspicious knapsack containing the bomb. But this new information from the feds gave us pause.

A satellite truck, a camera crew, a producer, and I were sent to literally camp out in front of Jewell's Atlanta apartment. We weren't alone. There were dozens of journalists and trucks. When FBI agents showed up with warrants in their hands to search his apartment, CNN—like many other stations and networks—went live. I simply reported what I saw, what was happening. When the agents finally left the apartment, we were again live. It was very uncomfortable to be reporting only what I was seeing, which wasn't much—"here they come, there they go"—but that is all I had *to* report. I was concerned, very concerned. On July 30, the *Atlanta Journal-Constitution* reported that according to their sources, Jewell was "the focus of the federal investigation." CNN's investigative teams were also turning up information about him and reporting what was on that newspaper's front page, attributing some of the information to the *Journal-Constitution*. At this point, Jewell's attorneys got smart and ordered us off of the private property. They could have done that from the first moment, but didn't—a big mistake on their part.

As we packed up our equipment and left, I called CNN executives to let them know what had happened. On our way back to CNN Center, though, we got a call from the national assignment desk with orders to set up in front of the Atlanta FBI office. Something didn't feel right about this decision, and I discussed it with my producer, Bettina Hutchings. Still, we headed to the FBI's office and began pulling out cables and deciding where the camera would be. My heart kept telling me this was wrong. It was one thing to report from Richard Jewell's home and say that the FBI considered him a suspect. But since he hadn't been charged, it was quite another to say the same thing in front of Atlanta's FBI office. Our mere presence there would add greater credence to the government's suggestion that he was the bomber.

I called CNN's National Desk again and did something I had never done before. I refused to do the story from that site. Beverly Broadman, who helped launch CNN (as one of the "Originals," as we know them) picked up the phone. She was the slot person, the hands-on person who ran all national news coverage for the desk. This is a woman for whom I had jumped through hoops, gone into hurricane eyes, and done just about everything humanly possible. And I did it, and would do it again, because I admire and respect her. Bev is, by far, the most accomplished, hardest working, brilliant national assignment editor in the business. She helped invent twenty-four-hour news coverage. Her news instincts are razor sharp, and her sense of humanity is equally amazing. So when she heard me saying that I would not do stories about Jewell from this location, she knew to listen. I had never before, in twenty years of reporting, refused to do a story.

She told me to call back in ten minutes. My producer and camera crew were very quiet during this time, though they let me know they supported my decision. Still, this was not a move many correspondents made. Within a few moments, Bev called me back. Without going into who she had talked to or the debates over my decision, she simply said, "You're right. Come back." CNN could do the rest of the stories from CNN Center, without our location adding undue credibility to a government suspicion. I was relieved.

It took a couple of years before we learned that this ethical decision saved CNN millions of dollars. It was determined that Richard Jewell had nothing to do with the bombing. He sued and collected a great deal of money from the *Atlanta Journal-Constitution* and received settlements (before suits were filed) from, among others, NBC, *Time* magazine and the *New York Post*. CNN also was involved with a settlement payment for, by my understanding, mainly rereporting the *Journal-Constitution*'s story. The amount CNN paid Jewell remains sealed, but it didn't come close to what the network would have been liable for had we continued to report from in front of the FBI office on Jewell being the prime suspect. The Jewell story is a classic example of what can happen in an extremely competitive news atmosphere in which journalists allowing themselves to be led by authorities cut corners and take what the feds and other news agencies report as the truth, with no independent confirmation.

In an after-the-fact investigation conducted by the Poynter Institute, writer Keith Woods agreed that the media had the responsibility to name Jewell and to say that he was a suspect. But "declaring that Jewell 'fit the profile' of a bomber went way beyond the media mandate. Describing him as all but a maladjusted mama's boy, as one print story did, is not what the First Amendment demands of journalists." Jewell, after all, had not been arrested. "This new pseudo-psychology journalism that we have seen in the past decade is anathema to informed, reasoned public discourse," wrote Woods. "It is sophisticated rumor-mongering. It encourages quick judgment and mob mentality. Worst of all, it happens every day in smaller, less dramatic ways, when the lives of 'suspects' are investigated and explicated by journalists single-mindedly seeking facts to validate the accusations."

While having sources with state and federal authorities is a must for journalists, we must always be vigilant and careful that we are not being used by them. In this case, the FBI was hoping the intensity of the media pressure would lead Jewell into making contradictory statements or worse. The media was equally manipulated by the police and state attorney in Union, South Carolina, during the Susan Smith case. In 1994, Smith drove her car into a lake and killed her sons, three-year-old Michael and fourteen-month-old Alex. She claimed they had been carjacked by a thirty- to forty-year-old black man of medium build and spent a week making televised pleas for the return of her children. The nation was captured by this sad tale. But Union police suspected her from the start and encouraged her to hold as many press conferences as possible. We later learned they were waiting for her to trip up, to change her story. They also had criminal psychologists on hand to read her body language during these press conferences. Among other things, apparently how often she blinked her eyes gave them a clue that she was lying.

In all three cases—the Cuban prisoners, Richard Jewell, and Susan Smith—most members of the media took as fact what government officials were saying. Rather than watchdogs, they were lapdogs. Officials justify it as one of the many strategies they have at their disposal to help them catch their suspects. But reporters are not government investigators or agents and should never allow themselves to be used as such.

WE GOT IT FIRST—AND WRONG

Even the most ethical journalists and news organizations can fall prey to the hazards posed by a major and truly exclusive news investigation. Unfortunately, enthusiasm and excitement can lead to all kinds of ethical and professional lapses which, in turn, result in the overlooking of important news-gathering steps. Shortcuts that aren't normally taken are approved by senior news executives who push their staffers to get the story on the air sooner. The information gathered may not be reviewed as carefully, scripts aren't vetted thoroughly, and in the thrill of the moment the project is given a bright green light by everyone including script approvers, producers, executive producers, vice presidents, the network's legal department, network presidents, and even news group chairmen. But equally unprofessional and unpardonable is what sometimes happens after the story runs, especially if the report's veracity is called into question. The senior executives often responsible for assigning the report in the first place, rushing the staff to get it done, and then approving the work for air refuse to be accountable for the decisions they made. Instead, they make scapegoats out of lower-level staffers who followed their instructions—a lose-lose situation for all but the senior executives. The public suffers, the network suffers in reputation (and quite often is too snakebit to launch other investigative endeavors), and the people directly involved with the project suffer, often losing their jobs. In major screwups or apparent screwups, journalism itself is sullied.

CNN's biggest debacle was a story now simply known as "Tailwind," although the actual name of the news segment was "Valley of Death." Tailwind was the name of a military operation during the Vietnam War that CNN alleged used nerve gas against U.S. defectors in Laos. The story was intended to be the investigative coup of the decade and ran on June 7, 1998, in the premier broadcast of a series of programs with the name *NewsStand* in the title. These almost nightly programs were created by then–CNN president Rick Kaplan at a time when Turner Broadcasting (CNN's parent company) and Time Warner were preparing to merge. The idea was to have Time Warner news outlets, such as *Time* magazine and others, join forces with CNN in television programs and vice versa. This is the so-called synergy that was aimed at saving money through shared resources. The Tailwind story, therefore, ran on *NewsStand: CNN & Time* and was also published in *Time* magazine with CNN correspondent Peter Arnett's name attached to both versions, TV and print.

CNN news executives were giddy with excitement in the days leading up to the airing of the Tailwind story. It was to be in the premier show of *NewsStand,* which would give the program immediate credibility. During a lunch with then–President of News Gathering Eason Jordan, he couldn't stop talking to me and other executives about what a major coup this story would be and how it would cement CNN's position as the "world's news leader."

The story instead became CNN's biggest disaster ever on just about every possible level. When the report aired, it generated huge publicity from current and former military people who said that what CNN reported was not true. Key interview subject Admiral Thomas Moorer, who had been chairman of the Joint Chiefs of Staff in 1970, was said to be an unreliable source because of his advanced age. CNN hired media attorney Floyd Abrams to conduct an independent investigation of the report at CNN's expense. According to Abrams, Admiral Moorer's words to producers Jack Smith and April Oliver did not conclusively support the thesis. He spoke in generalities. "The central thesis of the broadcast could not be sustained at the time of the broadcast itself and cannot be sustained now," Abrams wrote in his report, which was posted on CNN.com. "CNN's conclusion that United States troops used nerve gas during the Vietnamese conflict on a mission in Laos designed to kill American defectors is insupportable. CNN should retract the story and apologize." And that's exactly what CNN chairman Tom Johnson did. In addition, Smith and Oliver were fired, as was their direct boss, Pam Hill. Pulitzer Prize–winning correspondent Peter Arnett was disgraced, in more ways than one, and was allowed to quietly leave a few months later.

Writing about the Tailwind scandal, Neil Hickey has charged that CNN was blinded by a lust for ratings. Among his other criticisms: CNN didn't check the story out with its own military consultant. The network, he added, didn't give proper guidance to Smith and Oliver, the vetting process was faulty, too much emphasis was placed on the word of Admiral Moorer, and CNN had no documents from Laos or Vietnam to support its position that gas had been used. In addition, he claimed that *Time* magazine did not independently check the facts on the article that ran under Peter Arnett and April Oliver's bylines, even though staffers in Washington, D.C., were concerned about the story's accuracy. Hickey also charged that CNN's vetting process was inadequate, and he blamed Peter Arnett for not being more involved in the story.

Arnett defended his part in the fiasco by saying that he had not contributed "even a comma" to the TV script or the *Time* article. He said he simply read what he was told to read, a script written by the others. When I and many of my colleagues heard this, we were outraged. Peter Arnett, one of the most respected journalists in the business, was admitting he was a "news actor," something that immediately tainted all of us in the business. "News actor" is a term I use for people who put on makeup, appear on camera, and voice the story but have very little if anything to do with it. That a person can be highly paid for news acting and also be revered as a top journalist in this honorable profession is a disgrace. But it does happen, very frequently. In fact, very few television newsmagazine shows could afford to operate without having lower-paid producers do the reporting, the research, and the writing of questions for the star to ask in interviews and the script. The news stars fly in, conduct an interview or two, do an on-camera standup, perhaps change a couple of lines in the script, and then leave to their next news-acting job. It can easily take two to four months of work to produce one ten-minute story for such programs as *Dateline* or *60 Minutes.* If the correspondent or anchor were to actually lead the research effort, find the subjects to be interviewed and interview them, and write the script (even though a producer might log the actual video and the interviews) he or she would only be able to appear on air a handful of times each year. And that's unacceptable for newsmagazines that are celebrity-journalist driven, which is most of them. Still, in the final analysis, the anchor or correspondent can decide if he or she wishes to go along with this very common and irresponsible procedure. And if they do, then they will—as Arnett did for years—enjoy any professional profit from the kudos that accompany the vast majority of the stories they voice and put their name to. But if something goes wrong with a story they have conned the public into believing they actually reported, then they should accept the consequences. It is as simple as that. You can't have it both ways.

To the journalists at CNN, the Tailwind episode was also disturbing for other reasons. The fact that CNN chairman Tom Johnson hired a lawyer, and a team picked by that lawyer, to investigate the veracity of the story without including a single journalist sent a chill through the newsroom. Since when do news organizations have lawyers judge journalistic standards? I'm not naïve. I know and appreciate First Amendment attorneys who counsel reporters during the course of an investigation. Several have kept my butt out of jail. But a lawyer's job and a reporter's job are different. Journalists inform the public as fairly and completely as possible. Lawyers keep their clients from being sued. And if that means advising a network client to retract a story or not run it at all, not because it's true or false but because it will cost a lot of money to defend, then unfortunately that's sometimes the way it's done.

The other worrisome issue that Tailwind highlighted was the vetting process for scripts and investigative pieces. The Tailwind scripts were read and approved by a legion of journalists and in-house lawyers. The journalists included Chairman Tom Johnson, CNN President Rick Kaplan, President of News Gathering Eason Jordan (although he did not oversee this program's news-gathering efforts), several other vice presidents, the members of the ethics and professional standards committee, and others. The attorneys included the entire top tier of the CNN and Turner Broadcasting legal departments. All of them had access to the research, to the material, to the interview logs. And all of them approved the story.

Yet when the decision to retract the story was made, the only people held responsible were the producers and the correspondent. They lost their jobs. But the senior executives who assigned the story to them, hounded them to get it and get it in in time for a debut program, and congratulated them upon its completion continued to be gainfully employed. To underestimate the pressure senior executives place on correspondents and producers to deliver such a story is unwise. To make the lower-ranked people pay is even worse.

The Tailwind fiasco therefore left one other legacy behind: Fear. Why should correspondents and producers risk their jobs and their careers by embarking on dicey investigative pieces? The Tailwind staff abided by the guidelines for story and script approval by journalists and lawyers alike. They followed the rules and were given the go-ahead by senior executives who, theoretically, had the chops to know a solid story from a weak one. Yet they were sacrificed. For the rank-and-file staffers, the lesson was clear: investigative journalism, at CNN at least, is dangerous to your welfare. As a result, few if any truly controversial investigative reports are seen on CNN any more.

INVESTIGATE EVERYONE EQUALLY—UNLESS THEY'RE FAMOUS AND INFLUENTIAL

In the Tailwind episode, CNN management's decision to retract the story and blame lower-level employees had important, albeit indirect, ramifications. If the story was truly erroneous, then the public was not well served. The military's reputation was damaged, as were the reputations of some of the people interviewed or whose photographs were used—and CNN did pay settlements to several of them. At CNN headquarters, the only people truly punished were the hands-on journalists who followed orders issued by executives and aired work approved by them.

There are times, though, when management's unethical decisions *directly* injure viewers, when caving in to power endangers the well-being of the general public. In 1993, long before sexual abuse by priests was a major story, CNN chairman Tom Johnson personally assigned me to do a documentary on priest pedophilia. It became the most controversial story I ever did. During my in-depth research, I learned that a former seminary student planned to file a lawsuit charging Chicago's Roman Catholic Cardinal Joseph Bernardin with sexual abuse. The abuse, said Steven Cook, happened years earlier when both of them were assigned to the archdiocese of Cincinnati.

Once we learned that, producer Steven Springer and I followed the ethical and professional guidelines of the day to be as fair and impartial as we could, to safeguard our journalistic integrity, and to uphold to the utmost degree the highest standards of journalism. We would not report anything until a lawsuit was actually filed. And while CNN had the goods, after months of our research, we did not even air a report that day until we obtained Bernardin's side to the story. Again, this is how ethical news organizations function. In preparation, though, we did make contact with Steven Cook, and he granted us the only interview he gave until well after the suit was filed. When we learned that his memories of the alleged abuse had been retrieved through hypnosis—a process some people question—we also demanded to see the results of lie detector tests he had taken. We knew this wasn't admissible in court, but it did speak to his credibility. We saw the autographed gifts Bernardin gave to Cook. And the fact that another priest also implicated by Cook had admitted he had sexually abused kids also added weight to Cook's story.

There was a lot of information that we did not report because it was given to us "off the record," and we decided that with a story this monumental, we'd only go with material that was "on the record." Although Cardinal Bernardin had always declared that he had led a chaste life, we had not one, not two, but several sources telling us otherwise. These were people who had been in Bernardin's company in private situations. They included a long-time and well-respected priest in his diocese, a person outraged by what he was seeing. They also included the psychiatrist of a priest who sought therapy because he said he had been sexually abused by Bernardin, who at that time was a bishop. The psychiatrist told me about this information only after a great deal of soul-searching, and only because his patient was no longer alive. He had committed suicide. Still, the psychiatrist was too afraid of the power of the church to let me use his name. So rather than muddy the waters with an unnamed source, especially for such a serious accusation, I chose not to report this information.

Even before we heard about Cook and Bernardin, church sexual abuse therapists who welcomed us to their facilities and spoke very openly about priest pedophilia admitted on camera that their patients included "several" very high-level clergy, bishops and above. This was important information that Springer and I also passed on to senior executives. I was in Haiti for CNN when we learned that Cook had agreed to speak with us, and it was Johnson who ordered me back to do that interview. He read and approved the scripts, along with senior and executive producers, several vice presidents, the top three people in the legal department, and several others. Johnson was also in the studio the day we began our reports, giving me and Steven high fives for our work. That congratulatory attitude quickly changed, however, when his phone started to ring with complaints from cardinals, bishops, other high-level church officials, and even someone from the Vatican, he said. And while literally dozens of news organizations—networks, national magazines, and so on—had reporters camped out in front of Cook's home hoping for an interview, they simultaneously bashed CNN for having obtained the first interview. Johnson began distancing himself from the story he had encouraged and approved. In a meeting with a cardinal and some other high-level clergy who flew to Atlanta to complain, Johnson did not defend the story. When writers such as *Newsweek* columnist Margaret Carlson called for comment from Johnson and me, he refused to let me stand up for the reporting. Johnson also forbade me from submitting an article I had written to the *Columbia Journalism Review*. And one day when both of us were in the large CNN newsroom within earshot of many staffers, Johnson called out to me: "Bonnie, from now on the only cardinals we'll ever investigate will be little red birds."

Johnson was smiling, but the message he sent everyone that day was very serious. Lay off the church.

Months later, when Steven Cook was in the final stage of dying of AIDS and withdrew his charges against Bernardin, CNN led the media charge in reporting that Cook was now saying Bernardin *did not abuse* him. He said no such thing. CNN said he recanted. He did not. What Steven Cook said publicly was this: "I now realize that the memories that arose during and after the hypnosis are unreliable."

What he said to me privately was that he knew he had little chance of winning the lawsuit for several reasons. First, he could not prove what happened between two people in a room. He knew that the public's perception of repressed memories would not help his case. He had learned, after the fact, that one of his therapists was not licensed, and that would have had a very negative effect on the case. Cook also knew that the church was threatening to countersue if he didn't back off. Cook said he thought he'd probably die before the first suit went to court, never mind the second. But while the church was ordering him to completely clear the cardinal, Cook refused to deny Bernardin had abused him. So that is how the wording quoted previously was reached. Memories retrieved through hypnosis are sometimes unreliable. But sometimes they're not. Many, many perpetrators—priests currently serving lifetimes in prison— have admitted they abused children, but only after the children retrieved their memories through hypnosis.

Springer and I tried to explain all of this to the top CNN executives, but they ignored us. What's more, not only did Johnson have every news-cast for two-plus days, and I mean every one, report that Cook now denied the abuse, he also had anchor Bernie Shaw apologize to Bernardin on air on behalf of CNN. (When Shaw later heard our side of what had happened, he was furious that he had been used.) And then Johnson offered the cardinal fifteen minutes of live air time whenever he wanted, with whichever anchor he chose. This was the most absurd response any of us at CNN had ever seen. And it is when I truly experienced how power—political, religious, or economic—indeed can influence news reporting. CNN and I had been criticized for interviewing Cook, but the truly unethical behavior was what happened behind the scenes.

And was the public served? Absolutely not. CNN had been the first network to report in-depth about priest pedophilia. But then we dropped the ball, afraid of the religious power structures, afraid of bad press. It wasn't until eight or nine years later that the topic became front-page news again, forcing resignations of cardinals, bishops, and priests. I can't help but wonder how many kids were molested by priests during this period of time because a major network refused to stand up to a powerful institution. How many people are paying this high price, even to this day, for CNN's silence?

Ethical television journalism can have life-or-death consequences. It matters. When television news organizations shy away from reporting on influential people or institutions, they are forsaking their watchdog role and are, in effect, colluding with the power brokers at the expense of viewers. All of the examples of damaging, unethical behavior in this chapter are examples of public disservice of the ugliest variety. These should be seen not just as horrible lapses of the past but, also, as cautionary tales for the future. Despite very clear professional journalistic guidelines, these kinds of fiascos can—and will—happen again unless reporters speak up and viewers vote with their remote controls.

ALL PROFITS,
ALL THE TIME

THOUGH FEW PEOPLE knew it at the time, the world literally changed
with the flip of a switch on June 1, 1980. "I dedicate the news channel for America, the Cable News Network," said visionary Ted Turner.
That day, for the first time, 1.7 million homes in the United States had
access to twenty-four-hour news.

Less than a decade later, viewers around the globe watched events
unfold live at Tiananmen Square in Beijing. Then came unbelievable
images of the Gulf War, live, as it was happening. Journalists at competing news organizations, me included, immediately stopped making jokes
about the Chicken Noodle Network—and started making plans to join
the company.

The impact that live, twenty-four-hour-a-day global television had on
heads of states and governments, not to mention economies worldwide,

became known as the "CNN effect." In Washington, D.C., and across the United States, television sets in lawmakers' offices were kept on CNN nonstop so that elected officials would know what was happening as soon as possible.

. And when a major news story broke, ratings exploded as more and more U.S. viewers tuned in and stayed there. The standoff in Waco. The Oklahoma bombing. The Los Angeles earthquakes. Hurricane Andrew. The deaths of Princess Diana and Mother Teresa. Presidential elections and government scandals. *That* was CNN—then.

This was CNN in 2003: on CNN's *Inside Politics,* once considered the show to watch to learn about what was happening in Washington, D.C., anchor Judy Woodruff inaugurated a cooking segment called "Capitol Cooks." Her first guest was Senator Barbara Mikulski of Maryland.

> Mikulski: "Well, Judy, I'm thrilled to be able to do this. When it comes to talking about the Chesapeake Bay, I can talk longer than a filibuster. . . . But what I'm happy to do today is give you the recipe that really my mom developed [for crab cakes].

The senator went on to reveal ingredients in the recipe and answered a total of two questions Woodruff managed to ask about politics.

> Woodruff: "Now, what do you hear from your constituents? How comfortable are they with the idea that there could be military action soon?"
>
> Mikulski: "My constituents, from the conservative Eastern Shore to the Baltimore-Washington corridor, are saying, stick with the United Nations. Make sure that whatever we do is multilateral. If Saddam is that big of a threat, he's a threat to the world. And, therefore, we need to have international legitimacy and international support. . . . Now, Judy, we're at the next-best part of this. It's the actual making of the crab cake. What you do is, you take a little bit of crab. OK, in your hand. Some people use an ice cream scoop. I'm a hand-going kind of woman."

On March 10, 2003, Woodruff's guest was Senator Debbie Stabenow of Michigan. She was seen in her kitchen with her Greek husband, Tom

Athans, cooking up Greek food. During the entire segment, Woodruff asked only one question about the possibility of war with Iraq and another about health care. Two of the most powerful and intelligent women in the country—shown cooking on one of the most influential political shows on the air. Who else was given time on these same programs? Dick Cheney and Gary Hart. And no, they didn't cook a thing.

How did this proud network recognized around the world as the crown jewel of news wind up doing a cooking show?

THE BIRTH OF CEN:
CABLE ENTERTAINMENT NETWORK

Imagine high-powered senior television executives meeting behind closed doors to discuss potential programs for the future. They sit in luxurious, leather-upholstered chairs around a large, handsome hardwood table in a conference room on the executive floor. Against one wall, set into an expansive cabinet, are nearly a dozen television sets tuned to various channels, including their competitors.

The executives are all men, all white, all in their thirties and forties. But they are confident that they know exactly what everyone in America wants to see on television. Between bites of their catered lunch, they review a list of programs under consideration:

A cooking show

A quiz show

A humor program

An entertainment show

A crime show

A program about party planning and decorating tips

A late night "infotainment" show

A hunting and fishing program

A reality show depicting the lives of young interns at work and play

A newscast anchored by the host of the popular reality series *The Mole*

At most U.S. networks, this would be regular fare. In fact, it might even be considered a tad tame. But these executives weren't working for an entertainment network. They were in this hush-hush meeting to develop new programming ideas for the Cable News Network, CNN. Among those at the table were the president of the CNN News Group, the president of CNN news gathering, the president of CNN domestic networks (Headline News, CNNfn, and CNN/Sports Illustrated, among others.) They also included the boss of CNN/USA, the network seen in the United States and the company's main bread and butter earner. But the two men calling the shots, the men primarily responsible for CNN's dive into infotainment, were big Hollywood names hired to run Turner Broadcasting. They had enjoyed some success in programming entertaining networks and were convinced the same strategies, the same entertainment values, could make news more appealing to CNN viewers.

The time was early 2002. Advertising profits were down dramatically because of the weak economy, and to make matters worse, the Fox News Channel had overtaken CNN in the ratings and wasn't looking back. CNN and Turner Broadcasting executives knew their new bosses at AOL Time Warner were not pleased. So while they had already cut four hundred to five hundred people from the CNN staff, it was time to take radical steps to increase ratings and revenue. They made the decision to literally change the way CNN had covered and programmed news. High-paid, bigger-name news stars such as Aaron Brown, Paula Zahn, and Connie Chung were hired in the hope they'd attract a bigger audience. Several newscasts became fluffier and covered lighter topics and more local crime news than would have appeared on CNN before. For the executives sitting around the hardwood table at CNN Center, whose annual bonuses largely were tied to ratings, profit, and budget numbers rather than to journalistic standards, the only objective was to increase ratings, no matter how. If that meant sacrificing responsible editorial decision making and news ethics, and programming cooking, fishing, and humor programs, then that was what they'd do.

In all fairness, I should point out that a couple of those programming ideas were meant to actually include news anchors and newsmakers.

Veteran newsman Jeff Greenfield was the main person under consideration for the news quiz show. The cooking show envisioned Democratic
Party strategist James Carville whipping up some Cajun cuisine while chat-
ting with politicians. The intern show? Well, it would be about *news*
interns. The proposed humor show was designed around comic Dennis
Miller, who played the part of a news anchorman when he was on
Saturday Night Live. After that he hosted a monthly program on HBO—
which is owned by Time Warner—that dealt primarily with topical humor.

This would sound far-fetched unless you've watched CNN in the past
couple of years. Anderson Cooper, who had once anchored an overnight
program on ABC News but is best known for hosting *The Mole,* was
hired to anchor a prime-time newscast and even hosted a debate with
presidential candidates in late 2003. On Wolf Blitzer's weekday, prime-
time newscast, there is a daily news quiz.

If a cooking show, or segment, seems out of line for a serious news
network, consider this: on September 20, 2002, the staff of CNN
International (which is seen around the world) was informed that their
network would be airing a new program hosted by a well-known Comedy
Central celebrity. In a memo, CNNI head Rena Golden wrote, "*The
Daily Show: Global Edition with Jon Stewart* debuts this weekend on
CNNI (to 160 million viewers worldwide). It will air both Saturday and
Sunday. . . . Supervisors: In the event of breaking news, the show can and
should be killed." Also: "Insert CNNI Bug [the CNN International logo
on the screen] as usual, (Comedy Central branding will be upper right)."

At the time, Comedy Central was jointly owned by Viacom and
AOL Time Warner. (Later, in April of 2003, Viacom bought out AOL
Time Warner's stake in Comedy Central.) This was a blatant example of
cross-promotion and cross-pollination, and an embarrassing attempt to
lure viewers to what is, after all, a Cable *News* Network. But the damage goes beyond that. Stewart's comedy belittles the importance of news.
It is based on ridiculing the day's headlines and making fun of the stories. That belongs on an entertainment network and can even, sometimes, be amusing there. But to juxtapose it with real news, real death
and pain, and real traumas and tragedies, is an affront to journalism and

an insult to viewers. However, journalism wasn't the goal. In an interview with *The Guardian* (in Great Britain), Golden—whom I've always respected—was quoted as saying, "Jon is on because he hits our demographic. . . . young and intelligent . . . and because at the weekend our viewers stay with us for longer so we don't just give them rolling news." Again, making money ultimately drives every decision.

The promos that CNNI runs internationally also reveal the marketing strategy. In August of 2003, I was in a hotel in Brazil preparing to speak to a convention of journalists about ethical issues when I tuned into CNNI, as many English speakers traveling abroad are wont to do. What I heard, though, sent a chill through me. It was a promo, an ad, for the evening newscast anchored by CNN's Aaron Brown, which was simulcast—live—on CNNI in Latin America (and perhaps elsewhere, though I'm not certain of that). "He's smart. Insightful. Opinionated. Aaron Brown. For a unique take on each day's news." "Opinionated"? A "unique take"? They're promoting this as good news reporting? It took me a few moments to finally get it. Having been born and raised in Latin America, I realized that many viewers in the Southern Cone (including Argentina, Brazil, Chile, and Uruguay) and elsewhere in the region expected a network to have a slant, political or otherwise. This was good marketing in Latin America, a great way to draw in viewers. But it was also a huge affront to journalism. I heard the same promo there time and time again, always wondering if Brown—a journalist I'd always respected and first brought to the attention of CNN executives (for better or for worse, in retrospect)—knew about this. On November 5, 2003, just a short time later, I was in Atlanta watching a program on TNT (which is owned by Turner Broadcasting) and saw a similar version of the same promo. This time, Aaron Brown himself appeared on the screen inviting viewers to tune into his newscast "for a unique perspective on the news." It didn't mention that the very same program CNN promoted as "opinionated" in other countries was apparently not opinionated here. But it sure would offer a "unique perspective" on the news. If news is reported properly, fairly, and in a balanced manner, can it truly be unique?

That approach to programming and promotion, however, is increasingly being used by other so-called newscasts on CNN. In February 2004, the Web site for anchor Anderson Cooper's program described the show like this: "*Anderson Cooper 360°* does not shy away from strong opinions. . . . Regular features include Anderson's take on the world. . . . Cooper provides his unique view of the world." So two of CNN's prime-time weekday programs—supposedly newscasts— are offering the anchors' opinions, "unique views," and their "take" on the news.

As part of the Hollywoodization of CNN, one of the entertainment executives brought in to jazz up CNN's image suggested that the network interview celebrities on the first anniversary of 9/11. According to an e-mail David Neuman sent to senior managers, the names on his list included Britney Spears, Justin Timberlake, Whoopi Goldberg, Martha Stewart, Jim Carrey, Julia Roberts, Tobey McGuire, Joe Namath, Jay Leno, Bill Gates, Oprah Winfrey, Carlos Santana, Haley Joel Osment, Kristi Yamaguchi, Diana Ross, McCauley Culkin, Ted Danson, Whitney Houston, Mark Hamill, George Lucas, Adam Sandler, and Michael Jordan. Would these stars have helped increase public understanding of the lasting impact of 9/11? Of course not. But that wasn't the point. They would have drawn many more viewers than normal. Fortunately, journalism won out, and these interviews were not conducted that day.

That senior executives even considered using movie stars and other well-known celebrities to cover a major event, however, is further evidence that CNN is considering doing just about anything to attract viewers and rescue sagging ratings.

IN THE BEGINNING, THERE WAS ONLY CNN

For years, CNN was the only twenty-four-hour cable news outlet, and through the staff's hard work and dedication the network earned its reputation as the world's news leader. Though the company made a profit, it was not at the expense of news quality or quantity. When cable competitors started popping up in 1996, CNN executives virtually ignored them, believing none of them could possibly catch up. After all, between August 1997 and August 1998, Fox had a daily average of only 53,000 viewers, MSNBC had 113,000 daily viewers, and CNN had a whopping 426,000 (although it was down from 696,000 three years earlier.) It was business as usual—until Fox and MSNBC began narrowing the gap with CNN. Not only were these two new networks attracting new viewers, but the established cable news viewer pie was now also being shared by more companies. CNN's ratings continued to wobble, while the average age of the network's viewers rose above sixty years old. For advertisers—and people watching the bottom line—this was not good news.

But even before cable competition became an issue, CNN executives realized they needed a strategy to try to keep the hundreds of thousands of additional viewers who, unlike during ordinary news days, tuned in only for major breaking news coverage.

One answer was to milk the hell out of any potentially major story. That is why CNN decided to go with gavel-to-gavel coverage of the O. J. Simpson trial. The ratings justified that programming decision, even if the trial offered very little news on a day-in, day-out basis. For the twelve months prior to the trial, CNN's ratings had been down about 25 percent. During the O. J. coverage, millions tuned in—driving ratings up nearly 400 percent. The nonstop coverage of John F. Kennedy Jr.'s death gave the network an 800 percent ratings hike over the same day the week before. The Clinton-Lewinsky scandal was also a huge ratings draw. This type of programming worked.

This strategy is still being used today, especially when a celebrity story happens during a slow news time. The Kobe Bryant case is a perfect example. While it certainly deserved coverage, was it so important that every aspect needed to be reported live time and time again for days on end? What justifies this in the minds of many of the executives is that without good ratings, there are no good profits. Without good profits, they might be out of work. To them, appealing to the lowest possible denominator is the lesser of two evils.

As the cable news competition heated up, Turner Broadcasting officials began a series of management reorganizations. When veteran ABC
newsman Rick Kaplan was brought on board as CNN/USA president in
1997, he launched the second prong of the attack—an attempt to create
more "appointment viewing," to have people actually tune in for specific
shows and not just the latest news update. Kaplan created *NewsStand,*
nightly news magazines that would be produced jointly with sister Time
Warner publications such as *Fortune* and *Time,* as described in Chapter
Six. With the network's reputation at stake, more than $30 million, more
than the entire yearly budget of at least one CNN network, was spent on
this venture. But during Kaplan's three-year tenure, daily ratings dropped
36 percent, to 288,000 viewers. In June 2000, the ratings were lower than
they had been in nine years. Kaplan said, and few people dispute this, that
a main problem was that CNN did not spend the necessary money to
promote itself in other media.

When Kaplan was fired, there was yet another reorganization.
CNN/USA, the domestic network, was still run by a journalist, but a
sales-and-marketing expert was brought in and given control of the news
budget. That meant he also had influence on news coverage, something
that disturbed the journalists.

AOL "MERGES" WITH TIME WARNER

In 2000, on the day the AOL merger with Time Warner was announced,
CNN chairman Tom Johnson called an early morning meeting with senior executives, vice presidents and above. The thirty to forty people assembled in the sixth-floor conference room with excited whispers and
giddiness. Some, if not many of them, especially those who had been
receiving stock options the longest, had literally become multimillion-
aires overnight. The news of the merger had driven the stock price close
to $100, which for some of the executives was ten to fifteen times more
than the cost of their options. There was laughter and backslapping.
Within a short time after the merger, a few of these executives retired,
urging their colleagues to "keep up the good work," meaning "keep the

price of the stock up." In that and other meetings I attended, there was no talk about whether such a merger would have an impact on CNN's primary mission, which was to gather and produce news.

Over time, the stock price dropped to the teens and stayed there. Instant fortunes were erased, but what didn't vanish was the executives' lust for personal profits. Budget tightening and cuts demanded by the new parent company—steps most of these journalists would have fought in the past—were quietly accepted by many of them. If they did what they were told and stayed under the radar, they'd keep their jobs and earn more stock options.

And so there were more budget cuts. "The powers that be, the moneymen, have decided to eviscerate us," CNN's Christiane Amanpour charged in a speech to journalists that year. "It actually costs a little bit of money to produce good journalism, to travel, to investigate, to put compelling viewing on screen, and to give people a reason to watch us. But God forbid money should be spent on our news operations pursuing quality. For the most part, as we've seen, it's just a lot of demeaning, irrelevant, super-hyped sensationalism. And then we wonder why people are tuning out in droves. And I don't think it's just the new competition, which is obviously part of it. It's the drivel we spew into their living rooms."

As Fox continued to close the distance with CNN, there was another round of musical chairs in 2001, with the head of Turner Broadcasting and some of his top lieutenants replaced by men whose lives and careers had been defined in Hollywood, in the world of entertainment. From the chairman and CEO of Turner Broadcasting to the chief programming officer (an invented title never before used in news), they've spent their careers at Viacom, Orion Pictures, Fox, the WB, NBC Entertainment (and head of comedy series), and Walt Disney Television. They didn't just influence the path CNN would take, they led the charge. They were not shy about publicly stating they wanted more pizzazz, more glitz, more entertaining news, more "first person" stories from correspondents who would report from "their point of view." None of this, of course, was remotely connected to journalism.

Did it work? CNN's ratings did bump up a bit over the previous year, but, despite the huge, overwhelming audience CNN had had in the days following 9/11, Fox still moved ahead of it in January of 2002 and has stayed there. Perhaps that explains an apparently desperate attempt by CNN that same month to lure viewers. Under the new regime, the network released a promo—a television ad promoting the network—touting new female anchor Paula Zahn as sexy. In the background, viewers heard the sound of a zipper. Zahn, other CNN journalists, and many viewers exploded in outrage over the commercial, but every single one of the executives denied knowing anything about it beforehand. They blamed a new hire in the promo department. They also condemned the promo as irresponsible. Anyone who has spent time in network management, though, knows that an ad campaign about a network's new, high-paid, and high-visibility star can't sneak its way onto the air without a single high-level executive knowing. And whether or not this was the actual intent, the ad did garner a great deal of publicity for CNN. (Another sign that executives were pleased with the result: in June of 2003, when Zahn was on the set of her new evening show with the writer of *Sex and the City,* the camera lingered on wide shots, showing the two women's legs, when traditional news shows would have had close ups of the women speaking.)

Then there was another major reorganization of CNN (the fourth or fifth in as many years), and Jim Walton became president of the News Group. His main message was that CNN was going back to news, back to its roots. If only it were true. Walton had cancelled programs, including *Talk Back Live,* a news and talk-show hybrid program hosted by journalists with, for the first time in CNN history, a live audience, but they were replaced with other shows that haven't done as well. And he got rid of the first woman ever to head CNN's main network, Teya Ryan. Ryan was known as a strong producer who had created several popular CNN programs, including *Talk Back Live.* She had also helped to make CNN Financial a better network. Then, promoted to head up CNN Headline News, Ryan was behind the "relaunch" of the network that has gained it so many new viewers. When Ryan began to concentrate more on the look of the network than the content, it was clear she was following orders from the new Turner Broadcasting heads who had come from Hollywood. In return, they promoted her to the top news position in charge of the main domestic network, CNN/USA. It was a no-win job. The three previous heads of CNN/USA had all been let go after their efforts didn't bear enough ratings fruit within a short period of time. And soon after the show business executives left Turner Broadcasting, Ryan was also forced out.

Her boss, however, was not tainted by the fact that CNN was losing even more ground to Fox or that his leadership had resulted in the loss of tens of millions of dollars. Jim Walton's first job at CNN, an entry-level position he took in 1981, was as a video journalist. With sports as his interest, he worked his way up the ladder to become an executive producer in the CNN sports department. Walton then helped create the framework for a twenty-four-hour CNN sports network that included the experts at *Sports Illustrated*, a Time Warner magazine. (This was synergy before the merger happened.) The sports network would, Walton promised corporate executives, bring in huge returns. Look at the success of ESPN, he wrote. Even given ESPN's overriding head start, Walton managed to convince the senior executives that a twenty-four-hour sports network on CNN would be a good idea. As a result, the company invested well over $25 million just to launch CNN/Sports Illustrated, a huge budget in CNN terms.

From the start, though, CNN/SI had few viewers, far fewer than CNN en Español, which launched three months later, or any other startup CNN network. That wasn't the result of bad programming, it was the result of not being carried or offered to the public by enough cable companies. Carriage—just how many companies will offer your product to the public—is a major consideration when launching new programming. This should have been nailed down in advance before a single dollar was spent. So CNN/SI lost millions of dollars annually. Still, in 2001, Walton was promoted to president of domestic networks. That meant he was in charge of not only his failing sports network but also CNN/USA (the mothership), CNNfn, CNN Headline News, and the Airport

Network. Finally, in 2002, Turner Broadcasting (under the ownership now of AOL Time Warner) had had enough of CNN/SI's losses and decided to pull the plug. Yet Walton was then promoted to president of the CNN News Group, of *all* of CNN's networks and services.

What no one can contest is that CNN employees went through hell in 2001, 2002, and 2003 as a result of executives making the staff-reducing budget decisions they say for the most part "corporate" forced them to make. On Oct. 16, 2003, Walton decided to cheer up his staff. In a memo put into the CNN computer system, he announced that CNN would sponsor a talent contest, much like *American Idol* and other such "reality" programs. "Busy people need a breather, and the CNN News Group is in the financial position to provide just that." The first prize award was set at $12,000. The finalists from CNN's bureaus in New York, Washington, Atlanta, London, and Hong Kong were flown to Atlanta for the crowning of the champ on Dec. 3, 2003. The winner sang an original song about his job at Headline News. The second place finisher, who won $5,000, sang opera. Tens of thousands of dollars spent in travel costs, plus the awards, from the man who said he would turn CNN's reputation around, back to its original mission, by spending CNN's assets on news. Two weeks later, CNN's parent company, Turner Broadcasting, donated half a million dollars to the redevelopment of downtown Atlanta. This financial award was announced at about the same time Saddam Hussein was captured in Iraq. CNN saw a 336 percent spike in ratings that day—1.97 million viewers—but was still whomped by Fox, which pulled in 2.32 million viewers. Given the cutbacks at CNN, giving money away doesn't seem to be the best business decision at this point. But downtown Atlanta is sure going to look good.

ETHICS, SMETHICS—OR "YOU CAN MAKE MONEY AS LONG AS CNN DOES, TOO"

Ratings- and money-hungry network executives bear the lion's share of responsibility for CNN's decline. However, some on-air employees are often complicit, too. Some of the most obvious examples of CNN executives ignoring journalistic ethics and company policy in order to make more money involve anchor Lou Dobbs. His financial show, *Moneyline*, was a huge profit center for the network. At times, ads on this program cost 150 to 200 percent more than ads on other CNN programs. As a result, managers treated him like a golden goose and let him get away with ethical horrors that would have gotten other employees fired outright. One example was in 1992 when he was "strongly reprimanded" for violating ethics. He had taken money from several companies he and CNN report on ($30,000 alone from Ford Motor Company) to appear in videos shown to brokers and clients of Wall Street institutions. CNN's policy is very strict on this, clearly prohibiting people on staff from giving paid speeches to people in the industry they cover. This is a firing offense. But Dobbs simply had his hand slapped in a very public manner and then was permitted to continue earning huge amounts of money for CNN.

Other journalists in the company not only were outraged that Dobbs blatantly violated the most basic ethical guidelines but also were even more livid over the fact that CNN executives placed profit above professionalism. In a July 29, 1992, memo to CNN chairman Tom Johnson, a long-time senior manager wrote that when he joined CNN "no one person was ever, ever thought to be bigger than the story. The idea was that CNN was created to give a home to the news, and more news, and more news after that. When the network has been able to sign up good, reliable, professional journalists, it has made our mission that much easier. But times have changed. The news is no longer the star. The 'stars' are the stars. And even worse: the 'stars' are the news. Despite what are obvious violations of the company's various codes of ethics policies, it appears one man can get away with flaunting and violating these policies." The manager pointed out that two other CNN employees had been fired recently after committing less egregious violations, and were not given the chance to apologize for their actions. Continuing, the manager asked, "Why? Maybe it's because they were 'little people,' not someone who gets his or her name in the spotlight, not someone who has become a senior executive and is a big name in the CNN universe. By your statement and by his own statement, Lou Dobbs is undeniably guilty of violating company policy that governs the very foundation of our existence: our credibility. Why is his only punishment that he gets the moral equivalent of being sent to his room without his dinner?" The memo went unanswered.

In June of 1999, Lou Dobbs left the company over another financial spat. He had helped create space.com, and in addition to investing some of his own money, he was also the chairman. This, however, was a company that would compete with CNN's own Web interests. It was a very ugly public breakup. But a couple of years later, CNN executives went crawling back to Dobbs, begging him to return to CNN. None of the anchors they had used in his stead had been even a fraction as successful. They were willing to forgive and forget at the expense of CNN's journalistic credibility and reputation.

In 2002, however, he once again created an ethical stir. In his book about the media, Eric Alterman writes, ". . . Dobbs, who had been generously remunerated by Andersen [Consulting] for speaking gigs, whose previous show on CNN had been sponsored by the accounting firm, and whose company, Space Holdings (in which he held a minority interest), used Andersen as its corporate auditor, whipped himself into a near frenzy over the Justice Department's decision to indict the firm. He warned that 'the effect of the indictment will be to destroy the firm and the livelihoods of most of those 85,000 innocent people' and noted that neither Enron Corporation nor its executives, whose dealings with Andersen got the accounting firm in trouble, had yet been charged with a crime." Despite the clear editorializing, Dobbs's statements had no obvious impact on his career. In fact, he was promoted from financial anchor to his own prime-time news program, *Lou Dobbs Tonight*. And the editorializing continues unabated.

During coverage of Afghanistan and Iraq in 2003, Dobbs actually declared "war against Islamists" on air. He also began wearing an American pin in his lapel, just like his counterparts at Fox. For nonjournalists, this may not seem like a big deal, but journalistically it is very irresponsible. One of the main things that keeps journalists safe in war zones is their neutrality, the fact that they are there to report on all sides fairly. If a major anchor for a news network takes sides, that endangers the lives not only of that networks' field crews, but also the lives of staffers for all American news organizations. It also compromises CNN's hard-earned reputation around the world. "Under Ted Turner, Lou Dobbs would not be on the air wearing an American flag lapel pin," said Robert Wiener, CNN's Baghdad executive producer during the network's groundbreaking coverage of the first Gulf War. "What does that say to the viewers in Iraq or Lebanon, where [CNN correspondent Brent] Sadler is risking his life? It used to be that CNN was created as an international news organization based in the United States. Now I'm told [by people around the world that] CNN is looked at as nothing more than a mouthpiece of the U.S. administration."

Dobbs penchant for speaking his mind on air and ignoring the basic rules of responsible journalism was targeted further by several CNN employees who felt he was using his position to promote an anti-immigration agenda that slandered Hispanics. On February 5, 2004, staffers began circulating an e-mail petition addressed to CNN News Group president Jim Walton. "Some time ago, Lou Dobbs launched an on-air crusade against immigrants that staff feels is tarnishing our credibility and insulting our many viewers and employees. Top CNN managers and our Standards and Practices Department have responded to complaints by saying that Mr. Dobbs doesn't answer to CNN management nor does he apparently have to adhere to the journalistic practices guaranteed in writing by Time Warner employees and to which we adhere." The letter then reminded CNN of its stated mission: "Mr. Dobbs' show is billed on CNN as a news show with a business slant," the letter read. "Nowhere is it labeled opinion nor is there any disclaimer that tells watchers his views do not represent those of CNN. His show is not a talk show. . . ." Furthermore: "From his series on 'Broken Borders' to the more recent 'Great American Giveaway' and 'Exporting America,' Dobbs' show makes it appear CNN is on a campaign to demonize immigrants, most particularly Mexicans, without feeling any pressure to provide balance. . . . As far as Mr. Dobbs is concerned, undocumented immigrants have come here to abuse our health and education systems, steal our jobs while averting taxes, committing sex crimes, and clogging up our prison system—no room for any facts to speak otherwise." If the results of past complaints and letters to senior management about Lou Dobbs are any indication, this petition will have no impact whatsoever. Employee concerns about professionalism mean little next to Dobbs's ability to draw in viewers and increase CNN's earnings.

HEY! WE'RE "FAIR AND BALANCED" TOO! SEE?

That reputation mentioned by Wiener isn't completely unwarranted.

While Fox did not overtake CNN in the average daily ratings until January of 2002, CNN executives were very concerned even two years earlier about the conservative network's impressive gains in viewership. They were also very sensitive about being called liberal and about Fox managers claiming their network—unlike CNN—was truly "fair and balanced." So, very quietly, some Turner Broadcasting and high-level CNN officials began plotting how to go after some of Fox's conservative viewers without making it seem that the network was admitting a liberal bias. Among the first steps was reaching out to some well-known conservatives and gauging their interest, if any, in working for CNN. I was asked to check out Larry Elder, while others spoke with Allan Keyes and Rush Limbaugh. When CNN's romancing of Limbaugh was leaked to several newspapers, network executives were both angry and profoundly embarrassed.

Still, with Turner Broadcasting's television companies earning more than $1 billion in profits yearly, and with CNN as the company's crown jewel, CNN executives had their marching orders from Turner Broadcasting: do whatever it takes to lure old viewers back while also tapping into Fox's growing audience. And do it fast. CNN was so desperate to get on the right side of conservatives, pardon the pun, that network officials intensified their courting of right-of-center viewers, commentators, and legislators on and off screen. In mid-2001, CNN chairman Tom Johnson, who had been stripped of his budgetary authority by Turner officials earlier in the year, decided to call it quits. "One of the reasons that Tom Johnson resigned, and he told me personally about his resignation before he did resign, was he said because he would not preside over the

Fox-izing of CNN," said Wiener, a network veteran. "And that's precisely what happened to the network."

In fact, not long after replacing Johnson as CNN's chairman, Walter Isaacson actually traveled to Washington, D.C., for what turned out to be widely criticized—and lampooned—meetings with Republican leaders to let them know that CNN truly cared about covering them and their agendas.

The shift toward Fox-like programming has also been very evident on air. During the 1991 Gulf War, the network would never have used anything resembling an American flag in its onscreen graphics. That wasn't because CNN was anti-U.S.A or anti-anything. It was to preserve impartiality, an ethically responsible decision for an international news organization. But during the 2003 war in Iraq, on-air patriotism was the order of the day. Red, white, and blue graphics were prominent, while anchors and reporters routinely referred to U.S. servicemen and women as "our" troops. Identical displays of what was being touted as patriotic coverage could be seen on the Fox News Channel, which was trouncing CNN in the daily ratings.

The Iraqis certainly noticed something had changed with CNN's coverage. During the Gulf War, CNN was the only network permitted to stay in Baghdad because it was deemed impartial. But in 2003, the Iraqi government kicked out CNN correspondent Nic Robertson, his producer, and his photographer from Baghdad, saying that CNN had become even more conservative than the Bush administration. So at a time when U.S. servicemen and servicewomen were being killed and wounded, CNN could not independently inform viewers about what was happening in Iraq's capital city. By appeasing one side, the administration, CNN ticked off the other.

In an article published in *The New Yorker,* journalist Ken Auletta pointed out that CNN also was getting rid of older correspondents who specialized in in-depth reporting, in a further attempt to copy Fox. "Allan Dodds Frank, who is 55, had been a CNN correspondent for eight years, and before that he was a correspondent for ABC, *Forbes,* and the *Washington Star.* He was the investigative correspondent for *Moneyline,* and won the Gerald R. Loeb Award in 2002. He was laid off last December [2002], as was Brooks Jackson, an expert on campaign contributions and influence peddling in Washington. 'They are overreacting to Fox and deciding that everything has to be live, no matter how little sense it makes,' Frank says. 'The first rule of zoology, or journalism, is: You can't out-ape the monkey.'"

But for 2003 and at least part of 2004, CNN has still out-earned the monkey. Even though Fox's ratings have been higher since January of 2002, CNN has been pulling in two to three times more in advertising revenue. Tom Wolzien, the senior media analyst for Sanford C. Bernstein & Company, explains that earnings trail ratings. That means that even if ratings go up, it takes some time before advertisers accept that it is a dependable enough pattern that warrants paying higher advertising rates. Fox News Channel will probably be able to charge more for advertising some time in 2004, if it continues whomping CNN.

And CNN executives know that means fewer advertising dollars for their network. As a result, CNN is already looking at how it can further cut newsgathering costs in the future. In 1996, CNN spent $6 million to cover the major political events that year: the caucuses and primaries in Iowa and New Hampshire, and the two political conventions. In 2000, the conventions in Los Angeles and Philadelphia alone cost the network $10 million. According to well-placed sources, the people in charge of political coverage for 2004 are being ordered to spend no more than $8 million for everything.

(AIR)TIME, INDEED, IS MONEY

The drive for increasing earnings on a yearly basis has a direct impact on what news is covered and how it is covered at a network like CNN. Everything, including programming and staffing, is affected. This consideration has meant cheating American viewers of news they should have had immediately at times when the network could make more money renting its facilities and services to others. No one has yet documented how many times this has happened, but I can share two examples in which I had first-person experience with it.

The first time I watched CNN choose to make money over informing its own viewers happened in August of 1992, when I was a new employee, hired just two months earlier. Hurricane Andrew was headed toward the east coast, and because I'd lived in Florida for many years, my boss assigned me to cover it. This was precisely what I was supposed to do as CNN's new national correspondent. By the time I arrived at the CNN bureau in North Miami on Saturday morning, it was clear Andrew was going to make a direct hit somewhere in South Florida. Cameraman Jay Schexnyder, sound technician Kris Krismanich, and I did some pre-storm reports, including live shots as the hurricane was beginning to hit South Florida, and then—when windows from the higher floors of our building began to break—we took refuge in the stairwell of the building that housed the CNN Miami bureau. As soon as the worst passed, Jay, Kris, and I decided to head south toward downtown Miami, where radio reports said there was heavy damage. It wasn't as bad as I had anticipated, and I felt strongly that this wasn't where the eye had passed. So we continued south on U.S. 1, seeing more and more damage. In Cutler Ridge we found a nursing home that had lost most of its facade. Patients stood in hallways or walked around in a daze. I called this in. And we continued toward the Florida Keys. The highway, though, had become treacherous. Trees were down, as well as electric lines. Our rental van became an all-terrain vehicle. By 11 AM we had reached Naranja, just north of Homestead. I was shocked by what we were seeing. Migrant workers were walking and dragging one another to the fire department there, hoping to get some help and medical attention. On a stretcher lay a man whose throat had been sliced open by flying glass. The medics had no way of getting him to a hospital. We told them the route we had used to get to Naranja, but they said the hospitals weren't responding. This man later died.

With my cell phone running low on batteries, I called CNN from the firehouse and did a phone report, describing everything I'd seen. Then Jay, Kris, and I decided to go even further south. It was a joint decision; in dangerous situations, everyone's vote is equal. But we knew that we were the first news people in this area after the storm, and it was clear we were getting close to where Andrew had done its worst damage. Trees were sheared off at five to ten feet high. Buildings on either side of us were missing roofs and walls. Debris lay everywhere. When we got to Homestead, none of us could talk. Even though I knew the area well, I had a hard time telling Jay—who was driving—where to go. All of my landmarks were gone. All of them.

We finally found what was left of city hall, and we pulled up. Inside we found the city manager, in tears. "I've been in Homestead now for fifteen years, ten as city manager," he told me on camera. And then he started to choke up and look away. We kept the camera rolling. "You really . . . we've worked so hard in this community to build what we got. . . . and now it's gone."

Although one wall of his office was partially gone, miraculously his phone was working now and then. He let me use it for a phone report. I don't have the verbatim transcript of what I said, but I basically reported that Homestead was devastated by Hurricane Andrew, that thousands of homes were destroyed, that the city was in a real mess.

When I was done on air, I asked the National Desk when the satellite truck would be arriving.

"Oh, it's in Cutler Ridge, where the damage is really bad," a desk person told me. We had driven through Cutler Ridge earlier and knew better.

"It's worse here!" I said. "We need to get the truck down here as fast as possible! This city took the direct hit!"

"I'll get back to you," I heard on the phone.

Twenty minutes later, I called back. The governor and the president of the United States needed to see these pictures in order to declare the area an official disaster zone that would be eligible for immediate aid.

"What time is the satellite truck getting here?" I asked.

"It's not," the desk person said. "Newsource had affiliates yelling for live shots so they had to stay in Cutler Ridge to accommodate them."

Newsource is CNN's affiliate service. In return for affiliates each paying up to a couple of million dollars annually to CNN, Newsource provides daily feeds of material and live shots specifically for the stations around the country. It is a huge moneymaker, and the Newsource staffs are among the best in the business. Their job is to keep the affiliates happy so that they keep buying the CNN service and offer CNN live coverage of major breaking news stories that happen outside of a CNN bureau city.

In this case, though, by serving the Newsource affiliates, CNN was not serving its own viewers. We had wasted at least a couple of hours waiting for the truck so that we could feed the footage of the worst damage. We jumped back into our van and headed north. When we arrived back in Cutler Ridge, I was stunned by what I saw. Every local TV station and every network I could think of had satellite trucks parked in the same strip mall parking lot that CNN's truck had stopped in first. It was the classic herd mentality. If CNN was here, this had to be the place. So all of the other sheep set up shop there, too.

No one had a satellite truck in Homestead. And no other reporters had ventured further south. No one knew what my crew and I knew. But because Newsource needed the "bird," the satellite, it took over an hour before we could feed our video and report what we had seen in Homestead. Although the pictures we sent mobilized the governor's office to check out Homestead, the die was cast for that day and the next. The governor and President George H. W. Bush showed up at the parking lot in Cutler Ridge, where CNN had first stopped to do reports for our affiliates and where all of the transmission facilities were still set up. They toured around the immediate area, proclaimed it a federal disaster area so that the folks there could get federal aid, and then left.

My crew and I, however, continued to report out of Homestead. And, finally, near the end of the second day, CNN brought in another satellite truck and sent it to Homestead—and other news organizations followed suit. Finally, finally, the country was seeing live on television what I had been trying to show them for at least forty-eight hours. And many politicians had to make a second trip, to the real disaster area. The only reason there had been such a delay in getting help to Homestead was that the country's top twenty-four-hour news network had to stop to make money serving its affiliates, and other news organizations followed the leader. CNN's own audience lost out.

Years later, things were just as bad. I was managing editor of CNN en Español at the time, and we were covering the biggest story in Latin America since the launch of our new network. On December 17, 1996, leftist guer-

All Profits, All the Time 171

rillas belonging to Tupac Amaru took over the Japanese embassy in Peru, holding many people hostage (seventy-two of them to the very end.) The standoff lasted for four months. It was a hugely competitive story, which received major coverage from the start. As time went by, it became evident that no matter how it was resolved, we had to be there. That meant keeping reporters and camera crews on duty twenty-four hours a day at great expense. CNN even had a live, round-the-clock feed of one of the cameras that was trained on the embassy compound. On April 22, 1997, just over a month since we had launched our twenty-four-hour network for Latin America, we realized there was a military raid or rescue operation in progress. We immediately took the live images to air, having our Atlanta-based anchors do what they could to describe what was happening. But we were not allowed to simultaneously have a live shot with our own reporters. Neither was CNN. No CNN network, not the Spanish-language one, not CNN/USA, which is the domestic network, not CNN International. We watched helplessly as all other U.S.-based television news organizations had live, on-the-scene-while-it's-happening reports from their own correspondents in Peru. CNN viewers in the United States and worldwide lost out on information CNN correspondents who had been on the scene since day one could have provided.

Why? Because the minute the raid was under way, one of the two satellite paths CNN had set up in Peru was being used exclusively by TV Asahi, a major Japanese network. That meant that while viewers worldwide could see live pictures of the raid on one path, only TV Asahi's viewers could also see their Japanese reporter inset on their TV screens, since TV Asahi controlled the second satellite path. It wasn't until the raid was over that CNN was able to use the second path, which finally allowed CNN correspondents to report.

Why the delay? Why were CNN viewers forced to wait for coverage? Because TV Asahi has a contract with CNN to provide the Japanese network with international coverage. It is a contract that earns CNN between $11 million and $12 million annually. This was the first major international story that had a direct tie to Japan, so CNN executives chose to sacrifice informing *their* viewers to give TV Asahi the exclusive. The company chose money over informing the public. Eason Jordan, then–president of news gathering, justified it by saying that without TV

Asahi's annual payment, CNN wouldn't have had the money even to buy the satellite equipment needed for those transmissions. My response is, perhaps we couldn't have sustained round-the-clock coverage, but CNN's viewers could have seen the final outcome as it happened, using equipment we already owned. It might not have been fancy, but CNN viewers would have been served.

PLEASE WATCH US, WE'RE ALSO "FLY"

The Headline News network has always had a different personality from CNN's. The strategy from the start was that this network was aimed at busy news consumers, people who wanted brief news fast, while CNN targeted viewers with a bit more time and more interest in in-depth reporting. Headlines, as it's called by staffers, was seen as the *USA Today* of cable news and for years provided a very valuable news service.

As part of an attempt to appeal to younger viewers, however, Headline News was relaunched in 2001 with a faster-paced and more entertaining format and a new studio. Despite the critics, the new programming was a hit with viewers. But following a large drop in ratings between the end of 2001 and the end of 2002, this network attempted to appeal to an even younger audience so that it could regain lost advertising dollar ground. In October of 2002, a note was sent to the writers at Headline News urging them to be more hip. "In an effort to be sure we are as cutting-edge as possible with our onscreen persona, please refer to this slang dictionary when looking for just the right phrase." Among the terms in this dictionary: "fly" to mean sexually attractive, "ill" to mean acting inappropriately, and "jimmy cap" for condom. "Use this guide to help all you homeys and honeys add a new flava to your tickers and dekos." Dekos apparently means decorations, a less than professional way to describe onscreen graphics.

As soon as the memo was leaked to newspapers, CNN spokespeople claimed senior managers had known nothing about it. A few days earlier, though, the Associated Press had reported that Headline News head Rolando Santos said he wanted the network to speak "the lingo of our people."

That same year, CNN/USA inaugurated a new prime-time program with well-known news veteran Connie Chung as the anchor. To attract a younger audience to CNN's prime-time lineup, the program was designed to have a less conventional newscast feel. The *Wall Street Journal*'s headline on the story was "As Hard News Gets Even Harder, CNN Segues to Glossier Format." The first story on the premier newscast of the network's new big-name star? A "man with pedophile fantasies who had been turned in by Dear Abby," according to that newspaper. At the end of the first program, Chung then said good night to her husband and son, following the orders of the CNN's new talent recruiter, who publicly was encouraging on-air people to be more "first person."

Hiring Chung wasn't a bad idea. She has a following and brought in viewers, no question about it. Chung is a hard worker who *has* earned her stripes in journalism. But building a live show around her exposed her weaknesses and did not play to her strengths. Many in the news business recognized that. Many, that is, but not Turner Broadcasting's new chiefs and the guy handling talent at the time, all of whom came from Hollywood with no network news experience. So they hired Chung and "cast" her for a live news program that didn't work from the start. Within days, usually the only part that was shot live was the first few moments of the show that had her reading a TelePrompTer about the latest news update. She would then say something like, "and now our first guest" or toss to an animation. The control room would then run a tape of the rest of the program, which had been taped earlier in the day. This allowed Chung to do various takes on the same read and have editors and producers choose the best. Viewers turned away in droves. Her show was finally cancelled.

In November of 2003, CNN was still trying to manipulate how news is reported in an attempt to entertain and attract younger viewers. Along with the organization called Rock the Vote, CNN sponsored "America Rocks the Vote," a televised forum for college students from around the country to ask the democratic presidential candidates questions of interest to other young people their age. But in an attempt to duplicate a light moment during another *Rock the Vote* program years ago when President Clinton was asked if he wore boxers or briefs, a CNN producer strongly urged a student from Brown University to ask a specific question that she did not want to ask. In an article she later wrote in her school newspaper, the *Brown Daily Herald,* Alexandra Trustman said that she had prepared a serious question about future technology. "He [the producer] took a look at my question and told me I couldn't ask it because it wasn't lighthearted enough and they wanted to modulate the event with various types of questions—mine was to be one of the questions on the less serious side," Trustman wrote. "The show's host wanted the Macs or PCs question asked, not because he was wondering about the candidates' views of technology, but because he thought it would be a good opportunity for the candidates to relate to a younger audience—hence the 18-to-31-year-old audience of Rock the Vote." When Trustman's article was published, CNN spokeswoman Christa Robinson responded, "In an attempt to encourage a lighthearted moment in the debate, a CNN producer . . . went too far." They were caught this time because the student wrote about her experience. How many other times are they not caught?

WHEN DEFENDING CORPORATE PROFITS TRUMPS THE FIRST AMENDMENT

It is so rare that this following example may be the only case in which journalists have come to the aid of a company lawyer. When Eve Burton was hired to be CNN's First Amendment expert and lawyer, formally the "chief legal counsel," the CNN journalists quickly took note. She had a reputation of actually *defending* journalism and *helping* reporters go as close to the line as possible. She was very proactive, frequently filing documents and motions with courts demanding access to what should be public data. Despite tremendous pressure to toe the bottom line, she defended our right to information and did not shy away from going to court to force corporations and governments to hand over public documents. Most newsroom lawyers stop reporters from doing anything that could be dangerous—and that means anything that might lead to a lawsuit, even one that the reporter and news agency would obviously win. The lawyers are under orders to prevent lawsuits from being filed because defending them is expensive. Burton, though, was different. She was one of the only newsroom lawyers I've ever heard of whose advice was sought out by journalists. In fact, when she was given a desk in the CNN newsroom, there was no complaint. She was considered a colleague whose job was to help CNN employees do the best journalism possible.

So when Alice Randall, the author of *The Wind Done Gone,* was taken to court in July 2001 for allegedly infringing on the copyright of Margaret Mitchell's 1936 book *Gone with the Wind,* Burton had CNN join other news organizations in defense of the author and her right to use satire. This was very much in keeping with the First Amendment. Her actions were completely blessed and approved by Tom Johnson, the president and chairman of CNN. Yet Burton was fired. Why? Because Turner Broadcasting, the parent company of CNN, (and Time Warner, the parent of Turner), own the movie rights and sequel rights to Mitchell's book. While Burton was defending First Amendment rights, doing her job, she was also doing something that could have led to dollars leaving the corporate pocket. Some twenty women, mostly vice presidents and other well-known employees such as Christiane Amanpour, signed a letter of protest to the heads of CNN and Turner Broadcasting. The story even made the *New York Times,* but in the end, those of us who signed the letter were told to bug off by Jamie Kellner, the head of Turner Broadcasting.

THE CNN CUBA BUREAU: SELLING OUT JOURNALISTIC INTEGRITY, BALANCE, AND ETHICS

When CNN was given permission by the Cubans and the U.S. government to open a bureau in Havana, the first of any American news organization, I was a huge supporter of the project. As a Cuban-American, I felt it was important for Americans to see and hear the truth about Castro and Cuba. I did not expect nor did I want to see stories that only vilified him, his system of government, and the country. That would be poor journalism that would not serve the public. It would also hurt CNN's credibility and prompt people to think that everything they were hearing about Cuba was false.

What I did expect to see coming from CNN's Havana bureau were balanced, fair reports about the pros and cons of life in Cuba. The network could do stories about supporters of the revolution, but it should also cover the dissidents and the thousands of political prisoners still behind bars. Report on Cuba's rich musical history, but let viewers know about the many musicians forced to hang up their instruments to work in sugar cane or tobacco fields. Put stories about this closed society in full context; that, I believed, would truly be a public service.

But from the first stories to come out of the island, it was clear CNN was favoring the Cuban government and doing whatever needed to be done to keep the bureau open—which meant appeasing Fidel Castro. Out of the first twenty or so stories, one was done on dissidents, by correspondent Lucia Newman. But there was very little else that documented real life for most of the people in Cuba. CNN reported on education, saying that people on the island have the highest literacy rate in Latin America. That *is* true, but that's not the whole story. What the story neglected to include was that Cuba had the highest literacy rate in Latin America *before* Fidel Castro took over. The stories also did not explain that while the vast majority of people in Cuba can read and write, they do not have the freedom to choose *what* they read or write. If they are caught with anything—written by them or someone else—that is not deemed prosocialist and proregime, they *do* go to prison. It is as simple as that. But this was not in the story.

CNN's coverage of the Elian Gonzalez case was a prime example of how CNN neglected to report important information that would have angered the Cuban government. Rarely, if ever, did CNN spell out the kind of life Elian would have if he returned to Cuba: for example, the food rationing, which meant that in one more year Elian would no longer have access to milk. There were no stories about how Cubans are given a ration of meat, similar to a gristly hamburger patty, only six or seven times a year. No stories about how children Elian's age become "pioneros," young Communist "pioneers," and are sent to a camp with other kids for Communist indoctrination and work in the fields. Did CNN, the network with presumably the best access to information, delve into the lack of basic human rights this boy would have when he returned to Cuba? Did the stories explain about the block captains who tattle to the authorities if any family has more than a couple of strangers over to their home? No. And there were also no stories about the most obvious historical comparison that could have been made—East Germany and the Berlin Wall. Countless children made it over that wall only to have one or both parents die in the escape attempt. In case you ever wondered, not a single child was ever returned to Communist East Germany.

Rule Number One: Don't Piss Off the Cubans

The truth is that CNN was doing and continues to do everything possible to keep Castro and the Cuban government happy—in order to keep CNN's bureau in Havana. It is a symbol of prestige for the network. Prestige affects reputation, reputation affects ratings, and ratings affect the bottom line. Senior news-gathering managers will do whatever needs to be done to maintain it. For years, that job of placation went to International Assignment Desk vice president Larry Register. I was in Cuba with Register when Pope John Paul II visited the island in January of 1998. I was there as managing editor of CNN en Español to oversee the Spanish-language network's coverage of the trip. Register was there as the Cuba expert for the network. Part of his job was to help get all of the permissions needed to do our job.

The other part of his job was to make sure that we didn't piss off the Cubans.

As part of CNN en Español's coverage, our anchorman and I wanted to get guests that could talk about a variety of issues: Santeria (the religion that is a mix of African tribal rituals and Catholicism), dissidents, and so on. Two of the people I called to invite on our air both told me they were not allowed to speak to the media unless they had specific permission from the Ministry of the Interior. I asked them if they minded me trying to get that permission for them. They didn't mind, but they told me they didn't think I'd get it.

When the folks from the government dropped by CNN's workspace in the hotel later that day, which they did virtually every day, I asked them for permission to interview the two people. They reacted with tremendous surprise. "They don't need permission to speak," I was told. "Here in Cuba, people are free to speak if they wish." I knew that was absolute bullshit, but I thanked them, anyway. And after handling our live coverage for a couple of hours I called the two potential guests back. Both had been contacted by the Ministry and refused to speak with me. They had been ordered not to speak at all, and they hung up the phone. They were terrified.

When the Ministry people returned to the CNN workspace the next day, I made a point of talking to them about it. I asked them if they had called the two men. They denied it, and again said everyone in Cuba was free to speak. The conversation was tense. Although Larry Register only speaks a handful of Spanish words and couldn't understand a word the Cubans and I were saying, he was close by and immediately walked up. He then apologized to the Cubans and, in front of them, told me to drop it. Later, Register came back and ordered me not to do anything to "upset" the Cuban officials. He had been part of the team that won approval for the bureau, and it was his job to make sure the bureau stayed open at all cost, even if that meant not doing the job journalists are supposed to do. What he *was* doing was good for CNN and good for the Cubans.

When Cuban-Americans complain to CNN about the stories from Havana, and they do, the complaints are discarded as completely groundless. There's outrage when anyone suggests that CNN's coverage of Cuba is anything less than fair and balanced. Senior managers at CNN attribute the hatred Cuban-Americans have for CNN solely to the fact that the network has a bureau in Havana. The last thing they'd do is acknowledge that they have caved in to the Cubans to keep the bureau open.

When the Cuban government complains, however, that's a different story. I lost count of how many times President of News Gathering Eason Jordan, Larry Register, and even Ted Turner flew down to Havana to meet with Cuban officials and try to smooth ruffled feathers. Without exaggeration, there were more than twenty-five or thirty trips during the first two or three years alone. The Cubans knew they could yell "wolf" and

CNN would come running. The Cubans also knew that by constantly complaining, the so-called line of balance would slowly but surely inch closer toward the Cuban government's point of view. Each time they complained, they reminded CNN that the bureau was on that line. If CNN wanted to keep it, CNN had to keep the regime happy.

Fidel Isn't a Dictator, He's a Friend

As an extension of this policy, or perhaps as a result of it, CNN's stylebook was also affected. This is the manual that lays down the CNN law on grammar, word usage, titles that must be used for ex-presidents and the like, and the spelling of names such as Gadhafi (or is it Khadaffi or Ghadafi?) for all writers, producers, and correspondents. To this day, it remains completely forbidden at CNN to refer to Fidel Castro as a dictator. He must be called "President Castro," which is his preference. CNN's justification for this is that Castro was elected to the position, even though it is well known that Cuban elections are a sham and all political dissent is forbidden. If Fidel Castro isn't a dictator, what the hell is the definition of dictator?

Well, apparently to many executives at CNN, their definition of dictator is "friend." Displaying photographs in their offices of themselves posing with an arm around Fidel Castro is a big status symbol. CNN chairman Tom Johnson, President of News Gathering Eason Jordan, President of CNN Rick Kaplan, Executive Vice President Gail Evans, and virtually every other senior executive had such a photo in their offices. In the CNN headquarters building, this is politically permissible and absolutely seen as a badge of honor. Similar pictures of, say, Slobodan Milosevic or Saddam Hussein would not be politically correct, though. But someone who executed just twenty-thousand people and imprisoned just a couple hundred thousand others a short distance off our shores is OK. After all, he let CNN open an office there.

The mission to keep Fidel Castro happy also explains why CNN never gave serious consideration to any well-known Cuban-American anchors. In Chapter Three I told the story about *Good Morning America*'s newsreader, Antonio Mora, being virtually stood up by CNN executives when he came to Atlanta at our invitation for a job interview. In 2000, I got word from a major agent that newsman Jose Diaz-Balart was available. I was delighted. I knew Jose from the years we worked together at a Miami television station and knew him to be an excellent journalist and very strong anchor. He had just completed a stint as the news anchor on the *CBS Morning News.* He was well known, well thought of, experienced, Hispanic, and available. A perfect candidate.

Diaz-Balart was also very well connected. One of his brothers is a U.S. Congressman; the other was a Florida state senator. As Republican Cuban-Americans, the brothers often spoke out against Fidel Castro. That was their version of public service; his was to be a journalist.

I immediately informed Rick Kaplan, then–president of CNN/USA, and Rena Golden, the executive vice president and general manager of CNN International, who also was looking for anchors. They agreed to meet him, so I had Diaz-Balart fly in. He met first with Rena and did an anchor test. Rena was impressed enough to want to discuss hiring him with her boss, the head of CNNI. (They later decided not to offer him a job, saying he earned too much.) Jose then met with Eason Jordan, the head of news gathering, and other executives. And each one of them added to a chain of insults. Because of Diaz-Balart's heritage and his brothers, he was repeatedly asked if he could be balanced in reporting about Cuba. It may be hard for nonjournalists to understand this, but a question like that is a major insult. Diaz-Balart had been an award-winning journalist for nearly two decades, and no one had ever asked that question. Not CBS News, not anyone. His record of impeccable journalism spoke for itself.

When I later complained about that line of questioning, I was told that CNN was very concerned about the potential of having a Cuban-American anchor news about Cuba. I asked why. They looked at me as though I were crazy. CNN had assigned African American reporters to stories about the KKK and apartheid in South Africa. We had citizens from around the world reporting on the conflicts in their own countries. Most of CNN's Jerusalem bureau employees, who spend a great deal of time reporting on the Palestinians, are Jewish—yet they were never asked if they could be unbiased. Why this? No answer.

The biggest insult, though, was yet to come. And I can only believe it was aimed at discouraging Diaz-Balart from seeking a job at CNN. It worked. The moment I introduced him to CNN president Rick Kaplan, whose assistant had set aside a half hour for this interview, Kaplan said he was very busy and didn't have much time to spend with him. "I know you're not going to like this," Kaplan then said. "But I'm a good friend of Fidel's, and I think he's a good guy." Then Rick continued, talking about the good he believed Castro had done for Cuba. At this point, Diaz-Balart tried to get a word in edgewise. "Well, we don't have time for all of this now," said Rick. "Thanks for coming by. We'll have dinner some time." And he got up and escorted us out. "Even if they offer me a job, I can't work for a man like that," Diaz-Balart said to me later. "That biased thinking is reflected in the stories that are assigned and how they're done."

In May of 2002, a study by the Media Research Center (MRC), which admittedly promotes so-called conservative causes, confirmed what many of us (even liberal journalists) had been saying. After viewing 212 reports filed from Cuba since the bureau opened, the MRC condemned CNN as a "megaphone for a dictator" and a "propaganda tool for Fidel Castro."

Among other findings, CNN

- Gave "six times more air play" to Cuban government officials than to non-Communists

- Made Castro out to be a "celebrity rather than a tyrant"

- Gave American viewers "the impression that Castro's government is overwhelmingly popular among the Cuban public"

In news articles, CNN spokesman Matt Furman defended the coverage, pointing out that correspondent Lucia Newman had recently interviewed a top dissident. True, but what Furman didn't mention was that in five years, only seven other stories mentioned dissidents. When it comes to Cuba, though, it is unlikely that any criticism will prompt CNN to change the way it covers news on the island or about the island.

Keeping the bureau open, adding to CNN's prestige and bottom line, is far too important.

WHAT WE *DIDN'T* TELL YOU BEFORE . . .

In April of 2003, the same CNN executive responsible for the Cuba bureau admitted that the network had withheld horrific information for years in another country where it also had a prestigious bureau: Iraq. In an opinion-editorial-page story he wrote for the *New York Times,* President of News Gathering Eason Jordan revealed stories of atrocities that CNN had not reported because he said he feared doing so might endanger the lives of CNN staffers and others. He learned of these incidents during thirteen trips to the Iraqi capital, many of which resembled his trips to Cuba: the aim was to appease the government. There was no other reason for such a high executive in the company to return so many times. "Each time I visited, I became more distressed by what I saw and heard—awful things that could not be reported because doing so would have jeopardized the lives of Iraqis, particularly those on our Baghdad staff. The secret police terrorized Iraqis working for international press services who were courageous enough to try to provide accurate reporting. Some vanished, never to be heard from again. Others disappeared and then surfaced later with whispered tales of being hauled off and tortured in unimaginable ways. I came to know several Iraqi officials well enough that they confided in me that Saddam Hussein was a maniac who had to be removed. . . . An aide to Uday [Saddam's son] once told me why he had no front teeth: henchmen had ripped them out with pliers and told him never to wear dentures, so he would always remember the price to be paid for upsetting the boss." Jordan also wrote about an Iraqi cameraman who was tortured with electroshock techniques. "Again, we could not broadcast anything these men said to us. . . . I felt awful having these stories bottled up inside me. Now that Saddam Hussein's regime is gone, I suspect we will hear many, many more gut-wrenching tales from Iraqis about the decades of torment. At last, these stories can be told freely." He added that he believed that reporting about them at

the time would have automatically resulted in the death of many innocent people.

But *not* reporting this information allowed this regime to continue
killing, torturing, and repressing its people for many years. U.S. forces
are still finding mass graves. How did withholding this information affect
the longevity of the Saddam Hussein regime? We'll never know, but it is
clear that thousands of people continued to suffer while the world
debated just how bad this leader was, how much of a danger he posed
to Iraqis and the world. This information CNN chose not to report
might have galvanized the world into action sooner. And it may have
also been enough to convince other countries to pressure Iraq into more
civilized behavior. Perhaps the war in 2003 could have been averted, the
lives of American forces spared. But again, we'll never know. It was
the worst example of journalistic irresponsibility that I have ever heard
of. And I'm not alone. There was an immediate uproar among many
journalists, who felt CNN withheld these stories in order to make nice
with the Hussein government and, therefore, maintain its important
news bureau in Baghdad. An editorial in the *Washington Post* strongly
condemned CNN's actions, or lack thereof, and pointed out the impact
this sort of self-censorship can have. "This tale would be disturbing
enough on its own, but it is especially worrying because of CNN's special position in the Middle East. In the past, the network has been
watched avidly in the region, and nowhere more so than in Baghdad. It is
widely perceived around the world as a voice of the United States. If
CNN did not fully disclose what it knew about the Baathist regime, and
if CNN deliberately kept its coverage bland and inoffensive, that would
help explain why the regime was not perceived to be as ruthless as it in
fact was, in the Arab world and elsewhere."

In a memo to CNN's staff, Jordan defended his decade-long silence
about the atrocities by saying CNN had and continues to have a con-
tentious relationship with the Iraqi government and that several correspondents have, indeed, been kicked out of the country for months at a
time because they reported things the regime did not like. And again he
wrote, "Withholding information that would get innocent people killed

was the right thing to do, not a journalistic sin." But his reasoning that reporting the stories would have led to more deaths is faulty. Most journalists share the deep-seated belief that exposing such atrocities, shining a bright light on them, is the first step in making the government involved accountable. If the names of the CNN employees in question were reported throughout the world, it most likely would have offered them even greater protection, not the opposite. CNN also had the option of reporting the atrocities without naming the staffers, or even acknowledging that they worked for the network. Even this would have been preferable to the silence.

CNN made its name and became a worldwide phenomenon with its exclusive coverage of the Gulf War. Jordan, not much older than thirty at the time, was credited with much of that coup. He made it clear he wanted the bureau to remain open in a volatile place such as Iraq. But when does keeping a bureau open become more important than reporting the truth? Running a powerful international network's news-gathering operation requires making difficult decisions at times. But honesty and reporting the news should always outweigh lesser considerations such as merely keeping a prestigious bureau open.

All CNN staffers, by the way, were also forbidden from calling Saddam Hussein a dictator, because—just like Fidel Castro—he too was "elected." I can't help but wonder whether CNN has been withholding valuable information about atrocities in Cuba, too. Perhaps we'll find out when Castro no longer rules the island.

❏   ❏   ❏

In the end, who is to blame for the sorts of things that have been going on at CNN? Are multinational behemoth companies like AOL or Time Warner at fault? Can we blame shareholders who want to see their portfolios grow in value? Or how about news executives who sell out journalism in order to keep their jobs and get more stock options each year? Should a public that is increasingly taken in by so-called reality shows such as *Survivor* and *Big Brother* share some of the responsibility? Is the public simply getting what it wants? Did CNN and other such networks oversaturate viewers with hard news to the point where they just aren't interested anymore? Should we blame the Hollywood folks who applied strategies that work in the entertainment world to increase news viewership? The answer to most, if not all, of those questions is yes, to different degrees. At the heart of it all is money. That is the bottom line, the only line, for the corporations.

But at the heart of CNN there are still professional men and women who believe the value of good journalism is not measured in dollars and cents but rather in public service. As my colleague Robert Wiener says, "Despite the leadership, there are still a lot of good journalists at CNN who are struggling to maintain quality and standards." And they, too, are saddened by what they see happening at this network. If it is allowed to continue, it will be the death knell of solid, respectable, and honorable television journalism as we knew it. CNN was the last bastion of hope for the "old fashioned journalists," where morning news programs were about the news, not entertainment, and certainly not about perky anchors who chitchat with an ensemble cast of characters. For these journalists, many of whom went to CNN to get away from similar trends at other networks, there would be nowhere else to go. But CNN viewers, here and around the world, would be the biggest losers. That's why it's critical that the journalists remaining at CNN continue their efforts to rescue the network from greed and infotainment. That's also why former and current employees need to speak out, even though people still on the payroll who do so—such as correspondent Christiane Amanpour—are disciplined. You see, here's the biggest irony: if you work for CNN you are expressly forbidden by company policy to speak with reporters or anyone in the media. If you do so anyway, this news network could fire you for exercising your First Amendment right to free speech.

WE REPORT,
WE DECIDE

"Fiercely independent."

"Fair, balanced, unafraid."

"We report. You decide."

"Real journalism, fair and balanced."

When I hear these slogans, I don't know whether to laugh, cry, or applaud such unbelievable (and successful) audacity. The temptations to laugh and cry are for the same reason. To call what often appears on the Fox News Channel (FNC) "real journalism" is ludicrous. To claim that it is "fair and balanced" is equally preposterous. These catchphrases are laughable, but at the same time the damage this so-called news network has inflicted on the reputation, professionalism, and ethics of good journalism is devastating. Viewers, the First Amendment, and democracy are under attack. And that is the part that angers and saddens me and many, many other journalists.

If the other networks' decline into infotainment shows the lengths to which companies will go for larger profits, the Fox News Channel is the ideological poster child for what is wrong with American journalism. In fact, calling it a news channel or network is a misnomer. Run by Republican operative Roger Ailes, it is the mouthpiece of the conservative right, the propaganda wing of the Republican Party: biased and dishonest, it reports news with a right-wing slant, ignores stories that challenge its point of view, and violates nearly every principle of good journalism. Despite its slogans, it seeks not to report the truth but to shape public opinion. The so-called journalists at Fox, along with management, have an agenda and consistently cross ethical lines to force-feed conservative dogma to viewers, all in the guise of fair and balanced news reporting. Fox is setting the most dangerous precedent, one that threatens the very foundations of journalism.

Using what is reported, when it is reported, and who does the reporting to influence the outcome of an election, a war, or the public's opinion of an administration goes far beyond just crossing a line. During presidential election night 2000, Fox News was the first to make the call for George W. Bush's election, at 2 AM. The other networks followed. All had to retract their projections but the damage was already done. Who was behind the Fox effort? John Ellis, hired to be one of the network's election analysts. He also happens to be George W. Bush's first cousin, and was on the phone with George W. and his brother, Jeb, the governor of Florida, much of the night, passing on election information gathered by VNS, the news service created and funded by the Associated Press, ABC, NBC, CBS, CNN, and Fox. These unethical, behind-the-scenes maneuverings do not happen by accident at a network whose management also counsels Republican presidents. It is collusion between a political party and a part of the media at the highest levels.

This ideological strategy also explains why Oliver North was hired to be a so-called Fox News correspondent traveling with a Marine unit during the Iraq war. (That's about as nonsensical as my putting on a colonel's uniform and going out to command a unit of Marines in battle.) And why was it OK for Geraldo Rivera, who was brought to Fox by Ailes, to publicly proclaim he'd kill Osama Bin Laden if he had the chance? At one point, when Ailes was told that he might be accused of right-wing promotion, Ailes—according to *The New Yorker*'s Ken Auletta—said, "Good! That'll drive my ratings up!"

GIVE THEM WHAT THEY WANT, THEN TELL THEM THEY NEED MORE

From a business and political perspective, the creation of the Fox News Channel was pure genius. In 1996, the people at the helm of the News Corporation, which owns Fox News Channel, saw the beginnings of a political trend in this country and programmed a network to capitalize on it—as well as feed into it. When Fox launched in October of that year, it could reach only 17 million homes, whereas CNN had access to 70 million and MSNBC, 22 million. In just over five years, it became the undisputed ratings leader among cable news networks—a remarkable feat by any standard. "[Owner] Rupert Murdoch saw what he felt was a need in the business," said Joe Angotti, the former NBC News executive who now chairs the broadcasting program at Northwestern University. "He saw a perception on the part of the American public that the television media were liberal. And that they were biased, that a lot of conservatives out there were not getting news that they felt was, quote, 'fair and balanced.' So he made a very definitive decision to put on news with a political agenda, with a conservative view of the news." Veteran NBC News correspondent George Lewis agrees. "It says a lot about the brilliance of [Fox News president] Roger Ailes. He went after that same audience that listens to conservative talk radio. He captured that segment of the audience, and they are very loyal, stay with the network for long periods of time. It was very smart." In fact, Fox viewers tend to watch a lot more news than do people who tune in to CNN or MSNBC. An analysis of typical Fox viewers confirms what Angotti and Lewis say. Fox clearly offers programming that appeals to people with conservative points of view. According to a Pew Research Center for the People and the Press survey released in July of 2003, 41 percent of Fox's viewers said they were Republican, compared to 32 percent of broadcast news viewers and 29 percent of CNN viewers. Other findings include the following:

- Forty percent of Fox viewers thought coverage of the war on terrorism should be pro-American, compared with 26 percent of broadcast network news viewers and 29 percent of CNN viewers.

- Sixty-six percent of Fox viewers believe the media is liberal, compared with 54 percent of broadcast network news viewers and 47 percent of CNN viewers.

- Thirty-eight percent of Fox viewers believe the media is too critical of President Bush, compared with 21 percent each for the broadcast news divisions and CNN.

- Sixty-five percent of Fox viewers believe some news organizations are too critical of America, compared with 45 percent of broadcast network news viewers and 48 percent of CNN viewers.

- Forty percent of Fox viewers prefer pro-American coverage over neutral coverage, compared with 26 percent of broadcast network news viewers and 32 percent of CNN viewers.

- Sixty percent of Fox viewers believe criticism of the military weakens defense (versus keeping the military prepared). For the broadcast news divisions, that number is 38 percent; at CNN, 40 percent.

As the survey shows, Fox is giving the conservative audience what they want to hear—spinning news to benefit Republicans and others who share their conservative political views. Democratic presidents and candidates are fair game no matter when they were in the public eye. For example, on November 18, 2002, anchor Linda Vester delivered an ostensibly "objective" report describing President John F. Kennedy's health during his presidency. "It's rather shocking, the list of medicines he was on was rather long." Eight pills a day, she said breathlessly. "Today historians are criticizing these omissions. . . ." Whether the omissions were the supposed fault of the Democratic White House or the so-called liberal media was not made clear, but the implication was that it was one of them. A male anchor next to Vester then piped in, "His cholesterol level, get this, 410!" The next shot was a photo of FDR in a wheelchair, with yet another crack about lack of honesty. Democratic contenders who might threaten the Republican power structure in Washington are also singled out for special derision at Fox. During the 2000 presidential campaign, not only did the network flood the air with pro-Bush stories, but anchors and reporters spoke about candidate Al Gore "camplaigning" a lot. The reporters and anchors often concluded these comments with laughter.

There is no shortage of examples like these. During the war in Iraq, Fox anchors and correspondents routinely spoke of American troops as "our troops" and the war in terms of "us against them." At one point, anchors reported about "meat hooks where people were tortured" in an Iraqi warehouse. It turned out to be false. Howard Rosenberg, recently retired television critic for the *Los Angeles Times,* once quoted Fox anchor David Asman as saying, "There is a certain ridiculousness to that point of view" in response to a Fox reporter in Jordan saying that some people "on the street" may still consider Americans as invaders. And according to author and journalist Ken Auletta, who has written extensively about Fox, "On January 27th, [2003], John Gibson, an afternoon anchor, described a war protest in Davos, Switzerland, as composed of 'hundreds of knuckleheads.'" On February 11, Steve Doocy talked about those in Congress who favor some exceptions to strictures on immigration. "Guess who's giving sympathy to illegal immigrants linked to terrorists," he said, and showed a video of Senator Hillary Clinton.

Senator Clinton is one of the several Democrats Fox goes after with great frequency and, often, quite underhandedly. "When [her] book came out, they did an hourlong special called *Hillary's Tale,* but of course they were implying something else," said a former employee I'll name only as "G." (He asked not to be identified as he still works in cable news and is concerned Fox executives might retaliate against him.) Barbra Streisand is another target not seen as friendly to the conservative right. "They love to bash her, and it's usually done by Bill McCutty, the entertainment reporter," said G. He recalled an alleged Streisand quote from her Web

site that the *New York Post* ran, in which she seemed to complain about
how conservatives were attacking her. "It made her look very stupid. I
was supposed to package-produce [oversee the crafting of a taped report]
the story, and I went to the Web site to look for the quote, but the quote
didn't say anything like that. What was there was much less narcissistic.
I went and told them [news managers] that this was wrong, but they told
me to go with it anyway. It was so flagrant. The story was sourced to a
secondary source that they knew to be wrong."

THE FOX BIBLE

How can any news organization sustain an obvious political slant for
twenty-four hours a day, seven days a week? Were there truly that many
unhappy, available diehard conservative journalists—correspondents,
anchors, writers, producers—who were willing to turn their backs on the
very basis of ethical journalism? Well, management can lead by example
or it can manage by leading people by the nose. In Fox's case, both are in
play. Roger Ailes's politics are well known. He was a media consultant for
Richard Nixon, Ronald Reagan, and the first President George Bush. And
according to journalist Bob Woodward, Ailes advised George W. Bush after
the 9/11 attacks to be seen as using "the harshest measures possible" if he
wanted Americans to wait patiently for the U.S. government to retaliate.

Current and former employees say the boss's politics are at the tops
of their minds at all times. Charlie Reina is a former FNC producer and
copyeditor who spent six years at that network out of his twenty in broadcast news, which also included time at CBS Radio and ABC's *Good
Morning America*. In an article sent to Jim Romenesko of the Poynter
Institute and published on the Poynter Web site, he wrote

> [A]t Fox, if my boss wasn't warning me to "be careful" how I handled
> the writing of a special about Ronald Reagan ("You know how Roger
> [Fox News Chairman Ailes] feels about him"), he was telling me how
> the environmental special I was to produce should lean ("You can
> give both sides, but make sure the proenvironmentalists don't get the
> last word"). Editorially, the FNC newsroom is under the constant

control and vigilance of management. The pressure ranges from subtle to direct. . . . Everyone there understands that FNC is, to a large extent, "Roger's Revenge"—against what he considers a liberal, pro-Democrat media establishment that has shunned him for decades. For the staffers, many of whom are too young to have come up through the ranks of objective journalism, and all of whom are nonunion, with no protections regarding what they can be made to do, there is undue motivation to please the big boss."

G., the former mid-to-high-level Fox employee, agrees wholeheartedly. "There was a more than tacit acknowledgment among everyone that nothing remotely liberal would get on air," he said. "They (employees) would get in a lot of trouble if something appeared on air that wasn't 'fair and balanced,' which is openly acknowledged as doublespeak, meaning it makes the Bush administration look bad. So it's this weird thing, they're openly using their own catchline to mean the opposite."

But trying to please the boss doesn't, alone, account for the widespread and blatant conservative bias seen on Fox's air. There's a far more direct explanation: every day, news employees are told—in writing—how to slant and position stories that go on the air. The directive comes as an "editorial note" written by a member of senior management telling the staff which stories to cover, how to cover them, and to make sure they hype the Bush administration's position on various topics. "To the newsroom personnel responsible for the channel's daytime programming, The Memo is the bible. If, on any given day, you notice that the Fox anchors seem to be trying to drive a particular point home, you can bet The Memo is behind it," said Reina. From the March 20, 2003, editorial note, as quoted by Reina: "There is something utterly incomprehensible about [United Nations Secretary General] Kofi Annan's remarks in which he allows that his thoughts are 'with the Iraqi people.' One could ask where those thoughts were during the 23 years Saddam Hussein was brutalizing those same Iraqis. Food for thought.'"

Reina also wrote that right after the United States went into Iraq, "The Memo warned us that anti-war protesters would be 'whining' about U.S. bombs killing Iraqi civilians, and suggested they could tell that to the families of American soldiers dying there. Editing copy that morning, I was not surprised when an eager young producer killed a correspondent's report on the day's fighting—simply because it included a brief shot of children in an Iraqi hospital."

Orders to laud President Bush appear regularly in the note, says G. "It would say things like 'the President was amazing and brave and cunning in the Middle East today. Make sure we hit that note all day long.' And it would specifically say, 'On-air anchors please note,'" he said. "When Bush laid out his road map for peace, the exact words in the editorial note were, 'By laying out the road to peace in the Middle East, the Bush administration takes unprecedented action to bring peace to the Middle East.' A, it's flat out wrong. Every administration has tried to do that. It's editorializing, and it's not true. It read like it came straight out of Roger's [Ailes] mouth. It read like a piece of Republican Party talking points."

When accused Olympic Park bomber Eric Rudolph was captured in North Carolina in 2003, the editorial note warned staffers to stay away from certain parts of the story. "There was some talk that people in North Carolina had been aiding him," said G. "The note was in very plain English: There's a lot of speculation why people there supported Rudolph but let's be clear: No one in North Carolina supported Eric Rudolph's penchant for violence. The rest of the country would think it's repugnant and it won't look good for us, meaning conservatives."

RATINGS SUCCESS EQUALS MONEY EQUALS LOOSE PROFESSIONAL STANDARDS

Journalist and author Ken Auletta spent four months "embedded" with the Fox News Channel for a 2003 article he wrote for *The New Yorker*. This gave him unprecedented access to behind-the-scenes goings on at Fox—especially for someone not on staff. He chronicled how the Clinton-Lewinsky controversy helped the network find its supporters and how Ailes felt Fox "covered impeachment 'fair and balanced.'" The biggest test for the network, though, was the 2003 war in Iraq. For over a decade, CNN had always won the war ratings battle. Not this time.

"On March 19th, the first night of the Iraq War, Fox News bested CNN in the ratings, and did so every day for the duration of the war; according to Nielsen Media Research," wrote Auletta. "For the first time ever in a crisis, the audience for the network newscasts on CBS and ABC dropped—two and a half percent for ABC, nine per cent for CBS (NBC's rose slightly)—while the five cable news networks climbed by more than three hundred and fifty percent. Fox News set the pace."

Fox, though, started making a profit in 2000, long before it took the ratings lead. Former employees say that with an extremely meager news staff, the network has fewer expenses than does its competitors. G. estimates the entire news staff at around 150. But even at several times that number, it would still be dwarfed by the other networks. CNN, for example, has around 4,000 employees, although not all of them are directly involved in the news operation. "They do very little news gathering, so that entire operation is whittled down to just a few people," said G. "They don't have a person [correspondent] for state [department] or for justice [department]. They have someone at the Pentagon and at the White House and a general assignment type [correspondent]."

With so few editorial employees, how does a twenty-four-hour news channel fill its airtime? "There are five or six big Fox stories at any time, and that's where most of the employees are used," said G. For the rest of the news across the country and the world, say G. and other employees, Fox depends largely on reports from local affiliates, often simply replacing the local reporter's voice on the taped package with that of a Fox staffer. "Rarely do they have Fox exclusive material that is not from an affiliate," said G. The channel also relies heavily on the reporting and stories provided by video and print wire services. "Half the time a story will break on the AP [Associated Press] and they will go straight to air with it. When they say 'Fox has confirmed,' half the time they haven't confirmed it. They'll just take the stuff straight to air."

Although I hate to use unnamed sources, many former Fox employees still fear the wrath of Ailes and, like G., ask not to be identified. Another ex-Fox staffer offered yet another example of shoddy reporting that got on air. "When the Egyptian Air flight crashed off Long Island, in the rush to find a cause, Fox News reported on when the plane was manufactured and noted that there was a strike at Boeing at the time and that management had built part of the plane. There was little room to infer anything other than the plane was defective and Boeing was at fault for the crash." The investigation eventually proved otherwise; the pilot was blamed for the accident.

THE O'REALLY? FACTOR, A.K.A. "THE NO WIN ZONE"

Bill O'Reilly, a guy who earned his stripes on *Inside Edition*, one of the first programs to dishonor and destroy true journalism, now claims to be a journalist anchoring a show that is a "no spin" zone. This, a program that is spinning so fast it ought to be sponsored by a yo-yo company. On nearly any night, O'Reilly can be heard twisting information to either make the conservative right look good or the liberal left look bad. During a Dec. 4, 2003, show with Steve Young, a writer for the *Jewish World Review*, the two men discussed a meeting held in Los Angeles by Hollywood people opposed to President George W. Bush's policies.

"I mean, these people loathe the president. All of them," said O'Reilly.

"Nobody said that, though," Young tried to clarify.

"I don't care whether they said it or not, they loathe him," O'Reilly responded, interrupting his guest. "And they ought to be, you know, men and women enough to admit it."

Is it good TV? Sure. While you won't see a reasonable, measured, and fair discussion on any topic, it can be entertaining in a sadistic sort of way. It's the right-wing political talk-show version of *The Jerry Springer Show*, and it is very popular, getting a couple of million viewers a night, generally more than all of the other cable news networks get put together. But is it news? And is it balanced and unbiased? If a person agrees to be on the show, the cannon fodder for the evening, he or she will be made a fool of, scoffed at, belittled, cut off, and, well, who knows.

On Dec. 1, 2003, O'Reilly's guests were Tammy Bruce, an author who is self-described as a feminist, Democrat, and progressive, and

Katrina vanden Heuvel, the editor of *The Nation,* which O'Reilly made sure to mention is a liberal magazine. The topic of the night, and his first question to vanden Heuvel, was whether "the liberal strategy to gain power" would succeed. He then proceeded to interrupt her eleven times before cutting her off by saying, "I'm going to stop you now because your speech is lost on this audience. They know you're an ideologue." When she attempted to continue to answer the question asked, O'Reilly again interrupted, "This is an incredibly boring diatribe you're going through. This is incredibly boring." Moments later he threatened to cut off her microphone.

O'Reilly routinely riles up his guests. That's how he gets a response, and a huge paycheck. That's how others like him, on the left or on the right, get ratings. A lot of people who add to Rush Limbaugh's ratings, for example, are tuning in because they love to hate him. But they're tuning in, and that is what gives the Limbaughs and the O'Reillys a platform. Is there a place for these people on U.S. radio or television? Absolutely! I'll be the first in line to support their First Amendment rights. While we might not like what gets said, everyone—from the KKK to the Nazis—is free to take to the American airwaves and newspapers with their opinions. Just don't call it news or journalism.

Absurdly enough, O'Reilly claims to speak for journalism as a whole. In 2003, after news veteran David Brinkley died, O'Reilly had the gall to write an article that was published in many national newspapers saying that Brinkley's type of journalism has been dead for quite a while. Americans, he wrote, "want to know how the journalists they trust *feel* about things that are important to their lives. The news consumer is almost desperate for someone to define the truth of the matter. . . . The audience for dispassionate TV news is shrinking, the demand for passionate reporting and analysis is on the rise."

When I first read this article, the words "passionate reporting" stopped me cold. Isn't that an oxymoron? "That trend, of course, is like a cross in front of a vampire for the TV news traditionalists," O'Reilly continued. "Even though newspapers have editorialized from the very beginning of this republic, and print columnists are legion, analysis during a TV news broadcast is still very daunting for many network news types."

Well, then call me a news vampire. Comparing news analysis to an editorial is comparing apples and oranges. So is comparing a newspaper editorial to slanting stories within a newscast that is billed as "fair and balanced." Newspaper editorial boards and columnists don't pose as unbiased journalists. It is clear to readers that they are getting opinion when they read the op-ed page, the opinion-editorial page. If editors or columnists wish to analyze a news event from their particular point of view, that, too, is evident to readers. Responsible editorialists make no attempt to disguise their positions as straight news coverage. Readers are free to choose whether they agree with the particular opinion expressed or not. At the same time, straight news coverage can also include analysis and context without opinion. Analysis is not a synonym for opinion. And if what O'Reilly really meant to say was that having editorials or commentary during a newscast is an anathema to many companies, he needs to watch more TV. Many local television stations have included well-defined editorials or commentary in their news programs for decades. At the network level, NBC News included commentary from John Chancellor, once he left the anchor desk.

Furthermore, saying that Americans "want to know how the journalists they trust *feel* about things that are important to their lives" makes no sense, either. If the journalists are trusted, it is *because* they report the news in a fair and unbiased manner. They are trusted precisely because they provide as much information as possible and allow viewers to make up their own minds without attempting to sway them one way or another.

But O'Reilly is apparently capable of honesty on occasion. When author Ken Auletta suggested to him that a more accurate slogan for the network might be, "We report. We decide," O'Reilly responded, "Well, you're probably right." But it wasn't more than a few months later that Fox sued political satirist Al Franken in the New York State Supreme Court for using the company's trademark slogan, "fair and balanced," in the title of his 2003 book, *Lies, and the Lying Liars Who Tell Them: A Fair and Balanced Look at the Right*. Fox executives charged that Franken's use of those words would "blur and tarnish" the image of the network's news coverage. The case was swiftly dismissed by a judge who ruled "This is an easy case in my view and wholly without merit." Later, Fox publicists admitted they sued Franken to appease O'Reilly.

❏   ❏   ❏

So what does the tremendous success of this often unethical and biased network say for the future of truly fair and balanced journalism? Like many other broadcast journalists, George Lewis is worried. "Do we all become like Geraldo Rivera and say this is about me and my opinion rather than about the facts gathered in a fair way? It puzzles me and concerns me that we seem to be heading down this route. That objective news reporting is replaced by partisan shouting contests. I think we could become balkanized by this process. If everyone is programming for a particular niche and offering news tailored to a particular point of view, we lose the larger picture. We start coloring the news for the benefit of our audience. The truth is the first casualty."

Truth is already a casualty at Fox. But if informing the public in an unbiased way were the channel's true priority, it wouldn't have to be. Would Fox lose its core of conservative viewers if the network publicly proclaimed its conservative bias? Probably not. If rather than claiming to be "fiercely independent" the network acknowledged what it truly is, "fiercely conservative," it might even gain additional viewers. It still wouldn't be good journalism, but it would be far more honest with the public than it is now. That doesn't, however, seem to be on the Fox agenda.

This media company's agenda seems to be more calculating: using the false claim of journalistic integrity to influence as many American viewers as possible into supporting the current administration's politics and policies. "The most insidious thing about Fox is when its bias is subtle," said G. "They're not making up stories—yet. And when they do, it will be a good thing for everyone because they will be caught. It will be yellow journalism, and the public won't believe them." From business and political propaganda points of view, however, Fox has not suffered from any such obvious missteps. The public certainly has suffered, though, as has the integrity of professional, responsible journalism.

While this chapter has shown how this one ideologically-driven network manipulates what viewers are told, Chapter Nine reveals an even greater danger: what happens when all networks curry favor with an administration, abdicating their constitutional responsibilities and capitulating to a single political interest.

STRANGE
BEDFELLOWS

Picture a country where:

- Suspects tried and convicted in closed-door military tribunals may face a firing squad.

- The government denies its troops fired on one another, censors news stories, and locks up journalists in a warehouse to prevent them from reporting about soldiers who've died in battle.

- The president unilaterally decides not to share vital information with the legislative branch.

- It's permissible for government entities to secretly obtain a reporter's phone records.

- Police have the authority to monitor citizens' e-mails and tap their phones.

- Press conferences are rigged.

- The government encourages regular citizens to turn in fellow citizens they think are suspicious; in Cuba, an identical program is called the Committees of the Revolution.

But this country isn't Cuba, China, or Iran. It's the United States. Every one of these abuses has happened in a nation that condemns these types of actions in other countries, often by withholding diplomatic recognition and financial aid. It is an ugly double-standard that affects the United States government's credibility around the world and at home. Following September 11, 2001, the Bush Administration did more to muzzle the nation's free press, restrict access of American citizens to information about their government, and shroud once-open proceedings in secrecy than has any other presidency in recent history, if not since this country's founding—an all-out, sustained assault on the First Amendment to the U.S. Constitution. Never has there been a clearer example of the need for a free and aggressive press to challenge an administration's insatiable penchant for secrecy. And yet, we find broadcast journalism abdicating its watchdog responsibilities, even actively colluding with government, to satisfy its own insatiable penchant for profits.

THE WAR BEHIND CLOSED DOORS

The Bush administration's strategy for operating behind closed doors has been multifaceted—and remarkably effective, despite judicial reproach. At the administration's request, the Justice Department issued a directive to every federal agency and state's attorney general encouraging them to fight requests for information under the Freedom of Information Act (FOIA) and offering them support if they do. In addition, the USA Patriot Act gives government far more snooping power than ever before and allows secret searches by authorities. More than 1,000 non-American citizens were detained secretly—their names and locations kept from the public— as material witnesses or people facing immigration charges. Between 600 and 750 of them remain in custody as of this writing. Although in general immigration hearings are normally open to the public, Attorney General John Ashcroft ordered them closed for national security reasons. In a memo to all immigration courts, Chief Immigration Judge Michael Creppy said that under Ashcroft's new security procedures administrators could not even confirm or deny whether a particular person's case would be heard or not. Court officers were to avoid "disclosing any information about the case to anyone outside the Immigration Court." News organizations filed several lawsuits challenging the memo and asking courts to release the names of the detainees. Every court win, though, was followed by an appeal or a stay, leaving the U.S. Supreme Court with the final word on many of these legal questions. A ruling by the U.S. Court of Appeals (Sixth Circuit), however, openly and strongly chastised the Bush Administration. The court wrote that "the only safeguard on this extraordinary governmental power is the public, deputizing the press as the guardians of their liberty. . . . Today, the Executive Branch seeks to take this safeguard away from the public by placing its actions beyond public scrutiny. Against non-citizens, it seeks the power to secretly deport a class if it unilaterally calls them 'special interest' cases. The Executive Branch seeks to uproot people's lives, outside the public eye, and behind a closed door. Democracies die behind closed doors." The administration argued that opening the proceedings would jeopardize national security.

As these various court cases show, the rights of all people in the country are affected—even if terrorists may be the only intended targets of the administration's measures. It is critical for the news media to monitor what the federal government is doing at all times, but particularly during a time of war or when the United States is under attack from terrorists. Those are precisely the times when citizens need and deserve to know what their government is doing. Under no circumstances can an administration be permitted to redefine the meaning and intent of the U.S. Constitution. "The Constitution was designed to protect against abuses of power, even abuses taken for seemingly legitimate reasons," according to the Reporters Committee for Freedom of the Press. "The founding fathers know that power could be taken incrementally, used properly at first, but resulting in injustice when not checked. To prevent abuse and injustice, Americans must adhere to the principles in the Constitution even when—perhaps especially when—they are contrary to instinct."

And in the midst of these legal battles and the war against terrorism, President Bush signed Executive Order 13233 restricting public access to the papers and documents of former presidents, skirting the Presidential Records Act. What this also means is that President George W. Bush took extraordinary measures to keep his *own* papers out of the public eye. As a result, we may never truly learn the full extent of what went on following 9/11.

SO *WHO* DECIDES WHAT THE PUBLIC SHOULD SEE OR KNOW?

The American invasion of Afghanistan has been particularly shrouded in secrecy. During this phase of the war on terrorism, the Bush administration strictly limited press access. There were no reporters present to witness the buildup of forces prior to the October 7, 2001, attacks or to see the attacks themselves. In addition, the Pentagon signed an exclusive contract with a company called Space Imaging to stop that company for sixty days from selling to the media photos taken by the civilian *Ikonos* satellite. Reporters trying to cover Operation Enduring Freedom were not free to report alongside troops in actual battle for nearly a month. As a result, there was no independent confirmation of so-called victories until a small number of journalists were finally permitted to cover the action in November of 2001. All of them had to wait for permission before they could file their stories. Although more correspondents were finally given some access in 2002, they encountered tremendous resistance from U.S. forces. Some, as mentioned above, literally were locked in a warehouse so that they could not take pictures or report about fatalities. On January 11, 2002, CNN, CBS, and other news organizations were permitted to video-tape the departure of about twenty prisoners being flown from Afghanistan to the U.S. Naval Base at Guantanamo Bay, Cuba, but then were ordered not to use the pictures. In addition, "a dozen media organizations covering the military operations were several times prevented from doing their job by U.S. Special Forces troops and at least five journalists and media assistants were beaten or threatened with death by U.S. soldiers or their Afghan allies," according to Reporters Without Borders. On February 10, 2002, *Washington Post* correspondent Doug Struck was not allowed to report from a location where civilians might have been killed by American forces. On April 10, 2002, American troops watched without interfering as Afghan soldiers fighting with them beat up Ebadullah Ebadi, a translator and assistant for the *Boston Globe*. On August 23, 2002, *New York Times* photographer Tyler Hicks was detained by U.S. Special Forces who "demanded that the photographer clear his photographs from his digital camera and hand over a roll of exposed film."

"There has never been an American war, small or large, in which access has been so limited as this one," CBS anchor Dan Rather said in 2002. "Limiting access, limiting information to cover the backsides of those who are in charge of the war, is extremely dangerous and cannot and should not be accepted."

But the White House went even beyond simply restricting access to news events that U.S. journalists have the right, duty, and authority to cover under the U.S. Constitution. In October of 2001, National Security Advisor Condoleezza Rice placed a possibly unprecedented conference call to senior executives at the broadcast news divisions and cable news networks. She asked them not to air an unedited videotape they had all received of Osama Bin Laden, saying that the tape could contain secret messages to sleeper terrorists in the country. They all agreed to edit out portions Washington considered dangerous or inflammatory, one of the few times all major television news organizations have agreed to censorship.

Despite all of these obstacles, some broadcast journalists and executives have worked valiantly to inform the public. "It is journalists, not government officials, that have pieced together for the public how 19 hijackers assembled and completed their September 11 mission. Reporters, too, revealed details on how and why the military and the CIA failed to capture Osama Bin Laden in Afghanistan. And again, the journalists are the ones working to keep the public informed about the trials of detained foreign nationals and Taliban fighters," noted the Reporters Committee for

Freedom of the Press. CBS News executives should be congratulated as well, for announcing that they—unlike the other networks—would air parts of a videotape made of *Wall Street Journal* reporter Daniel Pearl, who was murdered by his Afghan captors. State Department officials say they were asked by the Pearl family to contact CBS News and request that the network not broadcast any of the tape in consideration of their feelings and their loss. The network did not back down. Parts of the tape would be aired, Dan Rather said, "to understand the full impact and danger of the propaganda war being waged." (It's not the first time this network and its main anchor stood up to White House pressure to not air a story. In 1972, at the beginning of the Watergate investigation by the *Washington Post,* CBS News decided to look into the story, too. When White House officials heard of CBS's intention to run a story or two, they placed intense pressure on CBS executives, which led to tremendous infighting at the network. Walter Cronkite stepped in and, using his power, prestige, and influence, managed to get the first of the two stories on air in its entirety. The report ran fourteen minutes, an eternity by television standards, and as a result emphasized that this was big, important news. The White House again intervened, leaning on top CBS executives, so the second story was edited down quite a bit. But the impact of CBS News following the Watergate story broken by the *Washington Post* had already been felt.)

With the video from Afghanistan, CBS again did the right thing. While there was no need to show all of the gory details such as the beheading of Pearl, it was responsible journalism to show part of what occurred so that viewers could know, understand, and feel the animosity many people in that country, and others, feel for the United States, its government, and its citizens. It helps make sense of 9/11 and could possibly even help avert another such nightmare. Pearl was a reporter, but he was also—in the eyes of many people in the region—simply an American target. His death, and the investigation of it, was having a large impact on developments in U.S. policy in the region. And we must also remember that Pearl chose to be there, to serve the American public, even to make the appointment that led to his death. I never met him, but I can't believe an esteemed journalist for the *Wall Street Journal* would have supported censoring any news story, much less such an important one. He was in Afghanistan to shine light—by telling and showing the truth—on the realities of what was happening in that country. I do feel compassion for the Pearl family, but they had the option of choosing not to watch CBS News that night. The benefit to the country as a whole, to freedom of the press and democracy in general, far outweighed the feelings of one family. It was important for viewers to know that if they watched the CBS newscast that evening, they'd see some of the real horrors and dangers of war and of terrorism and of journalism.

The federal government simply had no business and no authority to try to interfere with a decision taken by a news organization. And the interference didn't stop there. Some Internet sites that posted the Pearl video were threatened with criminal charges by the FBI if the video was not removed. One company, Pro Hosters, of Sterling, Virginia, removed it immediately but then re-posted it on their site, explaining that people in this country had the right to choose whether they wanted to view it or not. This company's actions should be applauded by all citizens. Not many people are game to stand up to FBI intimidation. Unfortunately, these kinds of acts of resistance to government pressure are increasingly the exception, not the rule. As recent events reveal, the networks have proved generally willing—sometimes even eager—to favor the Bush administration, at least as long as going along means higher ratings.

SECRETS OF THE RAH-RAH BROTHERHOOD

It's fair to say that most journalists are aware of the Bush administration's efforts to curtail or deny access to once-public records and information. Many journalists and their news organizations have chosen, for reasons described below, to go along with these new and unprecedented policies. Only a few, such as journalists Bill Moyers and NBC News correspondent George Lewis, have been brave enough to speak out. "Not only has George W. Bush eviscerated the Presidential Records Act and FOIA, he has clamped a lid on public access across the board," Moyers said. "I think it's a very dangerous trend," said Lewis. "The administration seems to be very intent on concealing information in a lot of areas, and I think that we have to keep pushing as hard as we can for openness and transparency in government." The free and open dissemination of the news is a powerful check on the forces of totalitarianism—any kind of totalitarianism.

There is no question that 9/11 contributed to the atmosphere that allowed the administration to employ such Orwellian tactics against the public and the media. The terrorist attacks gave rise to a level of public fear rarely if ever experienced before which, in turn, manifested itself in an overwhelming sense of patriotism. Executives at news organizations—the people with the most power and influence in news coverage—saw this and chose to ride that wave for higher ratings, even if it meant abandoning their basic responsibilities. "It's a very challenging time for journalists because . . . our role is to question government," said Barbara Cochran, the president of the Radio-Television News Directors Association (RTNDA). "That's why the First Amendment protects a free press, to be watchdogs on behalf of the public. But when Sept. 11 happened, the public was frightened, very frightened, and any kind of questioning of why weren't we better prepared, how did this happen, what are we doing to protect ourselves in the future, people didn't want to hear that at the beginning. The challenges to free press and to free speech are greater than they've been in years and years, and yet the public doesn't seem to raise questions, and journalists haven't been all that noisy either."

In fact, for the most part, the television news media seemed, if not content to go along with the administration's efforts, at least (with the exception of organizations such as RTNDA and the Journalists Committee for Freedom of the Press) not very defiant. Is this voluntary compliance or political collusion? "Since 9/11, journalists have assumed a role of cheerleaders of the administration," said veteran network journalist Robert Wiener. "And in many areas I blame the media for Bush's successful march to war."

At 8 PM on March 3, 2003, President Bush held one of his infrequent press conferences in the East Room of the White House. The commander-in-chief made an opening statement on the war and then took eighteen questions, all but two on Iraq. Many viewers might not have noticed, but the event was completely staged with the complicity of several members of the White House Press Corps. It was a performance: the reporters were told who was going to be able to ask questions and in which order. Generally, in White House press conferences for all the previous presidents, reporters were called on in random fashion. But even President Bush inadvertently let the cat out of the bag when he mistakenly allowed a question out of turn. "We'll be there in a minute. King, John King," he said, pointing at the CNN correspondent. The room exploded in laughter. "This is a scripted . . ." the president added before more laughter cut him off. Everyone knew the press conference was scripted. But was this truly funny? The so-called watchdogs were acknowledging with laughter that they had become lapdogs. "Not only were reporters going out of their way to make sure their softballs [questions] were preapproved, . . . they even went so far as to act on Bush's behalf, raising their hands and jockeying in their seats in order to better give the appearance of a spontaneous press conference," reported journalist Mike Taibbi.

The White House Press Corps, as well as many media representatives elsewhere, have literally become the Rah-Rah Brotherhood/Sisterhood. Some of their public support for the administration may be genuine, albeit unethical, but a great deal of it is simple capitulation. At least one journalist who asked a sensitive question was later approached by a White House official and told that higher-ups had taken note of his inquiry. That alone sends a chill through a press corps that could encourage compliance. As an example of the possible repercussions, consider veteran White House correspondent Helen Thomas, who had covered every president since John F. Kennedy in 1961 and was known as the dean of the White House Press Corps. By virtue of her seniority and stature, Thomas was permitted the first question during press conferences. But on January 6, 2003, she became persona non grata after the following exchange with White House spokesperson Ari Fleischer:

Thomas: "At the earlier briefing, Ari, you said that the president deplored the taking of innocent lives. Does that apply to all innocent lives in the world?"

Fleischer: "I refer specifically to a horrible terrorist attack on Tel Aviv
    that killed scores and wounded hundreds . . ."

Thomas: "My follow-up is, why does he want to drop bombs on
    innocent Iraqis?"

Fleischer: "Helen, the question is how to protect Americans, and our
    allies and friends. . . ."

Thomas: "They're not attacking you."

Fleischer: ". . . from a country . . ."

Thomas: "Have they laid a glove on you or on the United States, the
    Iraqis, in eleven years?"

Fleischer: "I guess you have forgotten about the Americans who were
    killed in the first Gulf War as a result of Saddam Hussein's aggres-
    sion then."

Thomas: "Is this revenge? Eleven years of revenge?"

Fleischer: "Helen, I think you know very well that the president's posi-
    tion is that he wants to avert war, and that the president has asked
    the United Nations to go into Iraq to help with the purpose of
    averting war."

Following this press conference, and after Thomas made a public
comment that Bush was "the worst president ever," she was relegated to
a back-row seat and lost her first-question privilege. The White House is
one of the most prestigious beats, if not the top one, for journalists. If
asking tough questions gets a reporter exiled to the Siberian back row and
cut off from all access to administration officials, that is the equivalent of
committing career suicide. It is good journalism and it serves the public,
but many journalists are not willing to pay that steep a price. White
House officials know this and took full advantage of the reporters' reluctance to risk alienating the administration. For the press corps, the message was clear: unless your reports are sympathetic to the administration,
you lose access. To further strike fear in the heart of the press corps, three
weeks later a senior administration official was quoted as saying:
"President Bush has 'some level of frustration with the press corps' for
accounts questioning the U.S. and coalition war plan in Iraq, and he finds

it 'silly' that such skepticism and questions were being raised just days into a conflict he says is going quite well."

The Bush administration also changed the rules about access to an American president when he is on an overseas trip. Unlike other presidents, including Ronald Reagan, George W. Bush never holds a press conference or participates in one if he is attending a summit with several other heads of state. He'll do what is known as a "news avail," which means cameras can take pictures, but other than that he keeps to a script. The only message that will come out, the only topics that will be reported, the only questions answered are all controlled by the White House.

And under the new guidelines, if the White House schedule states that there will be a press conference at some point in the day after Bush meets with another head of state, no questions or cameras are permitted when the leaders meet, not even impromptu questions yelled from the sidelines. The only other option offered to the television White House Press Corps on occasion is that they can send a camera but no editorial person, no correspondent. "They don't want him [President Bush] caught off guard with a question that makes him look like a boob," said a senior network executive who has organized his network's White House coverage for several administrations. (Despite going along with the administration on other coverage issues, such as presidential press conferences, the five networks drew a line in the sand over this *one* issue. ABC News, CBS News, NBC News, CNN, and Fox came together in a united front and told the White House they would not cover a presidential event this way. And they informed administration officials that they would tell viewers why they don't have video and questions with the president.)

If there is no official press conference scheduled later in the day, then White House officials do allow a correspondent or producer along with a camera to witness the meeting between President Bush and the other heads of state. But again, no questions are permitted. The president reads a prepared statement, and that's it. A frustrating case in point was when the president was in Africa in July of 2003 meeting with the president of Uganda and during a brief statement blamed the CIA for incorrect information he had given the nation during his State of the Union address months earlier. In that speech he gave outlining his primary reasons for attacking Iraq, he said Saddam Hussein had tried to obtain uranium from Africa in order to develop nuclear weapons. That information turned out to be false. After dropping this information bomb, however, President Bush then refused to take questions from any media on the trip, although the topic remained front-page news for several days.

President Bush's stealth visit to Iraq for Thanksgiving 2003 raised other issues of manipulation and collusion. Reporters and photographers were handpicked by the White House to accompany the president on the journey, in many cases defying the official pool rotation that was in effect. The major news organizations covering the White House rotate travel duty, and when it is their turn to go on a presidential trip, they share their material with the rest of the press corps. For Thanksgiving, the Bush administration dismissed the CNN crew that was on stand-by and took a Fox News Channel crew instead. Others invited to go along represented the Associated Press, *Bloomberg,* and *Time* and *Newsweek* magazines. They all acquiesced to the demand to give up the batteries to their cell phones during the duration of the trip to ensure confidentiality—even though they were handpicked for the job. The story would be told the way the White House wanted it told or not at all.

MY NETWORK IS MORE PATRIOTIC THAN YOUR NETWORK

After 9/11, the country—led by the White House—embraced a new, somewhat different, and, for journalists, unethical type of patriotism. Among many in the general public, if one opposed invading Afghanistan or Iraq, that was unpatriotic. If one criticized the White House and the president, that too was unpatriotic. This groundswell of patriotism was so powerful that even congressmen and senators found themselves in a political squeeze to support the wars, even if they didn't believe in them. And, as never before, the media also jumped on this new patriotic bandwagon, showing American flags on news sets, wearing flag lapel pins on air, and speaking of "us," the United States, versus "them," the bad guys and the terrorists. In fact, a survey by the Pew Research Center showed that 69 percent of the public believed the media was "patriotic," an all-time high. That statistic is alarming, given the definition of "patriotism" in the post-9/11 world. Whatever citizens choose to do within the law is their right, and a person who agrees with the federal government is no more patriotic than one who does not. They are both exercising their rights in this country.

Journalists, though, should meet a much higher standard. The U.S. Constitution grants the media very powerful authority, but along with that is the obligation to use it fairly and responsibly. Taking sides in any conflict, even one in which so many innocent American citizens were murdered in such horrible ways, does not serve or deserve the public trust. Journalists are duty bound to continue to strive for balance and fairness, even when the citizen within may feel and believe that one side is clearly in the wrong. When the country is reeling from immense attacks and is fearful of others, that is when it is most important that journalists do their jobs well and right, putting aside all personal feelings to provide Americans with the information they need and deserve. "The best way that journalists can show their patriotism is to do their job, ask questions, dig for facts, dig for answers," said Barbara Cochran, president of RTNDA. This is never easy, especially when a popular president whose approval ratings have gone up (as they have done for every president who declares war) says, "You're either with us or the terrorists."

And many, many journalists and news organizations crossed the line of balance to be "with us." I'll allow that some correspondents may have been simply swayed by the unprecedented attacks of 9/11. But I suspect the overriding reason was twofold: news organizations wanted to be seen as patriotic because that was politically correct at the time, and only that strategy would ensure keeping the viewers and revenue they had before the attacks, and possibly even gaining more.

As Chapter Eight, on the Fox network, showed, anchors and corre-spondents at that network virtually included themselves among the patri-otic troops, cutting down guests who did not agree with President Bush's assessment of the war, his strategy, or his politics in general. The broadcast networks were not as obvious. Another cable network, however, often was: CNN. On March 27, 2003, veteran correspondent Bob Franken, whom I've always respected, was in Iraq and reported, "We have moved here to capture an Iraqi air base." *We* moved to capture. As far as I know, CNN did not capture any bases but was only, theoretically, along to record what the troops did. It was a slip of the tongue, but one of the dangers of traveling with troops. Less than two hours later, CNN correspondent Jamie Colby reported from Fort Hood in Texas, "Everyone here has a vested interest in our country." To nonjournalists, this might sound like nitpicking. But remember that CNN is seen around the world. Using the words "our country" isn't ethical, but, more important, it also endangers CNN reporters elsewhere. On another day, CNN anchor Kyra Phillips's report from aboard the Abraham Lincoln aircraft carrier was so pro-U.S.A. that high-level producers had to "rein her in," a staffer familiar with the program told me. Her reports were being seen throughout the Middle East, where countless CNN employees were working with and reporting about Muslims and trying to survive while they did their jobs.

Not all reporters at CNN act this way. During that two-hour time period, CNN correspondent Ryan Chilcote, whom I've never met, delivered a very fair and balanced report while traveling with the 101st Airborne. Unlike his colleagues, he made certain to speak of American forces as American forces, not *ours,* and he attributed all of his information properly. It was a heartening thing to see, especially for a newcomer to network news.

Perhaps the most egregious example of behind-the-scenes news manipulating I've heard of was actually orchestrated by CNN chairman Walter Isaacson, who sent a memo to his staff in October of 2001 ordering them to remind viewers of U.S. losses *every* time they reported Afghani losses or gains. "As we get good reports from Taliban-controlled Afghanistan, we must redouble our efforts to make sure we do not seem to be simply reporting from their vantage or perspective. We must talk about how the Taliban are using civilian shields and how the Taliban have harbored the terrorists responsible for killing close to 5,000 innocent people." Again, this might seem harmless to nonjournalists, but it was clear political spinning to those in the CNN newsroom. This information was included routinely, but in nonstop coverage did not have to be mentioned every time there was a death among people fighting the United States. In terms of minute-by-minute balance, did CNN or the other U.S. news organizations mention how U.S. policy in the Muslim world had affected lives there every time they did stories about 9/11? Network news told the story of the day in context, but not balanced atrocity by atrocity, death by death. But to emphasize Isaacson's command, CNN vice president Rick Davis provided in a separate memo approved copy he strongly urged writers to use. Among the passages that were deemed acceptable: "The Pentagon has repeatedly stressed that it is trying to minimize civilian casualties in Afghanistan, even as the Taliban regime continues to harbor terrorists who are connected with the September 11 attacks that claimed thousands of innocent lives in the United States." Davis, a long-time CNN employee, is in charge of ethics and professional standards at CNN. The real message behind the memos, though, was even stronger: employees knew they were being told to toe the administration's line, to make sure stories were slanted to justify the invasion by the United States. One CNN cameraman in Afghanistan literally quit because he and the rest of the CNN staff there were being told that network headquarters was not interested in seeing any pictures of dead or injured Afghan civilians. "It was basic suppression," said former CNN producer Robert Wiener. "No news organization should tell reporters what to report or what not to report."

The American media not only went along with but helped fuel the story of Private Jessica Lynch as superhuman war hero, lying wounded but bravely shooting at the enemy until she was captured. It was one of the most celebrated and publicized events of the conflict but also one of the worst examples of untrue propaganda intended to galvanize the American public into supporting the war. Lynch's so-called rescue was blown out of proportion, but few people in the American media questioned why the U.S. military would send a photographer along to record such an apparently dangerous mission. All of the American television news agencies got hours of gripping live coverage and huge ratings upon her return. That their role in creating a national hero fueled greater patriotic support for the administration's war didn't seem to matter. It took a non-American news organization, the British Broadcasting System (BBC), to first report that the so-called dramatic and dangerous rescue of Private Jessica Lynch was a Hollywood-style screenplay, purposefully overblown by the U.S. government. Even Lynch, many months later, acknowledged that the government spread false stories about her going down shooting in an ambush. Her weapon, an M-16, jammed before she could fire a single shot. Lynch has also made clear she is disturbed by the over-dramatization of the rescue. In her book and in interviews, she said that Iraqi staff at the hospital she was "rescued" from did not offer any resistance and actually offered the rescuers a key to the door of her room. But that does not make as good a story as the administration wanted and needed at a time when some members of the public were beginning to question the wisdom of the war.

POLITICS MAKES STRANGE EMBEDFELLOWS

Strict regulations on how the media is permitted to cover U.S. military actions are a direct result of the coverage of the Vietnam War, when reporters' stories contradicted the far more positive assessments provided by the White House. Journalists then were free to travel with troops or not, could hop on military transport when space was available, and were not subject to government censorship or reporting regulations. The media exercised its own authority to decide what should be made public and what should not. While what the news organizations reported was, in effect, true, it resulted in a major public relations disaster for the military and White House. Since then, there have been various degrees of regulations placed on war correspondents, all in the guise of protecting the troops. Despite that charade, the truth is that not a single service person in Vietnam lost his or her life as a result of a journalist's report. And of the dozen or so violations of national security reported by the Pentagon, most were committed by non-American journalists.

Yet in recent conflicts such as the Gulf War, the rules virtually prohibited journalists from going to the front lines (other than CNN, which had permission by the Iraqis to remain in Baghdad). News organizations were forced to remain in Dhahran, Saudi Arabia, and other major cities and simply attend U.S. military briefings and report what was being force-fed to them. It was an unconscionable manipulation of the media, and as a result, of the public. The lack of media access led to intense negotiations between major news outlets and the Pentagon over a set of new rules governing how the media would be allowed to cover U.S. military operations. Those rules, however, were completely and obviously ignored during the invasion of Afghanistan. The ensuing "negotiations" with the Pentagon and the Bush administration resulted in the program that "embedded" journalists with military units. "This was so far superior to the system of the Gulf War and certainly than the absence of coverage in Afghanistan," said Barbara Cochran, president of RTNDA. "Was it the whole picture? No. Were there limitations? Of course. The reporter could only report what he was seeing. But that overview was added by everybody's Pentagon reporters." There is little, if any, question that the networks' Pentagon correspondents provided immensely important information during and after the invasion of Iraq. But that doesn't take the place of reporters on the ground free to report from the different sides of the conflict.

The embedding program did, however, provide the administration with the best day in and day out promotion possible. While the Pentagon appeared to have granted unprecedented frontline access to reporters, what the reporters filed was strictly controlled. As viewers saw every day, the reporters were able to provide more live reports for television and radio than ever before, but what they were reporting were simply snapshots of their particular slice of the war, from one point of view. With very little opportunity or access to independently cover the war, American news organizations—especially those in television news (despite their reluctance to admit their complicity)—became tools of propaganda for the Bush administration. Few news organizations reported or reminded viewers or readers of the thirteen pages of guidelines and rules their embedded reporters had to follow. Among them, for example, were rules that reporters could not reveal the names of military

installations or specific locations of military units. Other information forbidden to report included

> Anything regarding how U.S. troops were protecting themselves
>
> Information on U.S. tactical deployments
>
> Information about special operations units and unique tactics used
> by U.S. forces
>
> Information on U.S. aircraft that were either missing or downed,
> while search-and-recovery operations were under way
>
> Information about postponed or cancelled operations
>
> Information or photographs showing an enemy prisoner of war's face
> or name

All war journalists, especially smart ones, already follow these rules
without being ordered to. (Some of these rules are even spelled out in the
Geneva Convention, which details war rules.) But that's the point of con-
tention. It is the on-scene journalists and their news managers who have
the responsibility to determine what should or should not be reported,
and in the history of this country's military battles they have done a
good and responsible job of it. News organizations should not have
handed over that Constitutional freedom to the current administration
and Pentagon officials.

Among the ground rules were others that should give every viewer
pause. The only information reporters were allowed to file had to be
approved by each unit commander. That allows for many, many varied
points of view and personal biases by parties who have a vested interest in
a particular outcome. What one commander would permit, another might
not. U.S. embeds were also not permitted to report about the effective-
ness of enemy camouflage, deception, targeting, or security measures.
Information about previous conventional missions could only be released
in general terms. So, in general, journalists couldn't report advances or losses
by American troops or Iraqi troops. (That explains why the most common
live report—which was very visual, but offered no real information—was

about troops on the move, encountering or not encountering light or heavy resistance.) And then there was this regulation: "In instances where a unit commander or the designated representative determines that coverage of a story will involve exposure to sensitive information beyond the scope of what may be protected by prebriefing or debriefing, *but coverage of which is in the best interests of the DOD,* the commander may offer access if the reporter agrees to a security review of their coverage" (emphasis added). What that means is that the rules could be bent as long as bending them would result in positive military propaganda for U.S. forces. The result of this regulation is inevitably propaganda, pure and simple.

Did reporters remind viewers each and every time that what they were seeing and hearing was subject to these rules? No. If they had, it would have been far more honest. What the embedding program accomplished was the creation of close ties between reporters and individual servicemen and women. They were sharing the same space and, almost naturally, the journalists began to empathize with the soldiers. Many helped tend to wounded, and used terms such as "we" and "our country" when reporting on troop movements and activities. And many of the reports were extremely laudatory. None of this, by itself, is a bad thing. But the fact that these same journalists could not report about U.S. mistakes or how the enemy had actually won a particular battle, or that they were even prohibited from shooting certain incidents that would reflect poorly on U.S. troops—the fact that the U.S. press corps was forbidden to provide balanced news reporting—*that* is of great concern.

Following the invasion of Iraq, there have been many news "postmortems," as they're unfortunately called in this business. This is when journalists sit down to analyze what worked, what didn't, what could have been done better, and what should be done better in the future. Many embedded reporters acknowledged that they lacked the big picture; they could only report what they were seeing in front of them and that, of course, was subject to the coverage regulations. They could not offer anything having to do with the other side of the story, much less context of the overall conflict. There seems to be near consensus that the so-called "unilateral" reporters (who were not embedded) could offer more information. Mike von Fremd, an ABC News correspondent, agreed, saying he believes he got and was able to report a better overview of the action. But there were very few unilateral news teams. For example, of the twenty-plus correspondents CNN had in the war "theater," only four were so-called unilateral reporters—Jane Arraf, Kevin Sites, Ben Wedeman, and Brent Sadler. CBS News had about fifteen embedded reporters and only two or three unilateral ones at any given time. Jeff Goldman, who worked for CBS News in Kuwait, said that Pentagon officials "were much against independent journalists going in there."

It is true that being a unilateral reporter was far more dangerous than being an embedded one. At least fourteen of them, including ITV News correspondent Terry Lloyd, Paul Moran of the Australian Broadcasting Corporation, and BBC freelancer Kaveh Golestan, lost their lives trying to bring independent, nonregulated information to the public. In addition, two Spanish journalists were killed when a U.S. tank fired a shell at the hotel where most journalists in Baghdad were based. Many other journalists were harassed. Associated Press photographer Karim Kadim and his driver had weapons trained on them by American troops as they were forced to stand in the sun, handcuffed, for three hours. And two Portuguese journalists were held for four days by U.S. troops before being escorted out of the country.

But embedded reporters also lost their lives, among them Michael Kelly, the editor-at-large for the *Atlantic Monthly* and a columnist for the *Washington Post,* who drowned when the unit he was with came under attack and his vehicle rolled into a canal. German journalist Christian Liebig, a reporter for *Focus,* and Julio Anguita Parrado, a Spanish journalist, died in an Iraqi missile attack. Another who died was Jerry Little, an Austrian employed by NBC News.

All the same, administration officials, not surprisingly, given the control they could exercise, were very pleased with the embed program. The Pentagon, according to published accounts, considered the program a success. "We were dealing with a trained liar," Capt. T. McCreary, the public affairs advisor to the Joint Chiefs of Staff, said of Saddam Hussein. "By embedding the press, that would take most of the wind out of the sails of the disinformation program." One way to interpret that comment is to say that U.S. forces were using the American media for counter-disinformation. Torie Clark, the assistant secretary for defense for public affairs, added that "the net result is a positive one." Positive for whom? But even the majority (over 60 percent) of people surveyed by the Pew Research Center agreed that having journalists deployed with the troops was a good development. Most of those who were against the embed program felt so because they feared reporters were giving away too much sensitive information. The actual truth is that more often than not, the media reported far too little.

A lesson learned from the coverage of this war was that "better access than before" is far too low a standard. The new rules were accepted by the networks and other news organizations because they improved on what had happened, or didn't happen, in Afghanistan. The networks, in particular, were intimidated because they depend on visual images, and something was better than nothing. The most important aspect for the news agencies was access to live pictures of war, even if they didn't mean much. The images they were able to transmit—thanks to improved technology—were live and they were powerful, so networks looked the other way and broadcast virtually meaningless reports without proper context. This was good television, a good show. No Hollywood studio had the billions to put on such a realistic spectacle. And that's the key to why CNN, Fox News, MSNBC, ABC News, NBC News, and CBS News did not—as they did with the White House's coverage rules of presidential overseas trips—join forces and just say no. It was simply not good business to publicly challenge the Bush administration's war-coverage policies when public sentiment was running in support of so-called "patriotism" and this presidency. Moreover, journalists openly critical of the administration were likely to get excluded from any debate. Journalistic ethics and the responsibility to fight any and all attacks on the First Amendment were secondary, if considered at all. The news organizations knew that what was politically correct would lead to higher ratings. The new "embedding" policy provided sexy footage of soldiers and "brave" correspondents in an actual war.

THE TIDE IS TURNING

It has taken some time, but a few well-known journalists have come forward to admit that they and some of their colleagues did, indeed, feel the pressure to go along with the nation's patriotic mood. Even CBS anchor Dan Rather, who wore a flag lapel pin after 9/11 and told *The Late Show* host, David Letterman, that he'd line up wherever the president needed him, acknowledged that for awhile he, too, chose not to take on the Bush administration over the war on terrorism. And, in part, he blamed self-censorship. "It starts with a feeling of patriotism within oneself. It carries through with a certain knowledge that the country as a whole—and for all the right reasons—felt and continues to feel this surge of patriotism within themselves. And one finds oneself saying, 'I know the right question, but you know what? This is not exactly the right time to ask it.'" And why not? Because he feared he'd be ostracized as un-American. "It's an obscene comparison, you know I am not sure I like it, but you know there was a time in South Africa that people would put flaming tires around people's necks if they dissented. And in some ways the fear is that you will be necklaced here, you will have a flaming tire of lack of patriotism placed around your neck. Now it is that fear that keeps journalists from asking the toughest of the tough questions." And that, Rather now admits, is not being a good journalist or a good American citizen. "It's unpatriotic not to stand up, look them in the eye, and ask the questions they don't want to hear—they being those who have the responsibility, the ultimate responsibility—of sending our sons and daughters, our husbands, wives, our blood, to face death."

CNN's Christiane Amanpour says the outcome of the self-censorship was disinformation at all levels. "I think the press was muzzled, and I think the press self-muzzled. I'm sorry to say, but certainly television and, perhaps to a certain extent, my station was intimidated by the administration and its foot soldiers at Fox News," Amanpour said. "And it did, in fact, put a climate of fear and self-censorship, in my view, in terms of the kind of broadcast work we did." Ironically, Fox's response to Amanpour's comments underscored her message: "Given the choice, it's better to be viewed as a foot soldier for Bush than a spokeswoman for al-Qaida," said Fox spokeswoman Irena Briganti. The White House could not have said it any better.

❏   ❏   ❏

So, in reviewing coverage of the wars in Afghanistan and Iraq, along with events that have transpired in these countries afterwards, it is evident that most of the major television news organizations caved, exchanging ethics and responsible journalism for what now apparently counts most for them: riveting television images with true-life characters that increase ratings and, therefore, profits. Indeed, money can often be found at the end of the road where journalistic ethics and standards, beliefs, and responsibilities are tossed aside as relics of the world of "old" journalism.

Yet it is this concept of "old" journalism that has helped safeguard democracy in the United States for more than two hundred years. It is a concept born when the U.S. Constitution was amended to include the rights of people living in this country and it is far more powerful than the edicts of one presidential administration. Old? Yes, but also an immensely valuable tenet that has served Americans well and preserved our way of life. It will survive this assault; it must. It is the responsibility of the news media to ensure that survival, no matter how unpopular their efforts might be. But as representatives of the people, the media must have the support and encouragement of the public to wage a defense against any government usurping authority not granted it by the Founding Fathers. Patriotism is not blindly following one's government. It is being brave enough to stand up and say no, we don't agree, and we won't go along. It is reminding politicians who are more concerned about their time in office than anything else that they were elected to serve us, to address the needs of the people, and to protect our laws and our constitution.

The media need this support from the American people. And the people of this country need a media, a press free from government, corporate, and financial pressure. Our lives—both at home and overseas—depend on it.

CONCLUSION:
RX FOR TV JOURNALISM

Patriotism can be practiced in many ways. Some choose to defend the country by taking up arms. Others serve in diplomatic positions, smoothing the way behind the scenes. Still others become lawyers or judges who play integral parts in a justice system that helps prevent chaos and strives to protect the innocent. Many demonstrate love of country simply by waving flags. I and thousands of my colleagues have chosen the pencil, the pen, the computer, the camera, and the tape recorder to uphold one of the pillars that sustain a democracy, a free press. Democracy and a free press; you can't have one without the other.

All of us in the news business must endeavor to strengthen standards and ethics, to improve the depth, breadth, and quality of the stories presented, and to restore the institutions of a free press, a free media to the respected place they deserve in a healthy democracy. And we *can* improve the state of television journalism in this country while also recognizing the business needs of news corporations. *News Flash* is an optimistic call to journalists and all Americans to demand honest and fair news reporting, so that citizens can make informed decisions based on solid, unvarnished information.

We must begin with honesty. No more conning the public. No more pretending to be fair and balanced when there is a political agenda. In fact, no more political agendas in real journalism. We must keep news separate from entertainment and make the line between the two unmistakable. Cable news networks and broadcast news divisions are different from their entertainment counterparts. They can't be run the same way, nor can a newscast be expected to earn the same huge profits as a popular sitcom, although news can be a very good business. News organizations have a far more important role in this country, and the companies, along with the people who work for them, must be held to a higher standard. If reality shows and crime dramas were to disappear from television, the country would still function well. The same can't be said if we do away with what has been the fairest, most independent and balanced news institution ever seen. Preserving a free, responsible press—particularly the television news media—is critical and needs to become a national priority. We need to act now, before we get to a point where we can't remember what good broadcast journalism looks like anymore.

Let's give people what they need to know along with what they want to know. Let's make sure that Americans are never again blindsided by the type and intensity of hatred that brought about the attacks on 9/11. Let's have no more pandering to the liberals or to the conservatives, to the young, to the wealthy, to any particular segment of the population. All Americans deserve news coverage that is relevant to them, regardless of age, gender, ethnic background, political affiliation, marital status, religion, or degree of wealth, whether they live in urban areas or in rural ones. Many news organizations started down the slippery infotainment slope hoping to regain viewers lost through, in part, fragmentation, that is, to the many other news and entertainment choices available. Others chose fancy slogans to pretend they're fair and ethical. These are short-term measures that will only lead to a further evaporation of the news audience. And they don't provide the public service mandated by the U.S. Constitution.

It is time to challenge all television news organizations to focus on issues of importance that educate and inform, rather than merely entertain:

- Let the news be the star, what draws viewers, rather than hair-sprayed, attractive news actors being handsomely paid for their looks, not their experience.

- Encourage daily debates and discussions about ethical issues among employees. Let all voices be heard, and give all voices equal weight and consideration.

- Motivate the people on staff to aspire to the highest standards, even if they're not first with the news that particular day. Being first *is* good, but being fair, accurate, and balanced is better.

- Hire a journalist with impeccable credentials to be an independent ombudsman to monitor how news is gathered and how it is reported. Give this person the authority and latitude to step in and make major decisions, along with a long-term contract.

Pick an honorable, credible course and then stay with it. Don't expect overnight success; it won't be there. But with every day you will earn the respect and gratitude of more and more viewers who will be loyal to real news. They have been before. If you offer it, they will watch—no matter how many other news outlets there are, no matter what other excuses are used for the dwindling news audience. As my dear friend and CNN executive producer Steven Springer says (and he's one of the journalists I hold in the utmost regard): "There's got to be a TV news organization that will put its foot down and stand against the tide and say, 'Screw it, we're a news organization. Forget the crap and let's just do what we're supposed to do.'"

❏   ❏   ❏

So how do we get there? Well, by paying attention to four basic elements: the motives of the journalists on staff, the makeup of the staff, the actual programming, and the corporation's profit or bottom-line financial expectations.

MOTIVATION: THE HEART OF IT ALL

The people on staff, the journalists in front of the camera and behind—from the eager entry-level TelePrompTer operator to the beleaguered network president—are the key. News organizations need to identify, keep, or hire those who are driven by the right reasons: a sincere sense of public service and respect for the First Amendment, a commitment to take on the responsibilities inherent in becoming a journalist, and a deep-seated desire to help inform viewers in a fair, responsible way. Writes author James Fallows:

> If they recognized their purpose was to give citizens the tools to participate in public life, and recognized as well that fulfilling this purpose is the only way journalism itself can survive, journalists would find it natural to change many other habits and attitudes. They would spend less time predicting future political events, since the predictions are so often wrong and in many cases are useless. They would instead devote that energy toward understanding and explaining what had already occurred—and its implications for the future (which are different from guesses about who will win the straw vote in Florida). They would spend less time on sportscaster-like analysis of how politicians were playing their game, because they would realize that very few people care.

Those are some of the right reasons and the right things to do. I hope the wrong reasons are evident by now. The desire to become famous, to be a celebrity, to make a lot of money—these should all be huge red flags. People with these motivations will most likely not be guided by established professional standards and ethics, no matter how good they might look on camera.

Much of the direction news divisions and networks take is dictated by management. So it is essential that news managers, particularly the executives, be people who continue to respect news ethics, traditions, and the real purpose of solid journalism. Do they help create and nurture a company culture that encourages and rewards professionalism and a job done well? Have their increased salaries, stock options, car allowances, and expense accounts affected how they approach their responsibilities? Are they still as daring and willing to stand up for what is right? Or now that they have more to lose, have they become yes-men and yes-women? Bonuses and stock options are supposed to be incentives for managers to do the right thing even better. But all too often, the concept backfires.

Executives eager to stay on the gravy train deflect tough decisions and go along with corporate decisions they would have fought before. Too many of them have forgotten the days when they had the overnight shift, when they screwed up the feed from London, when they did whatever it took to make it right. But they have become the role models and, whether they like it or not, they lead by example. A vice president can't be permitted to violate the company's ethical guidelines while lower-level employees are punished for the same indiscretion. The rules must apply across the board.

DIVERSITY: MIRROR SOCIETY

I have always said that the day I rule a network the unfortunate souls in hell will be scrambling for ice skates and warm parkas. That's not because I'm not qualified or experienced enough to head up a major network or network group. I am, and so are many, many other women and minorities. In fact, I could name several who are either currently toiling in the business in lower positions or have retired in frustration. In all cases, they're as good as any of the men who've run the nation's networks. In many cases, they're better. But few women and even fewer people of color have been considered for the top jobs because they don't look like the people who have historically made those paramount hiring decisions. And the few who have gotten those jobs? They've never been given the time needed to truly make a difference.

Diversity isn't just about making up for the past. And it certainly isn't about making the company look good, or presentable, or "sensitive" enough to avoid boycotts from Jesse Jackson or the NAACP. Make no mistake; those threats help and they do make a difference, but only because they scare the hell out of the mostly white, male management. Changing the makeup of that senior tier of management will also change the company mind-set, and that in turn will have a lasting impact on any news organizations. By no means am I suggesting that we ought to just throw all the white guys out and hire women and minorities in their place. That isn't right, or legal, either. And at the same time it isn't smart business. Creating a senior management position with the intent that it will only be filled by a minority is also wrong, not to mention offensive. If the tables were turned, would these white men agree to be considered for a job where only white men in their forties were candidates? Doubtful. But this isn't a concept, a possibility, or an insult they've ever had to consider because they have never walked in a minority's shoes.

What news organizations should do is search out the best and brightest journalists in the nation and be committed to building a staff that represents a cross section of this country. Diversity will ensure that a network is able to present relevant stories to all viewers. The traditional idea of diversity should be broadened to include geographical backgrounds, economic status, religion, education, and cultures. We should take advantage of the experience of veteran journalists even as younger additions to the staff bring their energy and new ideas. Achieving true diversity is a long process that builds upon itself. People of different backgrounds and experiences moving into positions of authority will be more likely to be sensitive to diversity issues and proactive in hiring matters.

While I don't believe forced mentoring is effective, companies can still encourage veteran journalists to mentor the rookies. I can say with no hesitation that were it not for my two mentors, Guillermo Martinez and Don Browne, I would not have learned what I did so early on, I would not have been exposed to their high standards of professionalism at a time when I was shaping my personal set of ethics, and, as important, I would not have had access to the valuable opportunities that helped me grow as a journalist. Helping develop young journalists is one way we can ensure that journalistic standards remain high.

PROGRAMMING: WHAT VIEWERS WANT, WHAT VIEWERS NEED

Whether we're talking about a half-hour newscast or a twenty-four-hour network, the obligation is the same: to give viewers information they need to know to help understand events in their city, their state, their country, and the world. At the same time, there are many news stories that are informative and of great interest to the public. And surveys show that many viewers are drawn to opinion programming, in which topics are discussed or debated from different points of view. All of these mission objectives are very possible to achieve while maintaining the integrity of American journalism. The key is to differentiate clearly among entertainment, news, and opinion so that there is no question what the viewer is seeing. Newscasts should be solid news, but that doesn't mean they have to be boring. They can cover JFK Jr.'s death, Chandra Levy's disappearance, or the O. J. Simpson trial—but should cover them in a responsible and measured way that puts their importance in perspective to the rest of the news in the world.

A twenty-four-hour network should also be able to offer a range of news talk shows that explore major issues from different points of view. Instead of journalists voicing their opinions, however, these could have smart hosts (who are clearly not defined as journalists) and guests who can articulately and intelligently discuss the topic and their position on it. An op-ed-type program could give average people a chance to speak. But it must be clear that these are opinion shows, not newscasts. They should do news stories or even news programs on topics of interest to different segments of the population, for older people, for younger ones, for families, for students, for Christians, for Muslims, for Jews, and so on; in other words, offer programming that stretches knowledge. And given the important position the United States holds in the world today and how global politics and economics can result in life or death decisions for Americans, people in this country need to be kept informed about international issues.

During the 1990s, news divisions and networks closed down many international bureaus to save money and because surveys and focus groups tell executives Americans don't care about international news. "When you take a focus group and you say to them, 'Well, would you rather hear about some distant, irrelevant, ridiculous place on the other side of the world or about, you know, medical health care at home?' well, obviously they're gonna say medical health at home. I would," said CNN's Christiane Amanpour. "But if you ask, 'If we told you a story about the AIDS epidemic in South Africa or the little children starving in Ethiopia, or whatever, if we told you those issues and we made them compelling, would you listen?' I bet you they'd say yes. This is a country full of compassionate people, full of people who like to care. And I know from the reaction I get from my stories that people are interested if you tell stories well and relevantly."

International news coverage immediately following the terrorist attacks in the United States has proved that. Every news outlet experienced huge ratings jumps as Americans anxious for explanations and information turned to television. According to Nielsen Media Research, between January 2001 and January 2002 (after the attacks) Fox's ratings were up 109 percent, CNN was up 51 percent, CNN Headline News, 48 percent, and MSNBC, 28 percent. "9/11 was a major wakeup call for the news business as it was for the rest of the nation," said NBC correspondent George Lewis. "Our international coverage, particularly on the broadcast networks, has dwindled over the years, and we ignore the rest of the world at our peril, because there are people out there who do not mean us well. Now we're back in that game and again paying attention to what is going on in the rest of the world. Oftentimes international news was neglected in favor of national news, and some of that balance has been restored." In a way, yes. Responsible news organizations must maintain the current level of international coverage, if not expand on it. As we've seen, knowing what is going on around the world can also be a matter of life or death.

But we must do a better job of explaining international news than we've done before. Despite the heightened interest after 9/11, the public's viewing habits have returned to virtually where they were prior to the attacks. According to the Pew Research Center, about two-thirds of Americans with moderate or low interest in international news say they lose interest because they are not given the background they need to understand the current developments. Rather than reporting international news the way we've always done it, clearly we need to do a better and more thorough job of making it relevant and understandable to all. Whether the news is domestic or international, about sports or medical issues, it can be done in a compelling fashion without turning it into infotainment or selling out. Smart, updated graphics that are eyecatching will inform viewers and keep them tuned in. Crisp writing and clever story-telling are also draws. But none of these things has to lead to any sacrifices in journalism. They can work together, although news hasn't always been presented that way. Joe Angotti, who heads up the broadcast program at the Medill School of Journalism, produced *NBC Nightly News*. "I can't show my students old *Nightly News* programs that I produced. They look so dated, dull, boring that there's no way they can relate to them. And the reason is that the news and television in general has become so heightened visually that that's what they're accustomed to. This is a generation that grew up with computer games, so their televisions have always had a lot of action and things going on."

That doesn't mean that all newscasts must be geared toward young people who want multiple sources of data streaming toward them at the same time. There *is* a middle ground for basic newscasts and, at a twenty-four-hour network, the time to offer news presented in ways that different slices of the audience find relevant and compelling to watch. The content remains solid and pure; the packaging changes. At the heart of it all is good journalism, backed by good reporting and news gathering, good editing, and good writing.

THE BOTTOM LINE: WHEN PROFIT IS TOO COSTLY

Given the importance of a free press, a free media, just how big a role should profit play for parent companies? There isn't a simple dollar figure that would apply across the board. But there is a point at every news company beyond which cutting back on spending or not budgeting enough threatens the quality and integrity of the news gathered and programmed. Passing that point is counterproductive. If news divisions or networks don't have the budget to cover the news events they're responsible for bringing to the public, then the profit-pushers have crossed the line. "Selling" news to viewers is not the same as selling widgets, airplane engines, Internet service, or tickets to animated movies. The integrity of the news organization must be maintained for much more important and honorable reasons—for the good of democracy. Corporations that buy and run news organizations should treat these companies—and the profit they're expected to make—differently and protect what they do for the public good. And if they do, they can be profitable. "I think that there is some evidence that at the local level quality news operations do make money, that if you put quality first, you do attract an audience," said Lewis. "And a network based on those values of connecting with the audience, informing the public, can become must-see TV and attract an audience and have high quality and commitment to public service. It requires exceptional dedication and talent at the management level and a vision that goes beyond the next quarterly earnings statement. But it's possible."

For the shareholders of these corporations, it's an investment in democracy and in this country. It may not earn as many dollars and cents as other companies, but the dividend is far more valuable. As Amanpour says, news operations can and should be the crown jewel of the parent corporation. "Let us make you feel proud. Let us make you feel good about yourselves. Let us even bolster your credibility. Don't cut our costs. Give us more money so that we can produce real quality, so that we can produce work that will reverberate in all the right places, for all the right reasons."

❏   ❏   ❏

Like most of my colleagues who are equally concerned about television journalism today, I have not lost hope. My passion for journalism done the right way remains as strong as it has always been, perhaps even stronger. From the time I was a rookie reporter I've talked to people about the honor of being a journalist, the tremendous responsibility we have, and the absolute necessity of adhering to the highest standards of professionalism and ethics in order to protect this fundamental pillar of our democracy. These values are as relevant today as they were then.

Television journalism today is facing its greatest challenges on all fronts—from entertainment, the corporations that own the news organizations, the public, the federal government, and other political power brokers. It is my hope that *News Flash* will provoke debate about these critical issues. And while I've pulled no punches in my criticism, ultimately I hope *News Flash* delivers a positive message about the importance and power of journalism. This book seeks to inspire a generation of young journalists, and to renew the idealism of professionals and viewers alike who have grown complacent or cynical. It is my call to arms, a statement of my abiding faith.

NOTES

Preface

Page xi   "What we do and say and show really matters. . . ." Christiane Amanpour, keynote address to the Radio-Television News Directors Association, Minneapolis, September 13, 2000. Available at http://rtnda.org/resources/speeches/amanpour.shtml.

Page xiii   "As any actor would be, he was tuned in . . ." Joe Angotti, personal interview with the author, October 8, 2003.

Page xiv   "57 percent of those questioned watch local newscasts . . ." The Pew Research Center for the People and the Press, "People's News Habits Little Changed by September 11: Americans Lack Background to Follow International News," June 9, 2002, http://people-press.org/reports/display.php3?ReportID=156.

Page xiv   "Only 45 percent chose newspapers . . ." The Pew Research Center for the People and the Press, 2003.

Page xiv   "In 2000, the number dropped to twenty-eight minutes, . . ." The Pew Research Center for the People and the Press, 2003.

Page xiv   "On August 11, 2003, for example . . . ," Jim Ruttenberg, "Suffering News Burnout? The Rest of America Is, Too," *The New York Times*, August 11, 2003, p. C1.

Page xvii   "They state that the public's right to know . . ." J. Douglas Tarpley, "The Canons of American Journalism: The ASNE and SPJ Codes," August 11, 1998, http://www.gegrapha.org/resources/tarpley1.htm.

Page xvii   "An updated code of ethics, . . ." Tarpley, August 11, 1998.

Page xviii   "We do it because we're committed, . . ." Christiane Amanpour, keynote address, 2000.

Chapter One

Page 2   "And a 2003 survey revealed . . ." The Pew Research Center for the People and the Press, "Strong Opposition to Media Cross-Ownership Emerges: Public Wants Neutrality *and* Pro-American Point of View," July 13, 2003, http://people-press.org/reports/display.php3?ReportID=188.

Page 2   "In New York, from Fox affiliate Channel 5, . . ." From a Channel 5 employee who eventually left the station in disgust.

Page 3   "Baghdad is spelled B-A-G-H-D-A-D . . ." From a high-level CNN employee who
              was present in the control room for this embarrassing moment.

Page 3   "More than half of the people polled . . ." The Pew Research Center for the People
              and the Press, "Internet Sapping Broadcast News Audience," June 11, 2000,
              http://people-press.org/reports/display.php3?ReportID=36.

Page 3   "And the following survey results . . ." The Pew Research Center for the People and
              the Press, July 13, 2003.

Page 4   "It used to be that there was a different perception . . ." Robert Wiener, personal
              interview with the author, October 17, 2003.

Page 6   "CNN, he said, 'has become worldwide and skin-deep . . .'" Reese Schonfeld, *Me
              and Ted Against the World* (New York: Cliff Street, 2001), xv.

Page 6   " . . . the stars are often the news." A phrase first coined by a senior CNN producer
              who prefers to remain anonymous.

Page 6   "but nobody seemed to worry . . ." Barbara Matusow, *The Evening Stars* (Boston:
              Houghton Mifflin, 1983), 83.

Page 7   "And to make money, . . ." James Fallows, *Breaking the News: How the Media
              Undermine American Democracy* (New York: Vintage Books, 1996), 55.

Page 7   " . . . news rose from 'a 15 percent loss position . . .'" Matusow, 1983, 156.

Page 8   "One of our responsibilities . . ." Andrew Heyward, the president of CBS News,
              at a New York convention of the National Association of Hispanic Journalists,
              June 27, 2003.

Page 8   "According to author Ken Auletta, . . ." Ken Auletta, "Vox Fox: How Roger Ailes
              and Fox News Are Changing Cable News," *The New Yorker,* May 26, 2003.

Page 8   "Wolzien estimates that these news divisions . . ." Tom Wolzien, personal interview
              with the author, October 31, 2003.

Page 9   "Our parent companies and corporations are raking in the profits," Christiane
              Amanpour, keynote address to the Radio-Television News Directors Association,
              Minneapolis, September 13, 2000.

Page 11   "ABC in the '80s wasn't the plushest place to work, . . ." Tom Lubart, personal
              interview with the author, July 30, 2003.

Page 11   "Bob Wright raised all these questions . . ." Joe Angotti, personal interview with the
              author, October 8, 2003.

Page 11   "And what they determined . . ." Angotti, interview.

Page 12   "I think it took a long time . . ." Angotti, interview.

Page 12   "During 9/11 they knew they were going to lose . . ." Angotti, interview.

Page 12   "The old paradigm was that we were part . . ." George Lewis, personal interview
              with the author, September 17, 2003.

Page 13   "A CBS executive wrote to Lynch seeking an exclusive interview . . ." Gail
              Pennington, "Schwarzenegger May Have Terminated Line Between News and
              Entertainment," *The St. Louis Post-Dispatch, Everyday Magazine,* Aug. 12, 2003,
              p. E1.

Page 15   "I am not alone in feeling really depressed . . ." Amanpour, keynote address,
              2000.

Page 18   "Because we are more competitive now . . ." Lewis, interview.

Page 18   "A survey by the Pew Research Center . . ." The Pew Research Center for the People
              and the Press, July 13, 2003.

Page 19   "According to Nielsen Media Research figures . . ." Nielsen Media Research.

Page 19   "This is very worrisome, . . ." Lewis, interview.

Page 20   "Fox has two things going for it, . . ." Michele Greppi, "Fox Setting the News
              Agenda," *Television Week,* July 21, 2003. Available at http://www.craini2i.com/em/
              archive.mv?count=3&story=em463579562277728241.

Page 20   "lack of trust is a leading cause . . ." The Pew Research Center for the People and the Press, "Striking the Balance: Audience Interest, Business Pressures, and Journalists' Values," March 30, 1999, http://people-press.org/reports/display.php3?PageID=314.

Page 20   "Other findings include the following . . ." The Pew Research Center for the People and the Press, March 30, 1999.

Page 21   "The survey also highlights . . ." The Pew Research Center for the People and the Press, March 30, 1999.

Page 21   "The drive for profits and the drive for ratings . . ." Lewis, interview.

Page 22   "It's an example of companies trying anything . . ." Angotti, interview.

Page 23   "We, I believe, are in the fight of our lives . . ." Amanpour, keynote address, 2000.

Chapter Two

Page 26   "It pained me to watch . . ." From CNN.com, http://www.cnn.com/TRANSCRIPTS/0307/01/lol.04.html.

Page 28   "I don't think there are many instances anymore . . ." Joe Angotti, personal interview with the author, October 8, 2003.

Page 29   "Think of how much more of a contribution . . ." Christiane Amanpour, keynote address to the Radio-Television News Directors Association, Minneapolis, September 13, 2000.

Page 29   "Instead of informing the public more on international issues, . . ." Robert Wiener, personal interview with the author, October 17, 2003.

Page 30   "I shudder to think . . ." Angotti, interview.

Page 31   "One cannot fault Brokaw, Jennings, Rather . . ." Mitch Ratcliffe, "RatcliffeBlog-Mitch Thinking Out Loud," March 22, 2003, http://www.ratcliffe.com/RatcliffeBlog/archives/000951.html.

Page 31   "The press has abrogated its responsibility to be editors, . . ." Mitch Ratcliffe, March 22, 2003.

Page 33   "If it works well and we do it smart . . ." From a panel discussion at the June 2003 National Association of Hispanic Journalists convention in New York.

Page 34   "No sooner had the shock . . ." Howard Kurtz, "The *Times'* Left-Hand Man," *The Washington Post,* July 26, 1999, Page C01.

Page 34   "80 percent of the people polled . . ." The Pew Research Center for the People and the Press, "JFK Jr. Tragedy Attracts Huge Audience," July 27, 1999, http://people-press.org/reports/display.php3?ReportID=55.

Page 34   "We're operating in a world . . ." Barbara Cochran, personal interview with the author, November 6, 2003.

Page 37   "Reputations are made in war zones, . . ." Wiener, interview.

Page 38   "A majority (51 percent) . . ." The Pew Research Center for the People and the Press, "Strong Opposition to Media Cross-Ownership Emerges: Public Wants Neutrality *and* Pro-American Point of View," July 13, 2003, http://people-press.org/reports/display.php3?ReportID=188.

Page 38   "Four years earlier, another survey . . ." The Pew Research Center for the People and the Press, survey, 1999.

Page 39   "It wasn't just the conservatives . . ." Angotti, interview.

Page 39   "It's best for news when there's a diversity . . ." George Lewis, personal interview with the author.

Chapter Three

Page 42   "Still, the three broadcast news divisions have seen . . ." Nielsen Media Research.

Page 43   "H. L. Mencken once said . . ." Christiane Amanpour, keynote address to the Radio-Television News Directors Association, Minneapolis, September 13, 2000.

Page 44   "I was asked to do (the) Somalia (story) . . ." Tal Sanit, "The New Unreality," *Columbia Journalism Review,* May-June 1992, http://archives.cjr.org/year/92/3/unreality.asp.

Page 45   "You can't say you believe . . ." Sanit, 1992.

Page 45   "I am concerned, on a very basic level, . . ." Barbara Cochran, personal interview with the author, November 6, 2003.

Page 45   "When you do that [outsource], . . ." Tom Wolzien, personal interview with the author, October 31, 2003.

Page 46   "Talk is by far the cheapest thing to do, . . ." Wolzien, interview.

Page 46   "In terms of immediate breaking news, . . ." Cochran, interview.

Page 46   "What a good local TV station . . ." Wolzien, interview.

Page 47   "That's why a station needs to protect . . ." Cochran, interview.

Page 47   "According to a Pew Research Center survey, . . ." The Pew Research Center for the People and the Press, "Public's News Habits Little Changed by September 11: Americans Lack Background to Follow International News," June 9, 2002, http://people-press.org/reports/display.php3?ReportID=156.

Page 47   "Good journalism, good television, . . ." Amanpour, keynote address, 2000.

Page 49   ". . . according to a 2003 survey conducted . . ." Bob Papper, "Salaries Slide Backward," Radio-Television News Directors Association, survey available online to members only, 2003. Originally published in RTNDA's magazine, *Communicator,* in June 2003.

Page 49   "Journalism was overwhelmingly male, . . ." Quoted in Edward Alwood, *Straight News,* (New York: Columbia University Press, 1995), 9.

Page 51   "When questioned directly by minority journalists, . . ." From a panel discussion at the June 2003 National Association of Hispanic Journalists convention in New York.

Page 52   "While a 2002 analysis of network . . ." Annenberg Public Policy Center, *The Glass Ceiling in the Executive Suite: The Second Annual APPC Analysis of Women Leaders in Communication Companies,* University of Pennsylvania, August 2002.

Page 52   "It makes you wonder . . ." Barbara Ciara, personal interview with the author, November 10, 2003.

Page 52   "None of Fox News, CNN, or MSNBC . . ." David Folkenflik, "News Organizations Lack Diversity, NAACP Chief Charges," *The Baltimore Sun,* October 28, 2003.

Page 52   "Sadly, when it comes to news, . . ." "NAACP TV Diversity Report Yields Mixed Results on Networks' Performance," October 28, 2003, http://www.naacp.org/news/releases/tvdiversity102803.shtml.

Page 52   "According to the U.S. census in 2000, . . ." http://www.census.gov. For purposes of this report, the Census Bureau considered "Hispanic" to be a cultural distinction, rather than a racial one, hence the overlap in percentages.

Page 53   "a July-August 2003 report . . ." Bob Papper, "Women and Minorities: One Step Forward and Two Steps Back," *Communicator,* July-August 2003.

Page 53   "Part of [the reason for this imbalance] is short-term thinking . . ." Randall Yip, personal interview with the author, November 5, 2003.

Page 53   "I think that has everything to do with it. . . ." Ciara, interview.

Page 53   "The demographics of this country . . ." Art Rascon, personal interview with the author, October 31, 2003.

Page 54   "At stations in the twenty-five largest cities, . . ." Papper, July-August 2003.

Page 55   "What the NAACP's Mfume calls . . ." Folkenflik, 2003.

Page 55   ". . . although males outnumber females . . ." http://www.census.gov.

Page 55   "Television, our culture's most powerful . . ." The White House Project, "Who's Talking," www.thewhitehouseproject.org/research/who_talking_summary.html)

Page 56   "We must conclude that the nation's . . ." *Network Brownout 2002: The Portrayal of Latinos in Network Television News,* a report by the National Association of Hispanic Journalists. Available at http:/nahj.org/release/2003/pr121103.html.

Page 56   "Published reports peg the current . . ." Jeffrey M. Humphreys, "The Multicultural Economy 2003: America's Minority Buying Power," Selig Center for Economic Growth, http://www.selig.uga.edu; and Simon Applebaum, "Telemundo: Latino Buying Power to Soar," Multichannel News, May 5, 2003, http://www.multichannel.com.

Page 57   "When you consider that the joint buying power . . ." "Diversity Is Good Business," The National Association of Realtors, http://www.realtor.org/divweb.nsf/pages/divgood?opendocument.

Page 57   "The press has been basking in . . ." From various sources, including kpearson. faculty.tcnj.edu/Syllabi/rgn02.htm; and "The Color of Coverage," http://iml.jou.ufl.edu/projects/spring03/doucette/kerner.htm.

Page 58   "I don't think it would be wrong." Quoted in Herb Denenberg, "Hollywoodization of the News," *The Denenberg Report,* Oct. 5, 1998.

Page 58   "Older people face discrimination . . ." George Lewis, personal interview with the author, September 17, 2003.

Page 62   "Why are all these tapes you're showing . . ." From my spring 2001 meeting with Garth Ancier in his office.

Page 68   "Ninety-six percent of Americans believe . . ." *U.S. News & World Report* statistics quoted in Amy Standen, "Faith in America," salon.com, Nov. 20, 2000.

Page 71   "Flash may get you a momentary bump . . ." Cochran, interview.

Chapter Four

Page 73   "That illustrates that in a community . . ." Barbara Cochran, personal interview with the author, November 6, 2003.

Page 75   "The infidels are committing suicide . . ." Reported by hundreds of news organizations worldwide.

Page 77   "We were hated by both sides." Joe Angotti, personal interview with the author, October 8, 2003.

Page 80   "Simply the fact that we were out . . ." CNN producer Lisa Rose Weaver, on air.

Page 81   "Our 9/11 coverage was superb," George Lewis, personal interview with the author, September 17, 2003.

Page 81   "I was proud to be in the business . . ." Lewis, interview.

Page 82   "It looked as though the FBI . . ." John Miller and others, "Television Reporting—Network/Top 25," The Society of Professional Journalists, http://www.spj.org/awards_sdx_gallery/01_invest_5.asp.

Page 82   "There may be times in the future . . ." Steve Rogers, "National Television Academy Honors Broadcasters for Coverage of 9/11, National Television Academy, http://www.emmyonline.org/emmy/docu3.html.

Page 83   "There was some superb writing . . ." Robert Wiener, personal interview with the author, October 17, 2003.

Page 83   "Cameras recorded the critical meetings . . ." Tom Lubart, personal interview with the author, July 30, 2003.

Page 83   "I'm proud of the work . . ." Christiane Amanpour, keynote address to the Radio-
               Television News Directors Association, Minneapolis, September 13, 2000.
Page 87   "When I first talked to New York . . ." Angotti, interview.

Chapter Five

Page 98   "These are all judgment calls, and they are difficult to make." The ethical seminar
               I now give around the world is based, in part, on examples provided by Richard
               Griffiths, CNN executive producer, who has had several critical roles at the net-
               work, including—at one time—being the ethical conscience of CNN.
Page 104   "What really disturbed me was . . ." Robert Wiener, personal interview with the
               author, October 17, 2003.
Page 105   "On banners or crawls I see a lot . . ." George Lewis, personal interview with the
               author, September 17, 2003.
Page 106   "Steve Safran, an executive producer . . ." Steve Safran, *Things Viewers Never, Ever
               Say,* www.lostremote.com/story/viewers_never_say.htm.
Page 107   "You wouldn't believe how many people . . ." Christiane Amanpour, keynote
               address to the Radio-Television News Directors Association, Minneapolis,
               September 13, 2000.
Page 107   "When you think back about great editors . . ." Joe Angotti, personal interview
               with the author, October 8, 2003.
Page 108   "Interestingly, a survey of more than 800 viewers . . ." Stephen G. Gottlieb,
               "Media Ethics: Some Specific Problems," *ERIC Digest,* 1990-02-00,
               http://www.ericfacility.net/databases/ERIC_Digests/ed314802.html
Page 109   "His live television conversations . . ." From CNN transcripts on CNN.com,
               http://www.cnn.com/2003/WORLD/meast/04/04/otsc.irq.rodgers.
Page 112   "Certainly the O. J. Simpson trial . . ." Lewis, interview.
Page 113   "The need to latch onto a soap opera, . . ." Lewis, interview.
Page 113   "We didn't do a good job . . ." Angotti, interview.
Page 113   "You used to be able to pull off a wonderful . . ." Angotti, interview.
Page 114   "While CNN made a much larger commitment . . ." Wiener, interview.
Page 114   "For whatever reason, we, CNN at the time, . . ." Wiener, interview.

Chapter Six

Page 116   "She (Lewinsky) will get no money . . ." "Interview with Monica Granted
               to Barbara Walters," *The Holland Sentinel,* November 18, 1998,
               http://www.hollandsentinel.com/stories/111898/ent_monica.html.
Page 117   "On August 9, 2000, however, the *Washington Post* . . ." Paul Farhi, "ABC Paid to
               Secure Lewinsky Interview: Lawyer Lobbied Starr's Office," *The Washington Post,*
               August 9, 2000, Page C1.
Page 118   "Five years ago, when CNN or CNBC . . ." Tom Wolzien, personal interview with
               the author, October 31, 2003.
Page 119   "This is the meeting of journalistic need . . ." Wolzien, interview.
Page 120   "In addition, many of the hosts . . ." James Fallows, *Breaking the News: How the
               Media Undermine American Democracy* (New York: Vintage Book, 1996).
Page 124   "Do you think the public knows . . ." Joe Angotti, personal interview with the
               author, October 8, 2003.
Page 124   "When I see a morning anchor talking . . ." George Lewis, personal interview with
               the author, September 17, 2003.
Page 127   "but we had very good video of things flying . . ." Tom Lubart, personal interview
               with the author, July 30, 2003.

Page 128   "All of us in the field have seen examples . . ." Robert Wiener, personal interview
            with the author, October 17, 2003.
Page 129   "That was a gross violation . . ." Lewis, interview.
Page 130   "One of the things that drives me crazy . . ." Angotti, interview.
Page 132   "Matt, what's with all the heavy-handed questions?" Author saw this on air.
Page 132   "This is the continual blurring . . ." Lewis, interview.
Page 132   "CBS was 'using all its resources . . .'" Howard Rosenberg, "CBS Only Has Eyes for
            Survivor," *Los Angeles Times,* February 12, 2001, p. F1.
Page 132   "We've all got palm leaves in our hair . . ." Ann Martin, quoted in Rosenberg,
            August 25, 2000.
Page 132   ". . . a KCBS evening newscast devoted six minutes . . ." Howard Rosenberg,
            "Huge *Survivor* Ratings a Reality: To Promote Show, Newscasters Went Coconuts"
            Los Angeles Times, August 25, 2000, p. 1.
Page 132   "a manufactured *Survivor II* story and tie-in, . . ." Rosenberg, August 25, 2000.
Page 133   "When you start doing news . . ." Angotti, interview.
Page 133   "That's bad, for the business, for the people . . ." Angotti, interview.
Page 138   "declaring that Jewell 'fit the profile'. . ." Bob Steele, "Journalists and Jewell:
            Teaching Old Watchdogs the Right Tricks," posted on the Poynter Institute's Web
            site (Poynter.org) in October of 1996. Other contributors to the investigation
            included Keith Woods and Joann Byrd. Available at http://www.poynter.org/
            content/content_view.asp?id=5552.
Page 140   "The central thesis of the broadcast . . ." Floyd Abrams, "Report on CNN
            Broadcast," posted on CNN.com, July 2. 1998, http://www.cnn.com/us/
            9807/02/tailwind.findings.
Page 141   "Writing about the Tailwind scandal, Neil Hickey . . ." Neil Hickey, "Ten Mistakes
            That Led to the Great Fiasco," *Columbia Journalism Review,* September-October
            1998, http://archives.cjr.org/year/98/5/cnn.asp.

Chapter Seven

Page 150   "Her first guest was Senator Barbara Mikulski . . ." From the transcript of the
            January 24, 2003, *Inside Politics* program, http://www.cnn.com/transcripts/
            0301/24/ip.00.html.
Page 153   "*The Daily Show: Global Edition with Jon Stewart* debuts . . ." Rena Golden,
            memo sent to staff, September 20, 2002.
Page 154   "Jon is on because he hits our demographic . . ." Stephen Armstrong, "I Can
            Scratch the Itch," *The Guardian,* London, March 17, 2003. Available at
            http://media.guardian.co.uk/mediaguardian/story/0,7558.915409,00.html.
Page 155   "In February 2004, the Web site for anchor . . ." From CNN.com,
            http://www.cnn.com/CNN/Programs/Anderson.cooper.360/index.html.
Page 155   "According to an e-mail David Neuman sent . . ." David Neuman, e-mail sent
            to senior managers, date n.a.
Page 156   "After all, between August 1997 and August 1998, . . ." From Nielsen Media
            Research.
Page 156   "During the O. J. coverage, . . ." L. Brent Bozell III, "CNN's Turmoil: Not Good
            News," Media Research Center, August 31, 2000, http://www.mediaresearch.org/
            BozellColumns/newscolumn/2000/col20000831.asp.
Page 157   "In June 2000, the ratings were lower . . ." Gregory Boyd Bell, "Wanted: Ratings,"
            http://www.eye.net/eye/issue/issue_07.24.97/news_views/media24.html
Page 158   "The powers that be, the moneymen, . . ." Christiane Amanpour, keynote address
            to the Radio-Television News Directors Association, Minneapolis, September 13,
            2000.

Page 161   "Busy people need a breather," Jim Walton, memo to staff, October 16, 2003.

Page 162   "He had taken money from several companies . . ." "CNN Business Editor Did
            Video Work," *The Wall Street Journal,* July 24, 1992; and Howard Kurtz, *Hot Air
            All Talk All the Time: An Inside Look at the Performers and the Pundits* (Random
            House, 1995). Excerpted at http://www.pbs.org/wgbh/pages/frontline/shows/
            press/vanities/kurtz.html.

Page 162   ". . . no one person was ever, ever thought to be bigger . . ." Memo sent to then-
            CNN-Chairman Tom Johnson on July 29, 1992, by a senior manager who asked
            not to be identified, as CNN's policy forbids staff from speaking on the record to
            reporters or authors.

Page 163   ". . . Dobbs, who had been generously remunerated . . ." Eric Alterman, *What
            Liberal Media?* (New York: Basic Books, 2003), 137.

Page 164   "Under Ted Turner, Lou Dobbs would not be on the air . . ." Robert Wiener, per-
            sonal interview with the author, October 17, 2003.

Page 165   "Still, with Turner Broadcasting's television companies generating . . ." Jim
            Rutenberg, "Sparks and Stars Fly as CNN and Fox News Go at It," *The New York
            Times,* Jan. 13, 2002.

Page 165   "One of the reasons that Tom Johnson resigned, . . ." Wiener, interview.

Page 166   "In fact, not long after replacing . . ." Fairness and Accuracy in Reporting (FAIR),
            "New CNN Chief Trying to Please GOP Elite," Aug. 15, 2001, http://www.fair.org/
            activism/cnn-gop.html.; Maureen Dowd, "Foxy or Outfoxed?" *The New York Times,*
            Aug. 15, 2001.

Page 166   "Allan Dodds Frank, who is 55, . . ." Ken Auletta, "Vox Fox: How Roger Ailes and
            Fox News Are Changing Cable News," *The New Yorker,* May 26, 2003, p. 68.

Page 167   "Tom Wolzien, . . ., explains that earnings trail ratings." Tom Wolzien, personal
            interview with the author, October 31, 2003.

Page 172   "In an effort to be sure we are as cutting-edge . . ." Quoted in Karen Lurie, "News
            That Sounds Like Anything But," Bearings Web site, http://www.poppolitics.com/
            articles/printerfriendly/2003-01-06-tvlanguage.shtml; and confirmed by my sources
            at Headline News.

Page 172   "A few days earlier, though, the Associate Press had reported . . ." Columbia
            Chronicle Online, "CNN's 'Headline News' Tries on New Vernacular," Oct. 7,
            2002, www.ccchronicle.com/back/2002-10-07/arts11.html.

Page 173   "The first story on the premier newscast . . ." Sally Beatty, "As Hard News
            Gets Even Harder, CNN Segues to Glossier Format," *The Wall Street Journal,*
            July 5, 2002.

Page 174   "He [the producer] took a look at my question . . ." Alexandra Trustman, "Don't
            Shoot the Messenger," *Brown Daily Herald,* November 10, 2003. Available at
            http://www.browndailyherald.com/stories.asp?storyID=1867.

Page 181   ". . . the MRC condemned CNN as a "megaphone for a dictator. . . ." "Megaphone
            for a Dictator: CNN's Coverage of Cuba, 1997–2002," Media Research Center,
            May 9, 2002, http://www.mediaresearch.org/specialreports/2002/sum/
            exec20020509.asp.

Page 182   "Each time I visited, I became more distressed . . ." Eason Jordan, "The News
            We Kept to Ourselves," *The New York Times,* April 11, 2003, op-ed page.
            Copyright © 2003, *The New York Times.* Reprinted by permission.

Page 183   "This tale would be disturbing enough on its own, . . ." "Truth-Telling,"
            The Washington Post, Editorial, April 15, 2003.

Page 184   "Withholding information that would get innocent people killed . . ." Eason
            Jordan, memo sent to CNN staff, April 2003.

Page 185   "Despite the leadership, there are still . . ." Wiener, interview.

Chapter Eight

Page 189   "Good! That'll drive my ratings up!" Ken Auletta, "Vox Fox: How Roger Ailes and
            Fox News Are Changing Cable News," *The New Yorker*, May 26, 2003, p. 61.

Page 189   "When Fox launched in October of that year, . . ." Auletta, 2003.

Page 189   "[Owner] Rupert Murdoch saw what he felt was a need . . ." Joe Angotti, personal
            interview with the author, October 8, 2003.

Page 189   "It says a lot about the brilliance . . ." George Lewis, personal interview with the
            author, September 17, 2003.

Page 190   "According to a Pew Research Center survey . . ." The Pew Research Center for the
            People and the Press, "Strong Opposition to Media Cross-Ownership Emerges:
            Public Wants Neutrality *and* Pro-American Point of View," July 13, 2003,
            http://people-press.org/reports/display.php3?ReportID=188.

Page 191   "There is a certain ridiculousness . . ." Howard Rosenberg, "Objectivity Is Lost to
            Fox News' Barbs," *The Los Angeles Times*, April 11, 2003, p. E1.

Page 191   "On January 27th, [2003], John Gibson, an afternoon anchor, . . ." Auletta, 2003.

Page 191   "Guess who's giving sympathy to illegal immigrants . . ." Auletta, 2003.

Page 191   "When [her] book came out, they did an hour-long . . ." "G.," personal interview
            with the author, December 23, 2003. G. is a former mid-to-high-level Fox editorial
            employee who asked not to be identified. I spoke with two of his current and for-
            mer colleagues to assess his credibility. He was given very high marks. He currently
            has a very influential position at another network.

Page 192   "Ailes advised George W. Bush . . ." PBS Online Newshour, "Crossing the Line,"
            Interview of Bob Woodward by Terence Smith, November 21, 2002,
            http://www.pbs.org/newshour/bb/media/july-dec02/line_11-21.html.

Page 192   ". . . [A]t Fox, if my boss wasn't warning me to 'be careful' . . ." Charlie Reina,
            "'The Memo' Is the Bible at Fox News Channel, Says Ex-Staffer." Letter posted to
            Jim Romenesko's Web site column, October 30, 2002, http://poynteronline.org/
            column.asp?id=45&aid=53018.

Page 193   "There was a more than tacit acknowledgement among everyone . . ." G., interview.

Page 193   "To the newsroom personnel responsible . . ." Reina, 2003.

Page 193   "The Memo warned us that anti-war protesters would be 'whining' . . ." Reina, 2003.

Page 194   "It would say things like 'the President was amazing and brave and cunning. . . .'"
            G., interview.

Page 194   "There was some talk that people in North Carolina . . ." G., interview.

Page 195   "On March 19, the first night . . ." Auletta, 2003.

Page 195   "They do very little news gathering . . ." G., interview.

Page 195   "There are five or six big Fox stories . . ." G., interview.

Page 195   "Rarely do they have Fox exclusive material . . ." G., interview.

Page 195   "When the Egyptian Air flight crashed . . ." Former high-level Fox employee,
            personal interview with the author, November 2003.

Page 196   "During a Dec. 4, 2003, show with Steve Young, . . ." "What Happened at the
            Anti-Bush Meeting?", December 4, 2003,
            http://www.foxnews.com/story/0,2933,104851,00.html.

Page 196   "On Dec. 1, 2003, O'Reilly's guests . . ." "What Happened at the Anti-Bush
            Meeting?", December 4, 2003.

Page 197   "That trend, of course, is like a cross . . ." O'Reilly, June 23, 2003.

Page 198   "Americans, he wrote, 'want to know how the journalists . . .'" Bill O'Reilly,
            "Unchain TV Anchors, Let 'em Give Opinions," *New York Daily News*,
            June 23, 2003, http://www.nydailynews.com/news/ideas_opinions/v-friendly/
            story/94680p-85850c.html.

Page 198   "Well, you're probably right." Auletta, 2003.
Page 199   "Do we all become like Geraldo Rivera . . ." Lewis, interview.
Page 199   "The most insidious thing about Fox . . ." G., interview.

Chapter Nine

Page 203   ". . . the only safeguard on this extraordinary governmental power . . ." The
            Reporters Committee for Freedom of the Press, "Homefront Confidential: Access
            to Terrorism and Immigration Proceedings," September 2003, http://www.rcfp.org/
            homefrontconfidential/immigration.html.
Page 203   "The Constitution was designed to protect . . ." The Reporters Committee for
            Freedom of the Press, "Homefront Confidential: Military Tribunals," September
            2003, http://www.rcfp.org/homefrontconfidential/tribunals.html.
Page 204   "As a result, we may never truly learn . . ." The Reporters Committee for Freedom
            of the Press, "Homefront Confidential: Freedom of Information," September 2003,
            http://www.rcfp.org/homefrontconfidential/foi.html.
Page 204   " . . . but then were ordered not to use the pictures." Reporters Without Borders,
            "Press Freedom Being Tested by Bush Administration's Anti-Terrorist Policy,"
            May 23, 2002, http://www.rsf.fr/article.php3?id_article=2277.
Page 204   "a dozen media organizations covering the military operations . . ." Reporters
            Without Borders, May 23, 2002.
Page 205   ". . . correspondent Doug Struck was not allowed to report . . ." The Committee
            to Protect Journalists, "Attacks on the Press in 2002," http://www.cpj.org/
            attacks02/asia02/afghan.html.
Page 205   "On April 10, 2002, American troops watched . . ." Reporters Without Borders,
            May 23, 2002.
Page 205   "demanded that the photographer clear his photographs . . ." The Committee to
            Protect Journalists, "Attacks on the Press in 2002"; and Ian Fisher with John F.
            Burns, "U.S. Troops Focus on Border's Caves to Seek Bin Laden," *The New York
            Times,* August 28, 2002.
Page 205   "There has never been an American war, small or large, . . ." Matthew Engel, "U.S.
            Media Cowed by Patriotic Fever, Says CBS Star," *The Guardian,* May 17, 2002.
            Copyright © 2002 by *The Guardian.*
Page 205   "They all agreed to edit out portions . . ." The Reporters Committee for Freedom
            of the Press, "Homefront Confidential: Domestic Coverage," September 2003,
            http://www.rcfp.org/homefrontconfidential/domestic.html.
Page 205   "It is journalists, not government officials, . . ." The Reporters Committee for
            Freedom of the Press, "Homefront Confidential: Domestic Coverage," September
            2003, http://www.rcfp.org/homefrontconfidential/domestic.html.
Page 206   "to understand the full impact and danger . . ." The Reporters Committee for
            Freedom of the Press, "Homefront Confidential: Domestic Coverage,"
            September 2003, http://www.rcfp.org/homefrontconfidential/domestic.html.
Page 206   "The White House again intervened, leaning on top CBS executives, . . ." David
            Halberstam, *The Powers That Be* (New York: Alfred A. Knopf), 1979.
Page 207   "One company, Pro Hosters, of Sterling, . . ." The Reporters Committee for
            Freedom of the Press, "Homefront Confidential: Domestic Coverage," September
            2003, http://www.rcfp.org/homefrontconfidential/domestic.html.
Page 207   "Not only has George W. Bush eviscerated . . ." Charles Layton, "The Information
            Squeeze," *The American Journalism Review,* Nov. 4, 2002,
            http://foi.missouri.edu/terrorismfoi/infosqueeze.html.
Page 207   "I think it's a very dangerous trend," George Lewis, personal interview with the
            author, September 17, 2003.

Page 208   "It's a very challenging time for journalists . . ." Barbara Cochran, personal interview with the author, November 6, 2003.

Page 208   "Since 9/11, journalists have assumed a role of cheerleaders . . ." Robert Wiener, personal interview with the author, October 17, 2003.

Page 209   "The so-called watchdogs were acknowledging . . ." From CNN sources, my personal interpretation having seen a tape of the press conference, and a conversation with a person present.

Page 209   "Not only were reporters going out of their way . . ." Mike Taibbi, "Cleaning the Pool: The White House Press Corps Politely Grabs Its Ankles," *New York Press,* vol. 16, issue 11, http://www.nypress.com/16/11/news&columns/cage.cfm.

Page 209   ". . . after the following exchange with White House spokesperson . . ." The White House, Ari Fleischer press briefing, www.whitehouse.gov/news/releases/2003/01/20030106-1.html

Page 210   "President Bush has 'some level of frustration . . .'" John King, "White House: Bush Frustrated with Media Coverage of War: Officials Fault Reporters," March 28, 2003, http://cnn.com/2003/ALLPOLITICS/03/28/sprj.irq.bush.media.

Page 211   "The only message that will come out, . . ." According to a veteran high-level manager of impeccable honor who asked not to be identified.

Page 211   "They don't want him (President Bush) caught . . ." From a senior network manager who asked to not be identified.

Page 212   "President Bush then refused to take questions from any media on the trip, . . ." From a veteran high-level manager of impeccable honor who asked not to be identified.

Page 213   ". . . a survey by the Pew Research Center showed that . . ." The Pew Research Center for the People and the Press, "Terror Coverage Boosts News Media's Images," November 28, 2001, http://people-press.org/reports/display.php3?ReportID=143.

Page 213   "The best way that journalists can show their patriotism . . ." Cochran, interview.

Page 213   "You're either with us or the terrorists." Author heard the president say these words on the air.

Page 214   "We have moved here to capture an Iraqi air base." Author saw this on the air.

Page 214   "Everyone here has a vested interest in our country." Author saw this on the air.

Page 214   ". . . high-level producers had to 'rein her in,' . . ." From CNN sources.

Page 214   "It was a heartening thing to see, . . ." Author saw this on the air.

Page 214   "As we get good reports from Taliban-controlled . . ." CNN chairman Walter Isaacson, memo to staff, October 2001.

Page 215   "The Pentagon has repeatedly stressed . . ." CNN vice president Rick Davis memo to staff, October 2001.

Page 215   "It was basic suppression," Wiener, interview.

Page 216   ". . . the so-called dramatic and dangerous rescue of Private Jessica Lynch . . ." From television coverage of her capture and rescue; several published British news accounts; Lynch's interview on ABC; and accounts of her book, *I'm a Soldier, Too.*

Page 216   "And of the dozen or so violations of national security . . ." The Reporters Committee for Freedom of the Press, "Homefront Confidential: Covering the War," September 2003, http://www.rcfp.org/homefrontconfidential/covering.html.

Page 217   "News organizations were forced to remain in Dhahran, Saudi Arabia, . . ." Author's personal experience.

Page 217   "This was so far superior to the system . . ." Cochran, interview.

Page 218   "Other information forbidden to report included . . ." From federal government Web sites and various news sites.

Page 218   "Some of these rules are even spelled out in the Geneva Convention, . . ." Basic training information for anyone covering wars.

Page 219   "In instances where a unit commander or the designated . . ." Quoted in
               Homefront Confidential, Reporters Committee for Freedom of the Press.
Page 220   "Mike von Fremd, an ABC News correspondent, agreed, . . ." Radio-Television
               News Directors Association, "When War Breaks: RTNDA@CNAB Panel Discusses
               Coverage of Iraq War," April 7, 2003, http://rtnda.org/news/2003/040703b.shtml.
Page 220   "Associated Press photographer Karim Kadim and his driver . . ." Committee to
               Protect Journalists, Cases 2003: Middle East and North Africa, http://cpj.org/
               cases03/mideast_cases03/iraq.html.
Page 220   "Another who died was Jerry Little, . . ." Committee to Protect Journalists,
               Cases 2003: Middle East and North Africa, http://cpj.org/cases03/mideast_cases03/
               iraq.html.
Page 220   "We were dealing with a trained liar," Jennifer LaFleur, "Embed Program Worked,
               Broader War Coverage Lagged," The News Media & the Law, spring 2003 (vol. 27,
               no. 2), http://www.rcfp.org/news/mag/27-2/cov-embedpro.html.
Page 221   ". . . the net result is a positive one." LaFleur, 2003.
Page 221   "But even the majority (over 60 percent) of people surveyed . . ." The Pew Research
               Center for the People and the Press, "TV Combat Fatigue on the Rise," March 29,
               2003, http://people-press.org/reports/display.php3?ReportID=178.
Page 222   "It starts with a feeling of patriotism within oneself." Matthew Engel, "U.S. Media
               Cowed by Patriotic Fever, Says CBS Star," The Guardian, May 17, 2002. Copyright
               © 2002 by The Guardian.
Page 222   "It's an obscene comparison, . . ." Matthew Rothschild, "Propagandists for the
               State," The Progressive, September 17, 2003,
               http://www.progressive.org/webex03/wx091703.html.
Page 222   "It's unpatriotic not to stand up, . . ." Matthew Engel, "U.S. Media Cowed by
               Patriotic Fever, Says CBS Star," The Guardian, May 17, 2002. Copyright © 2002
               by The Guardian.
Page 222   "I think the press was muzzled, . . ." Rothschild, 2003.
Page 222   "Given the choice, it's better to be viewed . . ." Peter Johnson, "Amanpour: CNN
               Practiced Self-Censorship," USA Today, September 14, 2003, http://www.usatoday.com/
               life/columnist.mediamix/2003-09-14-media-mix_x.htm.

Conclusion

Page 227   "There's got to be a TV news organization . . ." Steve Springer, personal interview
               with the author, date n.a.
Page 228   "If they recognized their purpose . . ." James Fallows, Breaking the News: How the
               Media Undermine American Democracy (New York: Vintage Books, 1996), 269, 270.
Page 231   "When you take a focus group and you say to them . . ." Christiane Amanpour,
               keynote address to the Radio-Television News Directors Association, Minneapolis,
               September 13, 2000 (the last time she was allowed to speak her mind publicly
               without being reprimanded by CNN executives).
Page 232   "According to Nielsen Media Research, . . ." Nielsen Media Research.
Page 232   "9/11 was a major wakeup call . . ." George Lewis, personal interview with the
               author, September 17, 2003.
Page 232   "According to the Pew Research Center, . . ." The Pew Research Center for the
               People and the Press, "Public's News Habits Little Changed by September 11:
               Americans Lack Background to Follow International News," June 9, 2002,
               http://people-press.org/reports/display.php3?ReportID=156.
Page 233   "I can't show my students old Nightly News programs . . ." Joe Angotti, personal
               interview with the author, October 8, 2003.
Page 234   "I think that there is some evidence . . ." Lewis, interview.
Page 234   "Let us make you feel proud." Amanpour, keynote address, 2000.

THE AUTHOR

Bonnie M. Anderson is a twenty-seven-year news veteran who has won seven Emmy Awards and been a finalist for the Pulitzer Prize. She began her career as a print reporter for the *Miami Herald,* the *Miami News,* and *Gannett Newspapers,* and spent ten years at NBC and close to ten at CNN. At CNN she rose to become managing editor of the startup network CNN en Español and finally vice president for recruiting and talent development of the CNN News Group. As president of Anderson Media Agency, Inc., Anderson currently provides media training for executives, journalists, and other professionals. She speaks at schools, universities, corporations, and conferences in the United States, Europe, and Latin America on the subject of journalistic ethics and standards, and on journalism's critical role in a healthy democracy.

NAME INDEX

SUBJECT INDEX

LaVergne, TN USA
29 November 2009

165467LV00010B/26/P